Puff Piece

John Safran is a Melbourne writer and filmmaker. His debut book, *Murder in Mississippi* (titled *God'll Cut You Down* in the US), won the Ned Kelly Award for Best True Crime. His follow-up, *Depends What You Mean by Extremist*, found him lost among radicals and was shortlisted for the Australian Book Industry Awards. His television work includes *John Safran vs God*, *Music Jamboree* and *The Goddam Election!*, and has been recognised by the Australian Film Institute and Rose d'Or Festival.

ALSO BY JOHN SAFRAN

Murder in Mississippi
Depends What You Mean by Extremist

Puff Piece

JOHN SAFRAN

HAMISH HAMILTON
an imprint of
PENGUIN BOOKS

HAMISH HAMILTON

UK | USA | Canada | Ireland | Australia
India | New Zealand | South Africa | China

Hamish Hamilton is part of the Penguin Random House group of companies,
whose addresses can be found at global.penguinrandomhouse.com.

Penguin
Random House
Australia

First published by Hamish Hamilton, 2021

Cover design by Adam Laszczuk © Penguin Random House Australia Pty Ltd
Cover photograph (vaper) by Toshiro Shimada/Getty Images
Typeset in Adobe Caslon Pro by Midland Typesetters, Australia
Printed and bound in Australia by Griffin Press, part of Ovato, an accredited
ISO AS/NZS 14001 Environmental Management Systems printer

 A catalogue record for this
book is available from the
National Library of Australia

ISBN 9 781 76089 015 5

penguin.com.au

For Rose-Marie Weinberg, Judy Weinstein & Gitl Safran

THE DOOHICKEY

I pull into Doncaster Park 'n' Ride, in north-eastern Melbourne. The man told me to meet him here. The place sounded like a water-slide park, maybe with a few other attractions, like dodgem cars and a ferris wheel. But now that I'm here, 10.30 at night, I see it's a bus terminal. Powerful streetlamps render the view out my wind-screen dreamlike, drizzle sparkling up the asphalt, giant train-set trees bordering the carpark. You *park* your car here and *ride* a bus to work. No fairy floss.

You know those *Fast and the Furious*–looking cars? Where the dude can't afford a Ferrari so he's pimped up a Subaru? One of those slow-rolls into the carpark and pulls up alongside me. I wrap up the audio notes I'm recording: 'So anyway, when someone does a true crime podcast about my murder in Doncaster Park 'n' Ride, they'll be able to play this. It will be haunting.'

A man, I'm guessing university-student age, steps into the hyper-real light, continuing the film trailer vibe. He's Asian, so now it's the third instalment of the franchise, *The Fast and the Furious: Tokyo Drift*. Despite his eBay name – JapShop – he turns out to be Chinese. Makes sense: middle-class Doncaster is one-quarter Chinese.

JapShop is immaculately groomed. He wears a denim jacket covered in red words, giving the effect they've been painted on with lipstick. Later, typing up this encounter, I'll wish I could remember those words, but in the moment I'm disoriented – this being the first time I've bought contraband out of the boot of a car.

JapShop passes a white box through my window. I peel off the shrink wrap, open it at the hinge and there it is. My little baby Jesus, resting in a little manger: the IQOS.

'Like an iPhone,' JapShop tells me breathlessly. Right down to the *I*.

The packaging makes you think of Apple. The IQOS itself looks like a fat pen, which slides into a charger you can fit in your palm. This is Philip Morris's take on the future of smoking; importantly, they say it's not a vape.

This afternoon I sat with an old school friend, who knows science, and threw questions at him about the claims Philip Morris make about the IQOS. That's when I realised I needed the device itself – I can't just spend a whole book poring over sheets of paper with technical specifications. The problem was that it's illegal to sell the IQOS in Australia. I hit up Reddit, Craigslist and Gumtree, before finding JapShop offering one on eBay for $290. That's more than twice the price of buying one over the counter in New Zealand, where they're legal.

In the carpark, JapShop has something else for me. Through the drizzle, he passes me a box of HeatSticks. A HeatStick is what you slot into the IQOS and bring to your lips. The device is pointless without these – a turtle shell without a turtle. I pull one out, roll it about in my fingers, hold it to the moon.

That's when it hits me. Why nearly all of Philip Morris's promotion is about the IQOS, not these HeatSticks.

It's a classic magician's trick: misdirection. Making you look over there so you don't catch what's actually going on over here. Philip Morris want you to focus on the IQOS, ponder its shape, its feel, its electronics. Where does the USB cord go? What does the flashing light mean? This is like nothing you've quite seen before.

They don't want you to focus on the HeatStick, because you'll almost certainly ask straight away: 'Doesn't this look like a cigarette?'

IN THE BEGINNING WAS THE WORD

The European Parliament locks in the date. On Wednesday 20 May, 2020, Brit, Dane, Pole, Cypriot and Finn will wake up to a land where the menthol cigarette is forbidden. It's over. They're dodos. Not just the extinction of an entire category of smokes, but the ones that most often dangle from the lips of the young.

The world's largest cigarette company, Philip Morris International, most famous for the Marlboro brand, agrees to stop selling menthol cigarettes. Then they add that, by the way, they have a new product. It's not a menthol cigarette, they assure everyone. It's a menthol *HeatStick*. But a HeatStick is just tobacco rolled in paper with a filter at one end. You know, like a cigarette.

HeatSticks come in packs of twenty, the box emblazoned with the warning 'Smoking is a Major Cause of Stroke' and a nauseating photo of a damaged brain. Like a cigarette pack.

Slotting it into the IQOS, you puff on one of these HeatSticks like you'd puff on a cigarette, drawing nicotine and tobacco into your lungs. After you're finished, you flick the HeatStick into the bin or onto the ground. Like you'd flick a cigarette butt into the bin or onto the ground.

So why isn't this a cigarette? Because Philip Morris International says it's not.

Surely it won't be that easy? Wise lawmakers have spent years in committees, drafting legislation, determined to ban menthol cigarettes. Philip Morris agrees to abide by the new law, but then announces they have a new menthol ciga . . . err . . . HeatStick!

HeatStick. A brand-new word. A word that wasn't here last year.

I thought new words squeezed into the world from the ground up, grassroots and organic. That's from growing up with hip-hop blasting from a boom box bought with my bar-mitzvah money. *Def, b-boy, 24/7, cold lampin', gas face, scratching the wheels of steel* and *right up to your face and diss you*. Where did these peculiar and delicious words come from, before they ended up in the mouths of rappers? Nobodies-in-particular, patients zero slouching on a couch somewhere in America, impossible to track down now, shooting the breeze. Toying with language while not thinking about it. Crunching down words already in circulation. Brewing in-jokes. Verbing nouns and nouning verbs. These words either catch fire or they don't. The ones that do – their fumes float from a couch, up the street and spread all over town. Next thing you know, CNN's business correspondent is telling you the head of the Federal Reserve just dissed the airline industry and shares in Delta Air will plunge fo' shizzle.

'HeatStick' wasn't birthed this way. This word is not grassroots or organic, it's top-down and calculated. It's been created and deployed to change the meaning of what a cigarette is and isn't. Which, in turn, can change facts in the flesh-and-blood world. Soon, if things go Philip Morris's way, a Spaniard, otherwise prohibited from doing so, will be able to smoke a menthol cigarette that isn't one. A Fleming can go on phlegming.

Over the coming months I'll learn that this is not just a one-off tactic to try to slip by the European ban – warping language is Philip Morris's number-one wangle.

Words hold power. A phrase so overused it has itself lost much of its power. Still, it's no less true. I've been clobbered with this concept since Sunday School: according to kabbalah, the mystical branch of Judaism, God created the universe by breathing words. And, the Jewish mystics teach, we too can build and bend realities, like God has. Not with piping, mud and scaffolding, but with words.

Philip Morris, the Goliath of a dying industry, will either collapse and turn to dust or live to battle on. It all pivots on corporate kabbalah, breathing words into the world, hoping they catch alight and reshape reality.

Care factor zero

There's a layer to all this that's messing with my head. How do I know about HeatSticks in the first place? Not through the mainstream news or the counterculture news. Yes, they've (lightly) reported that menthol cigarettes are dead, but not that Philip Morris is poised to slink on through a loophole. I've set up Google News alerts for all the relevant terms, so, over the months, I've caught the only news outlets interested in this part of the story: trade magazines aimed at 7-Eleven and other convenience stores. They're telling owners to prepare to substitute in menthol HeatSticks for menthol cigarettes.

Philip Morris International is a Fortune 500 company, the biggest player in an industry that snuffs out 8 million lives a year. A Holocaust and a quarter per annum. Beyond that, a relentless strain on the health system; each year in Australia, 1.7 million hospital admissions are smoking related. Considering this, shouldn't someone be interested in Philip Morris's little word game besides the bloke behind the counter next to the Slurpee machine? I'm interested in why no one is interested.

The greatest story ever told

To understand all this, we need to wind back.

May 30, 2018. Philip Morris publicises a brand-new gambit. A galling gambit, it's a jaw-dropper – and not their usual one where they give you cancer of the jaw and it falls off.

I'm seeing their gambit through the eyes of a storyteller. That same day, a grey Sydney Wednesday, I have been hired to sit in a boardroom with ten other writers and plot out an action-drama television series. The Venetian blinds are snapped shut. A plate of chocolate minibars sits in the middle of the boardroom table and I am deciding if enough time has elapsed since I last reached in to grab another.

The key to writing action-drama is that the hero or the villain must be cornered into an impossible situation, where there is no apparent escape. In this writers' room, someone has determined that our villain, a skinhead, will be trapped down an alley, facing off with a cop with a gun. The skinhead has no weapon. He's screwed. There's no way out of this.

From there we, the writers, have to dig deep. Flex our imaginations. Draw on all our creative wiles to hatch an escape plan for him.

Something so ingenious, so lateral, that the audience never sees it coming.

I come up with it! The skinhead forces his fingers down his own throat. He throws up on the cop and, in that moment of disgust and confusion, he darts up the alley and escapes. Against all odds, he lives to fight another day. I pluck a Snickers minibar from the plate.

Back to Philip Morris's gambit. I see the creative minds there have also been plotting in a boardroom, squeaking fat black markers on butcher's paper. Philip Morris had also found themselves with a villain cornered in an impossible spot, where there was no apparent escape. That villain was themselves.

Philip Morris are part of a wheezing, dying industry. They're forbidden from advertising. Governments banished cigarettes from pubs around fifteen years ago, but if Philip Morris thought that would be the depth of their woes they were wrong. Smoking bans are reaching deeper into public and private space; the American company U-Haul will not hire people who smoke, full stop. Not after hours, not at home. Prospective employees must consent to drug testing for nicotine.

Shareholders in Philip Morris are noting news like this. And things are about to escalate. Significant dates loom. In Beverly Hills, Los Angeles, the council has banned the sale of cigarettes, effective 2021. It's the first city in the United States to do so. Philip Morris fears this could be the tipping point, that this is a new trend set to blaze through America then the rest of the world.

Philip Morris need to dig deep, flex their imagination. Come up with something ingenious.

And they deliver.

Philip Morris have come up with The Greatest Story Ever Told. A plot twist so audacious, no one ever saw it coming. The day they publicise this new gambit, 30 May, is significant. It's the eve of United Nations' World No Tobacco Day. Philip Morris have bought full-page advertisements in newspapers. Prepare to be dazzled but, more than that, befuddled.

In these ads, Philip Morris announce they plan to shut down as a cigarette company. They're going to relaunch as anti-smoking campaigners, dedicated to convincing the world's billion smokers to quit cigarettes.

'We're Moving Away From Cigarettes, What About You?' trumpets the bold blue headline. 'We've made the decision to build our future without cigarettes . . . No cigarette company has done anything like this before. But the vision is clear. And the benefits are clear too. For everyone.' Their clarion call is that they are going to 'unsmoke' the world.

'Unsmoke'. Another word that wasn't here last year that Philip Morris now whispers into the universe.

What they're planning sounds momentous. Historical. Smoking is the leading cause of preventable death; Philip Morris is the world's largest cigarette company. It's all coming to an end, and of their own accord? This begs comparisons to South Africa's apartheid regime throwing in the towel in 1994, conceding that their whole operation was an evil and unsustainable sham.

What on God's green earth is going on?

The next day – World No Tobacco Day – the writers' room rolls on. We've lost our inhibitions and are descending into an animalistic state, grabbing mini chocolate bars at twice the rate as the day before. Philip Morris are back today too, with another full-page advertisement. They tell us they're not going to be passive observers in the revolution. They're here to help.

'One billion people will start World No Tobacco Day with a cigarette. We believe people should stop smoking, and support measures to dissuade people from starting. That said, people who continue to use cigarettes deserve a better choice. They should be able to switch to alternatives that are likely to be less harmful than continuing to smoke. Why would anyone deny them this opportunity?'

That last line is a little passive-aggressive. Suddenly *we* might be the arseholes, not the cancer-bestowing multinational.

So, they *are* selling us something. Nothing wrong with that, if it helps. What is this alternative to smoking? Philip Morris says they have spent $4.5 billion, hired more than 400 scientists, engineers and technicians, and developed a new doohickey.

This doohickey is the IQOS. It's a – well what is it? I fold open my laptop in the writers' room. A photo online shows something sleek, blue and metallic-looking, roughly the length of a cigarette and a little fatter. It looks like a pen an astronaut would have, I suppose. Or at least a pen a model done up as an astronaut for a fashion shoot would have. It sits next to a matching charging device that's rectangular, with curved corners, also blue and metallic-looking. The pen slides into this charger and the whole package fits into your hand. If I saw a woman holding one on a red carpet I'd assume it's some sort of compact or tampon case that I'm unfamiliar with because I don't read *Vogue*.

'IQOS is a tobacco heating system,' Philip Morris explains. 'Thanks to sophisticated electronics IQOS heats specially designed heated tobacco units up to 350°C without combustion.' Combustion is one of those words where I think I know what it means until I have to explain it. If someone, right now, said 'Define combustion in the next thirty seconds or your father combusts,' he's combusting.

Okay, I looked it up. Combustion is the act or the process of burning. Philip Morris don't reveal it here but by 'heated tobacco unit' they mean a HeatStick, the item that looks suspiciously like a cigarette, only shorter. You slot this into the hole at the tip of the pen. The HeatStick's filter remains jutting out and you bring it to your lips and huff. Philip Morris says that the IQOS heats but never burns this HeatStick. As a result, it doesn't generate smoke, it generates aerosol. Your lungs draw in nicotine and tobacco, but because it's through this aerosol, 'the levels of harmful chemicals are significantly reduced compared to cigarette smoke'.

So, no more smoke, with its deadly carcinogens. Smoke is the villain of the cigarette and this has none. Imagine all the lives saved by moving smokers off cigarettes and onto IQOS.

'Our studies on IQOS are progressing rapidly . . . and indicate that it has the potential to present less risk of harm.'

A few days later, rereading this material, I realise Philip Morris don't quite say what I took them to say. They don't claim that IQOS will save lives – they've given themselves wiggle-room.

'Our studies on IQOS are *progressing* [so not completed] . . . and indicate that it has the *potential* [so something could be proven in the future but hasn't been proven right now] to present less risk of harm [So there's still some risk of harm. What type?].'

In fact, any more wiggles and Philip Morris could tour schools with Dorothy the Dinosaur.

Finicky

I don't trust Philip Morris to anoint new words – 'HeatStick'? 'unsmoke'? – but I trust the Scrabble dictionary. Two Scrabble associations, one representing the nerds of North America, the other the nerds of the rest of the world, update their dictionaries every few years. I snap these up from the bookshop on the day of release to see what the compilers have caught in their butterfly nets.

You can map the shifting world through Scrabble dictionaries. There's an influx of entries that rolled in with Muslim immigration to the West, from 'kiblah', the direction of Mecca, to 'cadi', an Islamic judge.

Later, as the new social justice spread, came the additions of 'manspread' and 'mansplain'. And 'cisgender', 'genderqueer', 'misgender' and the gender-neutral pronoun 'ze'. The tectonic plates of culture slip beneath our feet and so do our anxieties around language. At this point I'd feel safer drawing than misgendering Mohammad.

My Scrabble dictionary collection is tucked into the lowest level of my bookshelf, where eyes are least likely to wander, so I don't come across as a lunatic to visitors. In the Scrabble dictionary released in 2011, 'vape' and 'vaping' simply aren't there. They pop up in the next edition, released in 2015. Vaping devices had existed before then, available for purchase at the type of shops that sell dildos, bongs and Jimi Hendrix t-shirts, but they began to float into mainstream consciousness somewhere in that four-year gap between Scrabble dictionaries.

So one of the first questions that pops to mind is whether this new Philip Morris doohickey, the IQOS, is just a vape. Well, what is a vape anyway? Collins dictionary says a vape is a device that produces flavoured steam containing nicotine. You'll remember that Philip Morris says the IQOS produces aerosol. Is that the same as steam? And if it's different, does that mean the IQOS isn't a vape or does it mean Collins has screwed up the definition?

This sounds finicky, but I'll learn Philip Morris weaponises finicky. The IQOS is a shapeshifter. It is whatever Philip Morris needs it to be at any given moment, to accommodate lawmakers or draw in customers. It is sometimes an electronic cigarette, but it's *not* a vape when Philip Morris needs it to not be one. Philip Morris heralded its arrival as a better alternative to cigarettes but, slyly, the IQOS turns back into a cigarette whenever Philip Morris needs it to be one. Make no mistake, the doohickey, the physical object, remains the same in each incarnation – it is the word conferred upon it that bends it this way and that.

Let's pull out of this quicksand of slippery words and meanings and keep it simple for now.

A vape is a handheld inhaler, the battery inside heating up a metal coil. That coil vaporises liquid, which you draw into your lungs and then exhale, a cloudy afro forming over your head.

The IQOS doesn't heat up liquid, instead it heats up tobacco leaf. These are the HeatSticks, or 'HEETS' in some markets. Tobacco leaf is absent from vapes. Considering tobacco's awful reputation, this distinction strikes me as a big one. Philip Morris thinks there's a meaningful difference too. They tell punters the IQOS isn't a vape, it's a 'heat not burn' device.

Nonetheless, the vaping revolution is the backdrop to Philip Morris's supposed move away from cigarettes.

According to the infamous Westboro Baptist church in Kansas, God hates fags. However, He must really like *fags*, given that just as the cigarette trade had a real chance of being stubbed out, He's bequeathed Philip Morris a new playground to play in: the world of vaping. A world that is growing exponentially. Seven million vapers by 2011, over 40 million by 2018 and an estimated 55 million today.

People think the conflict is Big Tobacco and vapers fighting government regulations. But in fact one of the key battle lines in the future of smoking is IQOS versus vapes. Philip Morris, 175 years of smoke stained into their walls, are taking on the vaping industry, brand new and smelling a bit fruity.

Pitter-patter

I email Philip Morris Australia's Communications and Engagement department, asking if I can swing by.

Hi John, Absolutely – have always loved your work! We'd be very happy to chat and answer any questions you may have.

They suggest I meet Managing Director Tammy Chan.

A week and a half later, I've heard nothing more. I shoot them another message to firm up the details.

Hi John, we might have to give this a pass, sorry.

I write: *Is there anyone else at Philip Morris I could talk to besides Tammy?*

They respond: *We're going to leave it be for now, sorry.*

Philip Morris, did you even bother to think that between your first reply and the follow-up, I pitched a book on you and your Smoke-Free Future to Penguin Random House, premised on getting access to your company? And they bought it. You've really left my arse flapping in the wind.

DO PHILIP MORRIS
EMPLOYEES GO TO HELL?

It hides in plain sight: Philip Morris are plotting to slip past the menthol cigarette ban. Yet the story won't catch alight. Right now on Twitter, as I type, Martha Stewart is the trending topic that Philip Morris never is. What line did this American businesswoman and celebrity cross? She said, sarcastically, on a late-night comedy talk show, that she's holding her gardener and driver as detainees at her home. People are, unsarcastically, denouncing her for endorsing slavery.

I try to explain this to a friend who manages comedians. How we're living under a new moral code where Big Tobacco attracts less attention and fury than Big Sarcasm, the world of comedy. Being part of the Sarcasm Industrial Complex myself, I'd like to know what it all means.

But I explain myself poorly, I meander, so my friend misunderstands what I'm getting at. He thinks I'm questioning the morality of people who work for Philip Morris. That I'm asking how they can justify their work. He says I can't start pulling at that thread because where does it end? Nearly everyone with a job is complicit in something.

Complicity. Now that's an interesting subject. (You should know that much of what I write about comes from people misunderstanding me and answering a better question than the one I asked. I can't believe I've figured out a way to leverage my incoherence.)

I know complicity is a raw nerve. At parties and on trains, I've been a sounding board for strangers about this.

'I work at a bank, sorry.'

Sometimes I find it difficult to follow what they're feeling guilty about.

'Yeah, I'm an actuary . . . I *know*.'

I'm guessing they think my line of work – the noble arts – is not muddied by questions of complicity. I don't know about that. Regardless, book writers and ballerinas have a better reputation than those in Big Tobacco. Below a Philip Morris corporate video on YouTube, the public has spat the following comments.

'Simple. You work for Philip Morris, you're a murderer.'

'You guys kill millions of people. Everyone in that company is going to hell.'

Hell? I know just the man to talk to about that.

Jesus Christ

I've known Father Bob Maguire for a decade and a half. He's always tangled in some ruckus that's hard to follow. Right now, if I'm getting it straight, he's raising money for a camel sanctuary, where underprivileged kids can ride the animals, clomping around in fresh air and feeling a sense of purpose. But he's hit a hump. A nemesis, out for revenge over a bygone slight, keeps contacting the RSPCA, claiming the sanctuary is mistreating the beasts. Even though they always find nothing out of order, the RSPCA are obliged to drive down and check each time.

Bob began training for the priesthood at age nineteen, and was booted from his Catholic parish age seventy-six. That time his fight was with the Archbishop of Melbourne. There are half-a-dozen sub-fights to that fight, which I've never fully unpicked, one being that he sold off a church property to feed the poor.

The Archbishop tried to usher him off into an old people's home, and Bob did not want that. Instead he hit up trade unions and philanthropists, and set up the Father Bob Maguire Foundation. The organisation's shopfront office sits near a tram stop in inner-city Port Melbourne, along one of those well-to-do shopping strips where they still have a bookshop. Father Bob sleeps in a small room out the back of the office.

When I get there, his big black poodle bounces and slobbers around the boardroom table. Bob is old even for an old person. Each time I visit, his eyes are wonkier, his nose capillaries redder. He updates me on the sanctuary fiasco, but I'm not here about camels, I'm here about *Camels*. (That's not a Philip Morris brand, but how could I resist?)

'Aw, I know Philip Morris,' he tells me warmly, almost purring. 'The old days.'

The question of which circle of hell Philip Morris staff are heading to will have to wait – unprompted, Father Bob has rolled into the pleasure and the purpose of cigarettes. Another matter

I hadn't thought to interrogate until someone else did it for me. Yes, the reason people smoke is an important thing to establish.

He thinks viewing cigarettes through the lens of nicotine and addiction doesn't get to the nub of the matter. 'In the old, old, old days we *all* used to go around with bloody cigarettes hanging from our lips. The times were out of joint and you had nothing else to do. You couldn't suck your thumb at a board meeting, could you?'

So a Marlboro is a thumb substitute. 'But why do we want to suck our thumb?' I ask.

'It goes back to the womb and it goes back to the caves. We always needed something to reassure us that the bloody dragon was not going to come into the cave and gobble up the lot of us.'

'But how does a cigarette reassure us?'

'It virtually affects the brain patterns. *Do not be afraid. You are in control of this situation.* But you're not. Of course the dragon is still coming into the cave and it's going to gobble us all up, but in the meantime you'll be able to at least have your last smoke. A cigarette somehow suggests to you that you'll never walk alone.'

The poodle by his chair is panting in apparent agreement.

'It looks to be a trivial pursuit, but in fact it gets to the heart of the matter, which is how are we to live in what our animal nature says is a hostile environment? Imagine putting all your trust in a bloody cigarette – but that's all you've got, right?' He pats his suit jacket pocket. 'You've got your friendly Philip Morris in your pocket. Pat, pat, pat, pat, pat.'

I know Father Bob's smoking history. Maybe twelve years ago a man in drag slid up to me at a party. He said he knew a friend of mine. 'Who?' I asked. 'Father Bob,' he revealed. I thought I'd stumbled upon the priest's secret double life, but it turned out that the man ran a tobacconist and Father Bob bought his cigars there.

'I think I get the thing about the thumb,' I say to Bob. 'Is that like the mother's nipple?'

'Yeah, all of that.'

'So, the cigarette is a continuation of the mother's nipple?'

'Yes! *Mum! Mum!*' Bob cries, mimicking distress. 'Mum can't help him, or Mum's already been gobbled up by the bloody dragon.'

His explanation as to why folks smoke is packed with truth. The nipple/cigarette comparison spins another way though, moving from pleasure to consequence. The nipple giveth life and the cigarette taketh life away.

'If you work for Philip Morris, do you go to hell after you die?'

'Do you?' Bob volleys back.

'I'm asking you!'

'No,' he says but not with the conviction he had that dragons loiter outside caves. He ponders, then locks in a firmer no.

Bob says in the afterlife the Philip Morris employee will enter a portal, a waiting room of sorts. A tribunal of spirits will be awaiting them, and the Philip Morris employee will be able to give their side of the story. He says the backstory to why someone has been involved in a killing is important; if a woman is speeding and kills a person in a crash, it might come out in court that she was fleeing domestic violence.

'Have to tell the whole bloody story! We don't know everything. We like to think we know everything.'

He reckons the Philip Morris employee might argue to the spirits that they were just working for the cigarette giant to earn a livelihood. To me, that doesn't feel as compelling an excuse as fleeing domestic violence. But Bob won't pause and mull over this. He's moved on, riled up by a different set of moral questions: those arising when judging and punishing people. Justice should be restorative, making things right, rather than being driven by anger and retribution.

I circle back around again. 'I thought you had to pay the piper for your bad deeds eventually.'

'That's retribution. The detention centres are filled with refugees whose backstories the authorities can't be bothered working out.' *You* might compare Big Tobacco executives to murderers and monsters, but Bob has grouped them in with domestic violence survivors and asylum seekers behind bars.

I tell him it's a sensitive matter because of all the people killed by cigarettes.

'Terribly sensitive,' he agrees. 'We were rolling cigarettes for my old man at the Alfred Hospital.'

We've been talking for a while and Bob has only now revealed that his father died from smoking-induced lung cancer.

'He was a sailor, smoked all the bloody time. Those days, long time ago, they were smoking even in the cancer ward. It was considered to be a comfort.'

So strange. Cigarettes set your death in motion but then make your death less stressful.

Despite this personal stake, Bob doesn't harbour any anger for the cigarette companies. I tell him Philip Morris Australia reneged on their offer to meet with me, but I'm still hoping somehow to interview their company head, Tammy Chan.

'So, I can tell her she's not going to hell?'

'Yeah. She'll go through the door, the wardrobe door, into a new existence, into the portal. And her ancestors will be there to welcome her, to reassure her.'

Jew diligence

Bob wasn't worked up. He doesn't think a thunderous reckoning awaits Philip Morris employees in the afterlife. I decide to try my rabbi at East Melbourne Hebrew Congregation.

'Sorry, I just had a fishball, so I probably smell like a fishball.' Rabbi Dovid Gutnick dabs his mouth with a serviette. He's just wrapped a weekly Torah class, held in a long room attached to the synagogue. There are nibbles afterwards – cake, lox, herring and such.

'What commandment is "thou shall not kill"?'

'Number six,' he says. He doesn't smell like a fishball by the way.

'If you work for Philip Morris, are you breaking the sixth commandment?'

'No.'

'Why not?'

'It's not direct murder.'

Yes, kill versus murder. A rabbi has told me about this distinction before. By 'thou shall not kill', God actually meant thou shall not murder, leaving room for self-defence and accidents. And, apparently, flogging durries.

But self-defence and accidents aren't pre-meditated. Philip Morris workers know exactly what they're doing: pipelining bodies to the cemetery.

Rabbi Gutnick says it's too much of a leap to call Philip Morris employees murderers. 'It's not direct. It's not like you're walking up to somebody and stabbing them in the face. The warnings are clear. People still choose to do it to themselves. They purchase it, they buy it.'

He says the employees might be breaking a different law, one that doesn't make the top ten, Leviticus 19:14. 'Do not place a stumbling block before a blind person.' Don't make things difficult for someone vulnerable. Or, in the rabbi's Yiddish: quit being a nogoodnik. And Philip Morris workers are nogoodniks. They know their customers are schlemiels schlepping to the servo or schnorrers hitting up some schnook for a ciggie. Why place decks of cigarettes before these addicts, Philip Morris? Why not be a mensch?

Mixed feelings swirl within Rabbi Gutnick. The Lubavitcher Rebbe, kinda the pope of a worldwide Chassidic sect, told Rabbi Gutnick's grandfather to quit smoking. The science had become undeniable and the Torah commands that you should protect your body, your soul, your life.

But Rabbi Gutnick also remembers, from childhood, photos of great rabbis staring back at him from books and walls. 'I have images in my head: a cigarette in their hand gave them a certain calmness and it gave them a certain ability to think things through. I don't know if that's scientific at all.'

To him (and me) there are proofs beyond science. He knows a ninety-year-old mystic in New York, a revered man, who smokes as he takes in and teaches kabbalah scripture. That's another data point that smoking might dance with profundity in a way that can't be pinned down by some heathen in a lab.

As I leave the synagogue, he asks, 'Where are you going to draw the line?' He brings up Coca-Cola and obesity. If Philip Morris workers are to be condemned, why not the copywriters at Coke's advertising agency? 'I don't know why you're just picking on Philip Morris.'

What the hell? I'm picking on Philip Morris? *I'm* the bully?

Every year, across the world, 57 million people die. Of those, 8 million can be pinned on Big Tobacco. Fourteen per cent of all deaths in the world. Yet Rabbi Gutnick thinks I'm the whale and Philip Morris are Jonah?

Before speaking to Father Bob and Rabbi Gutnick, I was puzzled that the media aren't getting worked up by Philip Morris's plans. But it seems the clergy – the great judges of good and evil – aren't either.

Badgers

'I don't know why you're just picking on Philip Morris,' is still caught in my head, halfway home.

So that's one reason Philip Morris can cull the global population without the resistance you might expect: everyone's doing something bad. Why badger Philip Morris? Why not McDonald's (heart disease), Carlton & United Breweries (car crashes) and Crown Casino (suicides)? I mean, sure, but if you follow that logic, Supreme Leader Kim Jong-Un starves North Koreans, so why pick on warlords slashing throats in Tanzania? When everyone's guilty, no one is guilty. Everyone's off the hook. That's our collective state of mind. Very useful for Philip Morris.

When I get home, I google the phrase and find the exact wording: 'when all are guilty, no one is'. Hannah Arendt, theorist and author, who sat through the trial of Adolf Eichmann, Nazi, came up with that. Her other famous one is 'the banality of evil'. Both phrases circle around the idea that big crimes happen because little cogs turn. Don't just think of the goose-stepping Führer, think of the pen-pushing bookkeepers, keeping the trains and the camps running. There's something unspectacular and routine about systematic killing, and that lulls us into apathy.

Nothing's simple. When I look Arendt up on Google Images, I find a hint of what helped her churn this wisdom in her head and produce books and ideas that enriched the world. In the very first photo that pops up her palm is resting on her temple, silver streaked through her hair, and between her fingers a little ghost of smoke floats up from a cigarette.

I love everything about cigarettes except for the cancer.

Harry Potter and the Gauntlet of Ze

I click around, procrastinating.

What's this?

I see JK Rowling, the woman who conjured Harry Potter, and Daniel Radcliffe, the man who lived in his skin, are fighting over a word: 'woman'. JK says that transwomen are distinct from women because they were born with penises. Daniel is the revolutionary. He's says that transwomen *are* women. Because they're famous, JK and Daniel have taken this fight from gender studies faculties and Twitter bubbles to the mainstream news.

As a Scrabble dictionary yogi, I'm drawn in straight away. This is wild. I'm not sure how to score these things but what word ranks as more significant than 'woman'? It's equal first place with ones like 'death' and 'breath'. Certainly it's more important than 'bubble gum' or 'carpet'. Daniel Radcliffe and his side are committed to insurgency, overthrowing how this word has been understood by most up until this moment. This is a live argument; the ball is still in the air. Parliaments and sporting codes are being pushed into ratifying what 'woman' means.

Philip Morris aren't alone in their commitment to redefining a word, but nor are activists for trans rights. We're living through a fertile time for recasting words and meanings.

SLIPPERY

It's only the beginning of this investigation and I'm already learning to hate my audio recorder. I go about my day and think one thing has happened, then afterwards I play back the recording and it contradicts my version of events.

Here's what I thought happened. Vaping campaigners are in town and a sympathetic politician, Fiona Patten, leader of the Reason Party, is hosting a forum – past the neoclassical columns, the marble and the portraits of men in handlebar moustaches – inside a room at Parliament House in Melbourne.

'Couldn't be a better room to have this conversation, because this used to be the smoking room,' Fiona begins. 'The whole parliament was a smoking room, actually. They used to smoke in the chambers; port was allowed. Sadly, it's not anymore.'

I throw a curveball of a question to the panel that puts them on the back foot. They weren't expecting someone to have done their homework as thoroughly as I did. Dr Alex Wodak, a physician and campaigner for vaping, is forced to meander for a while, his mind ticking overtime, thinking how to dodge my interrogation.

But my audio recorder has a different version of events. This is what it says happened.

Fiona Patten asks for questions from the small audience. I raise my hand and mumble out a fumbling, barely coherent question to the panel. Actually, I'm flattering myself – it's not even clear it's a question. More a homicide of language, verbs and nouns laying mangled and strewn all over the carpet of the smoking room.

In fact, considering the sumptuous old-world setting, I half expect Agatha Christie's Inspector Hercule Poirot to wander in to solve The Case of the Murdered Rambling Run-on Sentence. He taps his pipe on the mantelpiece and begins speaking in his native Belgian, which is understood by those in the room more clearly than my English. Dr Alex Wodak, needing a moment to piece together what the lunatic in the front row was getting at, talks broadly for a minute before homing in on my point.

So those are the two versions of what went down. Who are you going to believe? Me or my lying audio recorder?

For clarity, I'll clean up my question for these pages. 'Is the difference between a vape and an IQOS significant? Might not the health consequences of one differ from the other? Do we confuse matters by scrambling the two together when discussing harm reduction?' I ask, dashingly.

Dr Wodak agrees there is a distinction. Yes, the IQOS contains tobacco and a vape does not. But he doesn't take this to where I expect. The IQOS's HeatStick, he explains, resembles and tastes like a cigarette – it even feels like a cigarette to the fingers. So smokers not willing to try a vape, because it's too unfamiliar, could be comfortable trying the HeatStick. A victory for the harm-reduction movement.

Philip Morris makes this point too. It's part of their can't-lose formulation, where what seems a mark against them becomes a green tick in their favour. You point out that the HeatStick resembles a cigarette, shouldn't that raise a concern it *is* a cigarette? They counter no, that's its genius, that's the point!

Dr Wodak relays a powerful statistic. 'When the IQOS was released on the Japanese market in April 2016, cigarette sales in Japan went down 31 per cent over the next three years.'

This is impressive, but it hinges on the presumption that a HeatStick isn't a cigarette. If it is one, cigarette sales didn't plunge 31 per cent – all those Japanese men and women kept on smoking them.

Rabbi Gutnick accused me of picking on Philip Morris, so I'll provide more from their side of the story. Seated next to Dr Wodak is David Sweanor, adjunct professor at the Centre for Health Law, Policy and Ethics, University of Ottawa. He makes it clear: the IQOS sits comfortably alongside vaping.

'We have to see it in context of what people are doing now, which is that they're smoking cigarettes. This is like having a discussion, "is it more hazardous to be juggling cricket balls, oranges or small stones?" when people are currently juggling live hand grenades.' The Canadian is waving his hands now. 'And the real answer is, I don't freaking care. Just get them to stop juggling hand grenades. We'll deal with the stone versus cricket ball stuff later.'

My new friend

Following the forum, strolling out past statues and busts, I meet a man with bushy arms.

Savvas Dimitriou is the Managing Director of Vapoureyes Australia, a vape empire.

'I'm trying to get them to understand where the science is,' Savvas says of politicians. 'But the difficulty is, what credibility do I have? I have a financial interest in this. Anything I say is automatically discounted.'

'I'm pretty obsessed with the IQOS,' I say, still caught in my own head. 'I love how they've decided it's not a cigarette. Like, why?'

'Do you mind if I vape while we talk?' he asks, and begins huffing on the steps of parliament.

I spotted another politician in the smoking room, Tim Wilson. He represents the federal Liberal Party, but left-wing people give him the side-eye for another reason too: he was once policy director for the Institute of Public Affairs, a libertarian think tank that has been funded by Big Oil, Big Mining and my stalking victim Philip Morris.

Savvas reveals that two men from Philip Morris were standing at the back of the smoking room too.

'Oh, really?' I chirp with delight and mope with regret all at once. Let's not forget, their Communications and Engagement department promised to hook me up, then ghosted. It seems that once again, Philip Morris has slipped through my fingers.

'This is a conspiracy theory,' Savvas begins.

My ears prick up way more than if he'd said, 'This is a fact.'

A clean conspiracy would run like this: Philip Morris is plotting to kill off vaping so they can rule the globe with IQOS. But not so fast. Philip Morris USA's parent company has bought a stake in Juul, that country's most successful vape enterprise. Sounds like they're not trying to kill off vaping but are instead embracing it? Not so fast. For Savvas, they've bought into Juul chiefly to buy a seat at the table in the vape industry. To what end? So they can lobby governments drafting vaping laws as an insider, not an outsider. And what are they intending to lobby for? Savvas thinks vaping laws that will kill off vaping, leaving IQOS to rule the globe.

I'm happy to follow the twists and turns of his conspiracy theory.

Savvas says he's not crazy; Juul lobbied the New Zealand government to ban vape juice flavours like Ice-Cream Cake, Chicken Corn Chips, Crotch Crickets and Nonna's Tiramisu. Wacky flavours are Savvas's bread and butter. (Bread and Butter Pudding is another vape juice.) It's not just his business model – if these types of flavours are banned, the antipodean vape industry will crumble (Honeycomb Crumble also available), leaving IQOS to fill that space. So maybe there is something to Savvas's conspiracy theory.

We exchange numbers; he tells me I should swing by his warehouse.

'It's all slipperiness,' he says of Philip Morris. 'And they're so damn good at it too. I'm envious. I'm jealous at how good they are at it, in fact.'

SHADOWLAND

A quirk stands out in the white supremacist belief system. They consider all other 'races' intellectually inferior, bar two: the Japanese and the Jews. They don't intend this as a compliment. The Jew, they contend, plies its sharp brain to screw over the white race.

What a tangle for the fight against antisemitism – you need to present the case that Jews are stupider than people think. When COVID-19 hits, a solid piece of evidence that this is in fact the case rolls in. Jews across the world, including here in Melbourne, are overrepresented in those who catch the virus, because they refuse to respect the science, insisting on congregating for prayer and social gatherings.

Then there's the anecdotal evidence. I live in Melbourne's Jewish hub, Balaclava, and despite the white supremacist claim of high Jewish IQs, no one here can parallel park. Jews jerk back and forth to the kerb like a Chasid rocking in prayer, blocking both directions of traffic along the shopping strip all day.

And here's a slice of personal evidence: my entire Jew brain is focused on catching Philip Morris out, yet time and again I read one of their claims about smoking or the IQOS and it takes me anywhere from a week to three months to realise that I've been duped.

Get this. *Gay Star News*, honoured as Publication of the Year by gay rights campaigners Stonewall, is hosting an event about smoking. 'Smoking is the secret killer of LGBTI people,' they tell readers in July 2019, after the British government singles out the community for their wheezy ways. '*Gay Star News* has decided to do something about this.' The event will be put on thanks to their new 'health sector sponsor', promising free drinks, canapés and a lively discussion.

I read on and learn that this new 'health sector' sponsor is Philip Morris International. Not only is a cigarette not a cigarette, now the company that produces more than 800 billion cigarettes a year is part of the health sector. Fair enough, I suppose. When I was younger I asked a woman how she became a film producer and she said she printed out a business card saying she was a film producer. Similarly, Philip Morris are part of the health sector because they say so. Fake it till you make it, Philip Morris.

But this is not the end of the matter, it's just the first Babushka to be twisted open. Those unable to make it to the *Gay Star News* event in person are encouraged to visit a site, *Hold My Light*.

'*Hold My Light* is about giving up cigarettes for 30 days. If you do it for a month, you're five times more likely to do it for good. Cigarettes are highly addictive, and every one you smoke causes serious harm and disease. Quitting cigarettes is the best decision you can make.'

It's hard to object to this campaign. In a reversal of collateral damage, here's some collateral *non*-damage. A message that's helpful, regardless of the yellow-stained fingers all over it. The campaign is pretty much identical to one run in my home state by Quit Victoria, a reputable, government-backed organisation. 'We're here to support LGBTIQ+ smokers to quit!' the Quit Victoria site promises. They want to 'support people who smoke to become tobacco-free'.

It takes a long while for it to click; another Russian doll twists open. A word central to Quit Victoria's campaign is absent from *Hold My Light*. Philip Morris has perfectly replicated an anti-smoking campaign but stripped it of the word 'tobacco'. It's nowhere to be seen. They're going wide with this strategy.

'We believe it's time to evolve World No Tobacco Day into World No Smoking Day,' their Chief Operating Officer, Jacek Olczak, has said.

World No Tobacco Day versus World No Smoking Day? They hit the ear as identical ideas. Yet the future of Philip Morris rests on them tippy-toeing in and swapping one word for the other.

In the world as it is, the IQOS is a nonstarter. The mission of public health bodies is to rid the world of tobacco. And the IQOS contains tobacco – the HeatStick. Their gambit, their doohickey, makes no sense. But in the reality that Philip Morris is quietly assembling, tobacco is innocent, a patsy for the real assassin, smoke. They insist the IQOS doesn't emit smoke. In this shadowland, the IQOS, and so Philip Morris, lives on.

The reality they're constructing is filled with what appear to be legitimate public health websites, train station billboards and social justice activism. And you have to squint hard to figure out what's going on.

Take Smoke-Free Future. The site promotes the Smoke-free program that's run by the British government's National Health Service, the NHS. You can see why someone fondling a dart over their keyboard, eager to quit, could think this an NHS-approved venture. It isn't. Philip Morris runs it. Jumbled in with the type of advice the NHS would offer smokers is the type of advice they wouldn't: it touts the benefits of tobacco devices like the IQOS.

You'd think gay rights campaigners Stonewall could regret awarding *Gay Star News* Publication of the Year once they learned Philip Morris sponsors them. Like true-crime favourite Jeffrey Dahmer, Philip Morris lures in gay men then kills them, which feels like a bad fit for a gay-rights group.

But they won't be rescinding that award. Screw open another Babushka doll. Philip Morris funds Stonewall, too, through Stonewall's Diversity Champions program. Here Stonewall trains you up on how to make your business more diverse, and then your business can promote its association with Stonewall.

If you're feeling chubby you can stand next to chubbier people to feel not so chubby after all. Similarly, Philip Morris, perhaps for the only time, look less maniacal standing next to some of the other members of Stonewall's Diversity Champions program. Also there is a company called AWE, Atomic Weapons Establishment, who manufacture warheads for nuclear weapons. You've got a problem with that? What are you, bombaphobic?

Locking lips

Philip Morris hasn't always been chummy with gay rights campaigners. Chunks of tobacco industry secrets are, theoretically, not secret anymore. Thousands upon thousands of in-house documents, too unwieldly to know where to begin, have been reluctantly tabled in courtrooms over the decades whenever Philip Morris has faced litigation. Lucky-dip in and you discover little histories.

One of those concerns Jesse Helms, who was a US senator for three decades, from the early seventies on. 'Think about it,' he opined in 1990. 'Homosexuals and lesbians, disgusting people, marching in our streets, demanding all sorts of things, including the right to marry each other.' A few years earlier he had complained about an HIV-prevention book. 'The subject matter is so obscene, so revolting, it's difficult for me to stand here and talk about it. I may throw up.'

Jesse Helms served North Carolina, a tobacco-farming state, so he locked lips with the tobacco industry, pushing their interests in the Senate. Gay-rights activists ACT UP discovered Philip Morris was, by far, Helms's largest corporate donor. They marched on Philip Morris's Washington DC office in 1990, to launch a boycott of Marlboro, demanding the company stop funding the senator. Philip Morris refused.

Not long after, a Jesse Helms museum opened, displaying the man's letters, speeches and baubles. The project's largest donation came from Philip Morris.

The world turns, seasons change. Today Philip Morris can boast a complete transformation. Now they're more than welcoming of gay voices. They sponsored America's Unfinished Business:

An LGBTQ+ Summit and tout an in-house advocacy group: 'Spanning 27 countries . . . the STRIPES group leads initiatives to support and celebrate LGBTQ+ inclusion within Philip Morris International's LGBTQ+ community.'

It's hard to square this with the company that once supported a man like Jesse Helms.

Who is the Jesse Helms of today? Perhaps Senator Marsha Blackburn. She argues employees should be able to discriminate against LGBTI people, fighting this cause all the way to the US Supreme Court.

Blackburn's views on gay people pushed singer Taylor Swift to break an oath never to talk politics to fans, speaking about her hometown senator in the *Miss Americana* documentary. 'If I get bad press for saying, "Don't put a homophobic racist in office," then I get bad press for that, I really don't care. I think it is so frilly and spineless of me to stand onstage and go, "Happy Pride Month, you guys," and then not say this, when someone's literally coming for their neck.'

Something else about Senator Blackburn. She serves Tennessee, a tobacco-farming state. Philip Morris USA's parent company always helps fill up her coffers. In 2017, to keep her in office, they donated ten times as much to her as they did to Tennessee Democrat James Cooper.

By the way, I don't think Philip Morris is homophobic or not homophobic, I think they're just gay for money.

Philip Morris have smuggled themselves into this world by not looking like Philip Morris at all. By the end of my adventure I'm going to have quite a sore hand from unscrewing all the Babushkas.

Vale

How can I not append this? Following a lifetime of smoking, Senator Jesse Helms underwent heart surgery in 1992 and quit cigarettes. He died in 2008 from vascular dementia, a form of dementia associated with smoking.

ARE VAPES LEFT-WING, RIGHT-WING, LABOR, LIBERAL, LIBERTARIAN, GREEN, FASCIST, CAPITALIST, NIHILIST, SOCIALIST OR ALT-RIGHT?

I need to work out which parties support vaping and which parties don't. And how Philip Morris will play this, to try to convince law makers to legalise the IQOS.

On the steps of parliament, Savvas Dimitriou, Managing Director of Vapoureyes Australia, looked bothered when politics came up, fidgeting with his Greek prayer beads.

Savvas told me he is left-wing but, almost exclusively, the politicians who'll advocate for vaping are to the right of him, sometimes far to the right, and often the ones seen as kooky. These politicians dip into their libertarian worldview: the government should back off telling people what to do and what not to do. The vaping issue slots neatly into this political position. People should be able to vape because people should have free choice.

Sounds simple. Why the anxious prayer bead fidget? What's the problem? These same politicians fear creeping sharia, African criminals and asylum seekers. And Savvas doesn't fear those things.

Fiona Patten is the one political joy for Savvas Dimitriou, his ray of hope, the solidarity he embraces, which is why he happily turned up to her forum. A libertarian streak runs through Fiona, but she doesn't mind burqas and Black people.

Fiona and Savvas both want to loosen the laws around vaping. Because vaping tumbled into town ten or so years ago, and legislators weren't ready, the laws around vaping (at the time of typing this sentence) aren't really laws around *vaping*. They're more like a piece of flypaper with bits of old laws stuck to it; laws drafted long ago that, coincidentally, overlap with vaping. Compounding this mess, these laws are different in each state. So it's hard to write about the state of play without qualifying statement after qualifying statement, asterisks raining down like snowflakes in a snowstorm.

I'll give it a go.

Nicotine is the stimulant that hooks you on tobacco. It occurs naturally in tobacco, and can also be extracted from it, but a very old law decided that nicotine could only be sold in the form of tobacco products like cigarettes. That law was passed to stop the sale of dangerous nicotine pesticides.

Later, the pharmaceutical industry developed nicotine patches and chewing gum, claiming these products could wean smokers off smoking. But because these products were tobacco-free, that old pesticide law made them illegal. Big Pharma set their minds to lobbying. A federal body, these days called the Therapeutic Goods Administration, rules on new medical products, and they agreed to green-light these gums and patches.

Which brings us to vaping. Thanks to that old pesticide law, vapes can't be sold in Australia, asterisk.

However, the components of vapes that don't contain nicotine *can* be sold in Australia. This means the actual vaping devices, like the pens and boxy doodads you see folks huffing in doorways, can be sold. And the juices you put in them, with their flavourings and chemicals, can be sold too, provided they don't contain nicotine.

A different law allows people – but not companies – to import small quantities of nicotine for personal use, asterisk. So, what happens is that a vaper buys the handheld device and nicotine-free juice in Australia, then orders a bottle of liquid nicotine from New Zealand and mixes it in. Or they'll buy the flavoured juice, like mango and strawberry, premixed with nicotine from New Zealand.

The flypaper approach to lawmaking leads to this. A vape shop sits a two-minute traipse down my street. I can wander in, buy a vape device, lean on the counter, pull out my phone, order Frozen Fruit Monster nicotine juice from the same shop's very website, and have it arrive on my doorstep, from New Zealand, in a day or two.

One more exhausting tangle. According to the law, you need a doctor's prescription to order that small quantity of nicotine juice. However, the law doesn't explicitly state that a vape company has to ask for that prescription. So, in practice, you don't need one.

So are vapes legal in Australia? To sound like a particularly infuriating Buddhist monk: No. *Gives wry curl of the lip.* And yes.

Savvas's ray of hope

'Adults should be allowed to be adults,' Fiona Patten tells me in her office in inner-city Brunswick, along a street filled with Lebanese cake shops. She serves in the upper house in the Victorian parliament. In 2017, the Australian Cyclist Party merged with the

Australian Sex Party. That's an image: cyclists merging into a lane with the Sex Party's shaggin' wagon. Together, they formed the Reason Party.

As the founder of the Sex Party, Fiona also ran the National Museum of Erotica, and artwork from the defunct museum has made its way onto her office walls. I cannot furnish you with more details of these artworks because I'm avoiding making eye contact with them.

Fiona says attention must be paid to how any behaviour affects others. 'However, if an adult chooses to drink or to take cannabis or to take MDMA, then that should be largely in the hands of the adult rather than the government. Vaping obviously follows from that.'

'People know enough about wine and MDMA,' I say, almost entirely not noticing the poster of a half-naked Jane Fonda behind her. 'So people can make informed choices about popping pills and imbibing bags of goon. Is enough known about vaping yet?'

'I think what we do know about vaping is that it is a lot less harmful than smoking.' She points me to a UK National Health Service endorsement of e-cigarettes. This endorsement is to the chagrin of bodies like the World Health Organization and Quit Victoria, who don't like vaping at all. Most claims that vaping holds health benefits are anecdotal; they come from people who are more likely to have self-tattooed their arms than spilled ink for a peer-reviewed medical journal. It's harder to dismiss the word of the NHS.

'99.9 per cent of people who choose to vape, it's because they no longer want to smoke. I don't think anyone actually disputes that it's less harmful than smoking,' Fiona insists.

I'm concerned that my interaction with Fiona is coming across as cold. In fact, we're laughing a lot. For instance:

'IQOS . . . They pronounce it "eye-kose". But I'm going to make it "I-cough", revenge for Philip Morris snubbing me.'

'Ha ha. Or "high-cost", because it costs so much.'

'Ha ha ha.'

I wish it was funny to read people laughing, because I'm just laughing up and down town all day. Call Fiona or Father Bob, they'll tell you. Yes, yes, I know laughter is as infectious as the self-tattoos on those aforementioned arms, but scattering conversations with 'ha ha ha' just doesn't work on the page.

Anyway, Fiona is saying vapes are less harmful than cigarettes. Let's dig into that. If a product touts that it's '99 per cent fat free', it may well contain several cups of sugar. If a product touts that it's '99 per cent sugar free', it could contain fourteen scoops of lard. Attention is drawn to the danger it isn't, not the danger it is. Is the same thing happening with vapes?

The WHO and Quit wouldn't dispute that vapes are less harmful in certain ways; they don't emit smoke, so they don't contain the carcinogens in that. But they could cause other respiratory problems. The vaper draws into their lungs water, nicotine, flavourings and propylene glycol or vegetable glycerine.

I ask Fiona about this. Putting aside that a vape lacks smoke, are there other health concerns?

Fiona responds that the news is awash with stories of vaping deaths. This is true. A number of American teenagers have died from vaping. But, Fiona points out, on the same day a person dies from vaping, 1300 Americans die from cigarettes. Where's the news about that?

Because, as we've discussed, the white supremacist's high Jew IQ theory is suspect, it's not until I'm back home, listening to my audio notes, that it twigs she dodged my question.

Oh well. I guess she's a better politician than I'm a journalist.

Next, Fiona hands me a book, *No Fire, No Smoke*, in which health experts present the case for vaping. She launched the book at Parliament House; Labor's then Minister for Health, Jenny Mikakos, called Fiona out for this. The subtitle of the book is 'Global State of Tobacco Harm Reduction 2018'. Squint and read the tiny print in the acknowledgments and you learn something called The Foundation for a Smoke-Free World funded the book. Shadowland builds. Dig deep into that foundation and you'll learn they are 100 per cent funded by Philip Morris International.

Fiona suggests she didn't dig deep. 'Unfortunately, there was some tobacco funding. That got me into a bunch of trouble.'

Ultimately, Philip Morris is in competition with the vape industry. Philip Morris wants IQOS to win the day, not vapes. But it's a complicated relationship. Philip Morris are like the US military, and the vape industry are the Kurdish rebels. The US will use the Kurds, so long as they're helpful, but throw them under the bus at any given moment. And vice versa.

In Japan, Philip Morris's dream has come true. There, the IQOS is legal, but vapes are forbidden.

In other countries, including Australia, where the government is uptight about both vapes and IQOS, Philip Morris is playing the long game. Stage one is helping loosen the laws around vapes, even though they're a competing product, because that will soften the path for legalising the IQOS.

The Greens tout a harm reduction policy. They admit that taking heroin and ecstasy is dangerous, but see that as a reason to support safe injecting rooms and pill testing at music festivals. So you'd think the Greens would support vaping, because while it's potentially dangerous it's less dangerous than smoking.

While the vape industry is mainly made up of small businesses, at least in Australia, the common perception is that Big Tobacco, the most maniacal capitalists in the world, are the secret force behind vaping. And the Greens hate maniacal capitalism; their voters are more likely than most to throw a brick through a Starbucks window. And those guys just do coffee and danishes. So, the Greens will not be supporting Fiona's vape push in parliament.

On the other side of politics, the Liberals tout free choice but, being conservative, scoff at hippie concepts like pill testing and safe injecting rooms. Fiona won't find many friends there, nor in the Labor Party. Our two major parties defer to the Australian Medical Association, and they'll not be canoodling with the vape industry anytime soon. They don't trust them one bit. You can see why vape activists kiss that golden ticket, the NHS endorsement. Very precious, very rare.

Fiona supports Philip Morris's professed mission to move away from cigarettes and towards smoke-free alternatives.

I say puffing an IQOS might affect the body differently to puffing a vape, but putting science aside, there is another distinction. The difference between Philip Morris and businesses like Vapoureyes Australia is that only one is responsible for cemeteries upon cemeteries of bodies.

'Can they never redeem themselves? Never, ever, ever?' Fiona says.

She points to other companies that changed course, finding their way back into our hearts. 'Our government does business with Monsanto, quite happily.' Monsanto developed Agent Orange, the chemical sprayed over civilians during the Vietnam War. They were recently acquired by chemical giant Bayer. 'Hugo Boss made the uniforms for the Nazis, quite happily. And yet I know numerous politicians who wear Hugo Boss suits.'

I reckoned with the question of when to forgive companies that cooperated with Nazis back in 1987, when Mike D from the Beastie Boys wore a crowbarred Volkswagen badge necklace. I wanted to look like him, so followed suit. How infuriating for Hitler, in the afterlife, to see the emblem of the company that built Love Bugs for the master race appropriated by the Beastie Boys, three Jews spitting Black music. Okay, two Jews and one half-Jew, for the hip-hop and/or racial purists.

Strolling out of Fiona's office, I pass a trio leaning on tripods and Pelican cases, ready to interview her next. They're from *Vice*, a media company that succeeded in a course correction as dramatic as the one Philip Morris is attempting. Decades ago, they were trailblazers in the field of button-pushing irony around race, sex and other cultural landmines. Like *South Park*, they were beloved by Generation X. But talk about a U-turn: now they instruct people on how to tread carefully and avoid setting off those very same explosives. When to use 'she/her', when to use 'they', when to use 'ze'. *Vice* disavows their past, clearly seeing the nineties as their period of sewing suits for the Nazis.

'Hey,' I mumble. 'Hey,' they mumble.

I wander out and head to a Lebanese cake shop, sip a coffee and take it all in.

Philip Morris benefits from the political movement fighting for vaping as a harm reduction tool. They can jump into this canoe, even though the paddlers already in there are paddling with different motives. Philip Morris lie back and let others row, a piece of straw between their teeth, temporarily holding off on their insistence that the IQOS is not a vape.

New moral code

A UK friend sends a photo from the London Underground. New billboards have gone up. 'Never Look Back' the headline reads, next to a handsome man. 'Watch now. How I Quit. ChangeIncorporated. com.' This a *Vice* project – their logo is stamped in the corner.

I check out the site. Change Incorporated wants you to stop smoking. The site serves you with punchy article and videos in the style of *Vice*'s main venture. The photos are squeezed full of young people – the least attractive more attractive than anyone in your friendship circle. The overarching message is: Quitting cigarettes full-stop is the best thing you can do. But, if you're not willing to do that, how about vaping?

A headline on this UK site captures my eye, 'If vaping is safe why is it banned in Australia?' I click through to a video and there's Fiona Patten. She's touting her pro-vaping message. That's what the *Vice* guys in her lobby must have been waiting to film.

Pull your magnifying glass out, then place your other magnifying glass in front of that, and you'll discover this *Vice* venture is funded by Philip Morris International. Shadowland.

Here's Philip Morris once again trying to normalise vapes, playing the long game that this'll ultimately help to normalise the IQOS.

But building a shadowland serves another special purpose for Philip Morris: outside parties, like *Vice*, can say things Philip Morris cannot. Philip Morris can't say that their new devices help wean you off cigarettes. That would be claiming these devices serve a medical purpose, which would set off a chain of consequences Philip Morris does not wish for. For one, government regulators would want to test these claims. Then they'd ponder: If they serve a medical purpose, should a doctor's prescription be compulsory to purchase one? Should they only be for sale at pharmacies?

But an outside party, not selling the product, in this case *Vice*, can be looser with language. They can make woollier claims.

I'm beginning to understand more deeply the contours of the new moral code. The rules we must abide by to move smoothly through the world. They're different from those when I came of age. It's a very good time to be Philip Morris. You can give people heart palpitations, but only if they're literal ones (respiratory disease) and not figurative ones (offence). *Vice* got wind of what's up and adapted. They sheared off their old fleece, no longer offensive like in the nineties, these days really putting the *ze* in emphysema.

CAN PHILIP MORRIS EVER
BE FORGIVEN?

'I voted for the Sex Party once,' my dad reveals over coffee in my kitchen. I've been telling him about my meeting with Fiona Patten. 'I used to be a poll clerk at the elections.'

Australian-born, to parents who escaped the Nazis, I want to know what he makes of Fiona's view that people should forgive Philip Morris like they have Hugo Boss, the makers of Nazi uniforms. (My mum cut it finer, born in Uzbekistan while her parents were fleeing Poland for Australia.)

My dad says he met a Sex Party pamphleteer one election. 'It was this young woman. She was wearing a tracksuit. It wasn't a normal tracksuit, it was a harlequin tracksuit, a diamond pattern, red and white. And I thought, *Oh God, that looks really good*. And I voted for the Sex Party purely because I was influenced by what she was wearing.'

Yes, but what if she was wearing a Hugo Boss suit?

'Well, I'm now driving a German car. And that would have been considered a cardinal sin for someone in the Melbourne Jewish community, say, in the 1950s.' He hoons the streets of Balaclava in a BMW. 'I feel pleased that I've got a German car that was not particularly associated with the Nazis.'

'Would you do a Mercedes?'

'Yes.'

'Would you do a Volkswagen?'

'Less so. The Volkswagen was particularly associated with Nazism.'

'So you *do* draw the line somewhere.'

'It's not a case of I wouldn't get it,' he clarifies.

He lists German car options, from guilt-free to dicey, based on their proximity to Hitler. BMW is guilt-free. How convenient, my BMW 320i–cruising papa. Then Audi, then Mercedes and, rounding off last place, the Hate Bug makers, Volkswagen. Car listings should cover this. Too much talk of mileage, not enough on the Jewish Question.

Should Philip Morris be forgiven, I ask, if we take them at their word that they are phasing out cigarettes for healthier alternatives?

He rubs a temple on his nearly bald dome and puts down his coffee. He is wearing a wrist support that he says is just from getting old.

'Well, I think you've got to be careful that you don't carry prejudices forever. Otherwise you'd say, "God, I should never go to Spain, they had the Spanish inquisition there."'

(My dad, later that day, emails me a photo of actor Timothée Chalamet: a still from the film *Dune*. 'THE GUY IN THE TOP PHOTO HAS THE SAME WRIST SUPPORT AS ME – I'M SUCH A FASHIONISTA!')

49

Critics of Philip Morris say that even if we accept that their Smoke-Free Future mission is a positive thing, what about the fact they are still selling cigarettes? How to reconcile the two, that they heal and they kill?

The pickle of this is the same as the pickle my father's father had to carry – his life was saved by the Nazis.

One day, my dad noticed a scar on the back of his father's neck, hidden in the folds. He asked him about it.

'He said, "Oh, I used to get these terrible headaches."' This was in the late 1930s, in Germany.' He was operated on; my father says it must have been a tumour. 'It was obviously very successful, the operation, because it never played up again. He would have had what was probably the most technologically advanced medical treatment in the world. And he got it for free, because it was part of the national social-service system that the Nazis had introduced.'

His father had slipped into the hospital system just in time, either in 1938 or 1939; by 1941 Jews had had their citizenship revoked and, with it, all rights to social services like medical care.

'I had this vision that here's my dad in the hospital, and he's getting the best possible medical surgery in the world, and downstairs the Nazis are beating up other Jews in the street.'

He asked his father whether the surgeon thought it was odd, this dichotomy: save Jew in the hospital, beat Jew in the street.

'My father said Germans were funny people and if something was the law, they obeyed it to the nth degree.' The surgeon in question was held in such regard, he toured Melbourne in the 1950s to lecture here. My grandfather popped over to one of his talks to say thank you.

So, reflecting on this story, and assuming IQOS is safer than cigarettes, do we prevent Philip Morris from saving a few because they kill so many others? I don't know how to answer that, although both my father and I were only born and now sit at this kitchen table because that other pickle played out the way it did.

I get greedy. I recall a photo atop a piano, growing up. My father and his father, cigarettes resting between their fingers. His father died of emphysema, I think? A horrible way to die, but perhaps this book lacks personal stakes. It doesn't get more personal than Philip Morris killing your grandfather. What a logline: 'Saved by the Nazis, killed by Philip Morris.' This can be a tale of revenge, modelled on those Quentin Tarantino films I love. *Kill Phil* boings into the ear as pleasantly as *Puff Piece*.

My dad confirms his father smoked, and that emphysema is inked on the death certificate. But the story is more tangled. He worked as a toolmaker in a plastics factory, cutting metal moulds. How can we separate the fumes from that factory with the carcinogens from his Craven A (not a Philip Morris brand)? Either way, whatever was destroying his insides, it destroyed them enough that he could no longer work. He lost his job and fell into a funk; a deeper funk – his wife had died a few years earlier.

My dad was enrolled at university at this time.

'One day I came home from the lectures and he said, "I tried to hang myself, but it didn't work." And he showed me his telephone cable that had broken. Couldn't hold his weight.'

A doctor said he should try an aged-care home. My dad arranged this.

'He'd been there two days and he threw himself down the stairs. He didn't die immediately, but he must have suffered fairly tremendous brain damage because he was in a coma. It must have been for the best part of a year, till he finally died. And on his death certificate they gave as cause of death: emphysema.'

This is the first time I'm hearing this; I'm goosebumped and horrified.

What to make of it all? Does it have anything to do with cigarettes or did that float away somewhere during the story?

Maybe cigarettes helped calm my grandfather's troubles somewhat, like they did for Father Bob's dad on his deathbed. Maybe the carcinogens amplified his pain, adding to the cholent of malaise.

One more question I don't know how to answer. But with this, I can't go anywhere else to ask. Life doesn't roll out stories in simple, cordoned-off ways.

Philosophy

My dad has his own smoking history. Age seventeen, he decided to become a beatnik. 'I had my goatee beard and I smoked a pipe and had these big floppy jumpers.' He procured a second pipe somewhere along the way, a corncob one. I know because in Grade 3 I grabbed it from the mantelpiece, donned a sailor's cap, drew an anchor on my arm, and wandered the schoolyard as Popeye for a whole term. The taste from that unlit yet long smoked pipe was tart, but I enjoyed it, in the same way I enjoyed sticking my tongue on a 9-volt battery.

This beatnik talk propels me out the kitchen to fetch a yellowing volume of poetry. 'Ah!' My dad smiles. 'Kerouac, Jack Kerouac.' He opens it to the fountain-penned inscription. 'Oh! Look at that. *Alexander Safran, 1961.* Isn't that wonderful, I'm glad you've got it.'

See? He likes me.

'Kerouac was almost like a god for wannabe beatniks like me. He and Søren Kierkegaard, who was a Danish philosopher.'

My antenna twitches as he says the word 'philosopher'.

'I tried to read him,' he goes on, meaning Kierkegaard, 'and got as far as about page two before I had to put him down.'

My dad beats himself up for not finishing the book. Says it reflects poorly on him, shows him up to be lazy.

'That's not true.'

'Yes, it is.'

I tell him if he's lazy, good grief, what am I? The word count of my manuscript hardly budged this week.

'If you've felt lazy – I cannot tell a lie – the gene would be from me.'

He mightn't have finished Kierkegaard, but he did study philosophy at university. I ask him to dig into that discipline for the question at hand: 'When a cigarette company has done awful things, if they do a good thing, how are we meant to process it?'

He says he read Plato's *Republic*. 'He had this idea that there was some pure form of red and every other red was simply a variation of this totally pure form. And similarly, with a chair. There was some concept of a perfect chair and any other chairs, well, they varied from this perfect notion.'

'How does that help me with my cigarette book?' I ask. What about the question at hand?

'Well unfortunately Plato isn't around to answer that. Nor is Aristotle.'

The consequentialists

I know a philosopher. I met Peter Singer at the Kadimah, a Yiddish library and playhouse four minutes from my home.

I email him at Princeton University, where he is a Professor of Bioethics. The *New Yorker* has called him the most influential philosopher alive. He focuses on ethical arguments that push the case we should be kinder to animals; that we shouldn't eat them, for a start. He raised eyebrows when he said of bestiality, 'It's not wrong inherently in a moral sense.'

'I'm a consequentialist,' Peter emails back to my questions, 'which means I think about the future, not the past, unless the past is going to have an impact on the future, as sometimes it does. If Tyson, one of the world's largest factory-farmed meat producers, starts marketing plant-based alternatives – they are putting quite a lot of money into developing them – I will be happy to encourage people to buy them.'

So that's how a consequentialist sees it. *If* (and that '*if*' needs to be bigger and redder than the *It* on the cover of the Stephen King book – but *if* Philip Morris starts to help lives, what applies to Tyson also applies to Philip Morris.

That all makes sense. Don't throw out the baby with the psycho-path water. If the Nazis will cut out your tumour or a cigarette giant helps you quit cigarettes, sure, why not?

I'm noting something else, though. The list is growing: Father Bob, Rabbi Gutnick, Fiona Patten, my dad and now the conse-quentialists. They all have one thing in common. *None* of them are worked up like I am by Philip Morris and their brand-new hustle.

Am I barking up the wrong tree? Is it bleeding obvious that Philip Morris should be free to pursue their Smoke-Free Future without meddling? Why is this rankling me? Am I mad? Is this not a thing?

A WORLD WITHOUT CIGARETTES

What might this utopia, this world without cigarettes, look like? That is the goal of health departments around the world and also the professed aim of Philip Morris.

We don't have to use computer modelling or host a panel of futurologists to find out. Victorian prisons banned tobacco in 2015. At the time, a prison source told the *Herald Sun*, 'All hell is going to break out when they are stopped from lighting up.' Back then at least 80 per cent of prisoners smoked.

Nigel, whom I've known for sixteen years, works in a prison. So his name is not Nigel – that's me, at his request, throwing people who know him at the prison off the scent.

Nigel sits on a telephone book in the café down my street. He was born a dwarf. (Nigel is insistent I disguise his identity thoroughly. He's brought it up three times already.)

Before I can ask him about the ban, he rolls into a story about a guy he knew who used to chew tobacco.

'It's not a thing anymore, but thirty years ago it was. You just chewed on this shit and then you spat it out,' Nigel says in his thick Romanian accent. (Now his bosses will be searching their minds for a worker who is a Romanian dwarf.)

'It rots all your teeth, then it rots the gums,' he continues, the bell atop his velvet cap jingling. 'And then you get cancer of the mouth. You don't get cancer of the lungs, you get cancer of the mouth.'

His friend ended up dying of cancer that ate away his mouth. Nigel's point is that this man didn't *smoke* tobacco, yet he died a tobacco-related death. So the fact the HeatStick doesn't emit smoke doesn't discount the possibility its tobacco could still kill.

I didn't come to Nigel for this, I came for prison stories, but it's an excellent point. If someone from Philip Morris ever agrees to talk to me, I'll have to ask them about that.

Nigel has his own tobacco history. He quit cigarettes after a medical check-up years ago. The nurse told him her brother-in-law, a heavy smoker, had the same birthdate as him and he had died of heart disease a week before. Nigel took this as an omen. People are strange – the fact that it was a nurse who told him this distracts from the fact that it was numerology, not science, that convinced him to quit.

'And I'd been quitting for years. It's highly addictive. In the prisons, the most trafficked drug is tobacco. All the other drugs have gone down, down, down. A pouch of tobacco, what does it cost now, forty or fifty bucks? It sells for $1300 inside the prison.'

I wow. He says no other narcotic hits anywhere near that price. Nigel's point, another good one, is that the prison economy is the ultimate when-push-comes-to-shove proof. Tobacco, above even heroin, holds uniquely addictive properties. 'Everybody in prison's had every drug that exists. What's the one they want? *Just give me another Philip Morris, will ya?*'

Craftsman Sailors Rum, Bond Street, Choice, Longbeach and Peter Jackson are all roll-your-own tobacco brands sold by Philip Morris.

Nigel says the stench of cigarettes is as much a feature of a prison as metal bars. Far from the 2015 tobacco ban working, the black market runs like clockwork. The guards are eager to supplement their income. But unlike with heroin, they don't have to deal with drug dealers on the outside, just tobacconists or convenience store attendants. TAB accounts are set up and girlfriends on the outside pay money into them in exchange for the tobacco. And if a guard is busted supplying tobacco to a prisoner, they won't go to jail – at worst they'll be fired.

'The prisoners roll these really skinny cigarettes,' Nigel says, picking a poppyseed from his ruby-encrusted teeth. 'What's the thinnest paper you could get in prison?'

'Toilet paper?' I try.

'Bible paper. They're tearing up the New Testament. There's Bibles everywhere in prison, so everybody's rolling their own Bible cigarettes.'

This image appeals to me so much that I want to forgive Philip Morris for everything.

Nigel hops down from the telephone book. He pays the bill, handstands and cartwheels out of the café.

I asked at the top of this chapter: *What might this utopia, this world without cigarettes, look like?*

I have an answer now. A world without cigarettes is a world with cigarettes. To misquote poet Emily Dickinson, the heart-disease wants what the heart-disease wants. People will procure cigarettes by any means necessary.

This helps Philip Morris's case. If people will smoke no matter what, it makes sense to offer a lower risk alternative. Legal note: I explicitly forbid Philip Morris from using that sentence as a quote on promotional material. Because, it must be made clear, the premise of that sentence is that the IQOS holds a lower risk of harm. And we don't know that. At least, not yet.

Prisons are teetering on anarchy and violence at any given moment; men and women determined to bash the staff, hang themselves, hang others. This is another reason Philip Morris can steam on without resistance. People in authority, in this case prison guards, have concluded that there are bigger fish to fry. More so, there's a buck in it. Thirteen-hundred clams, in fact.

The Second Epistle of Bob

I swing by Father Bob's again to talk this through.

'I have a question for you about prisoners.'

'Christmas?' Father Bob says.

'No, prisoners.'

On top of his eyes turning wonkier, and his nose capillaries redder, his ears become harder of hearing each visit.

His big black poodle springs about the boardroom table, youthful and lively as ever. I tell him about jailbirds using pages from the New Testament for rollies.

'Yes, I can imagine that.' He thinks for a moment. 'Well, it's got to be used for something, you know what I mean? "The word of God enters everyone's mouth."'

He's paraphrasing a Bible verse: 'The word that God puts in my mouth, that I shall speak.'

'But is Jesus or God getting angry if you're tearing a pa—'

'Nah. One of them told us – I don't know who's the one who told us – *eat the word of God*.'

'But maybe you're not allowed to desecrate a holy book or the word of —'

'That's your lot.'

Yes, my lot – the Jews, the People of the Book – don't use the Torah for rollies. Although, thinking about it, the Torah is a scroll, so it might be better for the job than the New Testament. It is true Jews treat holy books reverentially, burying worn out and damaged ones in the cemetery.

'What about the – what is it? – the thurible?' I ask. I always get 'thurible' – the metal ball filled with burning incense, swung by the priest, spreading smoke throughout the church – confused with 'theremin', the musical instrument played throughout The Beach Boys' hit 'Good Vibrations'.

I point out that spreading smoke is an existing Christian ritual that pleases God. Bob sees where I'm heading with this and he likes this apologia, this ecclesiastical defence of the prison rollie. Yes, a prison rollie, spreading smoke, is pretty much a thurible. We talk it through and end up agreeing that Christians who *aren't* smoking Bibles might be the ones in the wrong. Why aren't they as committed to God as the prisoners?

Bob is suddenly distracted: 'There's a nice man walking past the door with his little Mecca cap on.' I turn and see a Muslim guy strolling by the shopfront window of the Father Bob Maguire

Foundation. We agree it would be inadvisable to tear pages from a Qur'an and light them on fire. Bible cigarettes should be limited to the holy book of the smoker's own faith, in the interest of community harmony.

I move on to other matters. 'And if you're a guard, are you allowed to take tobacco in to sell to prisoners?' (The automated transcription service I use for my audio notes transcribes 'guard' as 'God'; artificial intelligence wryly commenting on the power dynamics in a prison.)

'I presume it's against the law,' Bob says.

'What about God's law? What's Jesus thinking, looking down on this?'

'Jesus would say they shouldn't be in prison anyway.' Here we go. For Bob the crime is never the crime. Bob decides Jesus is cool with guards smuggling tobacco into prison, although he can't back this up with a scriptural citation. Bob's wrath is finally aroused when I tell him about the mark-up. Thirteen-hundred bucks for a pouch.

'That's taking advantage! But *that's* capitalism!' he snaps. 'Even in the prison, the wardens are capitalists. Disorderly capitalists. Unthinking capitalists. Wanton, W-A-N-T-O-N capitalists,' he preaches, exclamation points exploding everywhere. 'And we should have gone beyond that by now, after 200 years. But we learned it all from our origins here as bloody convicts. And the wardens learned how to take advantage. Prison wardens will have to learn to put the prisoners first.'

'Yeah,' I say, coming around to his way of thinking. 'They should just have a little mark-up, like maybe five or ten bucks.'

'Why?'

'Oh, no mark-up at all, you're saying?'

'Bloody tobacco should be provided.'

Bob believes prisoners' smokes should be paid for by the state. His old-school Labor Party values sort of scan here, but they sort of don't. We are talking government-funded cigarettes, after all, not chickenpox vaccinations. But Bob's brain is living in an alternative, contorted reality, where Prime Minister Cough Whitlam is granting universal ruin-your-health care for all.

I wander past Bob's Collingwood Football Club memorabilia, the photoshopped portrait of Pope John Paul II in a Magpies guernsey, the several rickety Archibald Prize paintings Bob has sat for, because he can't say no to anyone, and out onto the chilly Port Melbourne street.

I think back to Nigel the Romanian dwarf; his Bible cigarette tale brought me here. So much is projection, I realise. I had called Nigel strange because what pushed him to quit cigarettes was numerology, not science. How's he different from a Haitian whistling past a Red Cross medical tent on his way to visit a voodoo doctor about his sore foot? But then, how am I different? I've tasked myself with understanding tobacco, smoke, nicotine and addiction, yet so far I've not spoken to a single scientist or doctor. But I have visited a rabbi and, twice, a priest.

SMOOTH CRIMINALS

After another day spent poking around Philip Morris material, I lie on the couch and go on a *Rage* binge. No wonder I had a Michael Jackson poster stuck above my bed. He's on one side of the stage . . . what? . . . how's he? . . . he's moonwalking. Good Lord! Now he's in a speakeasy, done up like a thirties gangster. Feet fluttering hither and thither. Now he's somehow anchoring his feet and leaning forwarder and forwarder without tipping over. If I was the Annie in that song's refrain, the answer would be, 'No, I'm not okay, I broke my nose – I shouldn't have leant forward like that.'

But I've come to a new conclusion. Michael Jackson, you ruled the roost during your lifetime, but it's finally time to hand over your crown, there's a new king of fancy footwork: Philip Morris.

A vape differs from an IQOS, being free of tobacco leaf. Yet both can be classed as e-cigarettes, so whenever there's any good news around those, Philip Morris soaks it up.

Philip Morris tweets: 'There's a lot of noise surrounding e-cigarettes at the moment. We stand by claims that using science backed smoke-free alternatives is less harmful than continuing to smoke. As do Public Health England.'

That's a government agency that reports to the UK's National Health Service. The NHS indeed tells doctors that 'patients should be advised that e-cigarettes are deemed to be substantially less harmful than smoking'. But they go on to clarify that by 'e-cigarettes' they mean vapes, not devices like the IQOS. 'Because [those] devices contain tobacco, they come with all the long-term health concerns of tobacco, so we recommend these should not be used.' In fact, the NHS has kicked them out of the building. The actual building. 'These products should not be allowed on NHS premises and grounds.'

But Philip Morris has taken the NHS's explicit rejection of the IQOS and, through the nimblest of moonwalks, spin turns, heel pulls, whisks and pirouettes of the English language, given the impression that the NHS *endorses* their flagship product. Well done on that remarkable fancy footwork, Philip Morris.

I look up and see that *Rage* has moved on to 'Thriller'. Michael Jackson is gyrating around a cemetery. In a reversal of the Philip Morris experience, people are coming out of graves.

IT CAME IN A DREAM

One bugbear of vapers is this. (Bugbear, another vape juice: Fuji apple mixed with pumpkin spice. (I can't slow down each time this happens; just assume every word that isn't 'and' or 'but' is a kooky vape juice.))

One bugbear of vapers is this: there's a myth that vaping is a plot cooked up by Big Tobacco.

So, how *did* vaping come to be? It turns out religion and mysticism were key. Ha! So it hasn't been off-point that I have been drawn to a priest and a rabbi for answers.

The Scythians are Iranian nomads who find themselves, in 5 BC, in what is roughly modern-day Ukraine. They communicate with gods by consuming mind-altering plants. The Greek historian Herodotus writes: 'The Scythians take some of this hemp seed, and, creeping under the felt coverings, throw it upon the red-hot stones; immediately it smokes, and gives out such a vapour as no Grecian vapour-bath can exceed; the Scyths, delighted, shout for joy.' So, vaping.

Circa 1600, under the Mughal Empire in South Asia, either physician Irfan Sheikh or Abu'l-Fath Gilani thinks up the hookah pipe. Tobacco is squeezed into a compartment within the pipe, which is heated (not burned!) by a bowl of water, with the vapour inhaled through a tube. (Like many, my intrigue with hookah pipes began with the drug-fiend caterpillar in the *Alice in Wonderland* picture book.)

In 1927, American Joseph Robinson files a patent for an 'Electronical Vaporizer'. You can google it, but don't do it at work because it looks like a penis. An electronic element heats a compound, which is to be inhaled through a cylinder. His proposal makes no mention of nicotine or tobacco, and nothing comes of his dildo, I mean vaporizer.

In 1963, 40-a-day-smoker Herbert Gilbert, a Pennsylvanian, files a patent for a 'Smokeless Non-Tobacco Cigarette'. It never goes anywhere, not least because his prototypes are burned-not-heated in a warehouse fire.

By the late seventies, NASA space engineer Phil Ray is begging his doctor to help him quit smoking. They squeeze nicotine-soaked paper into plastic tubes that have the same dimensions as a cigarette. They take their idea beyond the doctor's office; their 'Favor' smoke-free cigarettes make it all the way to TV commercials, where you titter at the actor's eighties haircut and *Greed is Good* suit. Favors are a flop – the nicotine evaporates before the packs are sold. Plus the Food and Drugs Administration is incandescent that they went through with all this without so much as a phone call to them.

All this history wends its way to a city boy and intellectual from Northern China, Hon Lik. In the early seventies, around age eighteen, the Communist Party sends him to work with farmers as part of their 'ideological remoulding' program, to ensure Hon Lik doesn't stray from communism. The anxiety of his new reality drives him to smoke. When he returns to the city, he becomes a Chinese-medicine pharmacist, but he can't quit his two- to three-pack-a-day habit. On top of this, his father has developed lung cancer from cigarettes.

One night, Hon Lik falls asleep after forgetting to peel off his nicotine patch. 'That one night I had continuous nightmares,' he later tells a tech conference. 'And those nightmares were very monstrous.' He is drowning in the sea, pulled deep beneath the waves. A flash of light. The sea vaporises and now he's floating in a fog. He awakes, thoughts of science and reflections on the dream intertwining.

Hon Lik built radios in high school and knows his way around circuit boards, so he knuckles down at his workbench and begins vaporising food additives by ultrasound. This is 2001. Within two years, he's honed his idea, employing a high-frequency, piezo-electric, ultrasound-emitting element to vaporise a pressurised jet of nicotine liquid. (I fear you suspect I don't know what I'm on about here. A gun expert once told me you can tell when a crime writer doesn't know about guns: they go overboard describing the gun.) The first vape hits the shelves in 2004.

The history of vaping is driven by addicts, not tobacco company executives. Men impelled by the anguish of their compulsion and self-hatred; shame is underrated as a driver of human progress.

Eerie morning of the soul

'So, we're driving down Nepean Highway,' I report to my traitorous audio recorder. 'And there's clouds hanging over. Gum trees. Are they gum trees, you reckon?'

'They look like gum trees, don't they?' says Savvas, the man you met on the steps of parliament. He's tightly clasping the wheel of his black SUV.

'Some guy walking his dog,' I continue. 'Some of the streetlights are on, some of the streetlights are off.'

Perhaps tiring of my shopping list approach to setting the scene, Savvas laments, 'It's not so much the dark night of the soul but the eerie morning of the soul, because this weekend has been awful and today is going to be very difficult.' The clock has not yet struck 6 am; he's driving me to go see his warehouse.

He says fewer orders than usual have come through to Vapoureyes, both for vape devices and juices.

'This weekend was a precipitous drop. More than enough to pucker my arsehole.'

What does he think drove this drop, this sphincter tightener?

'Fear.'

Vaping tragedies are popping up in headlines for the first time. At this point around a dozen American kids have died and over a hundred have been hospitalised. The fear is percolating out there.

Groups like the WHO say these deaths prove their point: the vaping industry needs to be shut down. Folks like Savvas suspect there's more to the story; that the deaths weren't caused by the devices and juices sold by people like him. They speculate that kids are buying black-market juice laced with THC, a mind-altering ingredient found in cannabis, and that an additive to THC, vitamin E acetate, is the real killer. Savvas reasons that these deaths prove *his* point: governments need to smooth the path for legal and well-regulated vaping.

Savvas regrets that the media won't cut his industry a break. A large part of that is they don't see vaping as I've described it – the story of NASA space engineers and Chinese dreamers, men on a hero's quest. Those men who slay a dragon outside the cave (in this case, addiction), who venture through the forest, battling demons and monsters (faulty prototypes and self-doubt), capture the boon (invent an e-cigarette) and return to the village to save others as they have saved themselves.

Rather, the media sees the vape story as all about Philip Morris – *Lord of the Smoke Rings: Return of the Finks*. And they can piece together that story easily enough. In 2017, Juul becomes an independent e-cigarette company; by the close of the following year, Philip Morris USA's parent company buys in, becoming co-owners.

And what about Hon Lik and his fever-dream inspired vape? In 2013 he sells his intellectual property to Imperial Brands, famous for Peter Stuyvesant and Drum. Tobacco multinationals didn't hatch vaping, but they've swooped into the nest.

I'm sounding so Generation X, snarling against selling out. But I've got to be honest, when I read that Hon Lik sold to Imperial for a rumoured $7.5 million, I thought, *Hey man, didn't they lowball you?*

Born again

A decade-long cigarette addict, Savvas wandered into a pub on the cusp of thirty and spotted an old friend of his with a hefty black contraption squeezed between his lips. He had no idea what it was. The friend flicked him a business card for some bloke's shop, which ended up being a shed in said bloke's backyard in Salisbury, Northern Adelaide.

Savvas, driving me to his warehouse, puts on his anthropologist hat and declares Salisbury 'the go-to-suburb you'd name if you wanted to generalise about bogans'. A hundred-and-fifty bucks bought Savvas a homemade vape and a bottle of Chinese juice. Since that day, late October 2013, he has never touched another cigarette.

'People don't realise, unless they've been a tobacco addict, just how all-encompassing it is. Catching a flight – it consumes you. All you can think about is, *I need to get off this plane and get a cigarette.* You wake up in the morning, first thing, you have a cigarette. After you have a meal, you have a cigarette. And if you don't do those things, something feels wrong. Not just mentally but also physiologically, because you're not having the nicotine hit when your body expects it. That addiction, trying to break it . . . And the worthlessness that you feel when you fail?'

Savvas looks weighed down, sinking further into his body the more he talks.

'You tell everybody, I've quit smoking and this is the time I'm actually going to do it. I'm using the gums, I'm using the patches, I've got my willpower. And then you fail and your friends will see it. You'll be at the pub, you have a cigarette, and they'll know. And you'll know that they know you fucked up, that you couldn't beat this thing. And everybody thinks it should be so simple. Why can't you quit? Why are you so shitty, that you can't give up this thing that you know is going to kill you. That's genuinely what it's like for smokers, that self-loathing.'

The darkness begins to wash away.

'So when you find something that can finally break it – when it finally releases you from it – holy shit. It's like a religious experience.

You just want to stand up and shout to the world about it. You want to tell everybody that you ever meet. I did this, I did this! I found this thing that saved my life and it can save your life as well.'

The vape world is a confederacy of subcultures, one being the vaper as born-again evangelical. The thing is, I'm the rare bird who buzzes Mormons up into my apartment for a chat and who takes Scientologists up on their offer of a free personality test. So I love this subculture of vapers, but I'm a poor judge as to whether the wider community would cross the road to avoid them.

'Quite literally what we're doing is saving people's lives,' exclaims Savvas, gripping his vape like an E-meter, soaring down the highway. 'I know it sounds like puffery. But spend five minutes with the customers we've serviced in our time, and you hear their stories and the struggles that they've had.'

But every religion needs a devil, and for evangelical vapers that's Simon Chapman. He's been awarded a medal by the WHO, and another by the National Heart Foundation (they give out medals?), for his campaigning against Big Tobacco over the decades. When vaping moseyed into town, he declared to the public and governments – with his considerable clout – that vaping is nothing but more Big Tobacco shenanigans.

'We make a real big difference to people's lives,' Savvas says, no longer chipper. 'To think that that's being taken away from us to satisfy the whims of a turd like Simon Chapman, so that that fucking arsehole can retain his own personal sense of accomplishment . . . It's sick. It is absolutely sick.'

The candy shop

Vapoureyes has just set up in Dandenong South, in Melbourne's industrial south-east. There's not a scuff mark in the shiny, brightly lit warehouse. We tootle up lanes stacked high with colourful bottles that look like they could be sold at Toyworld with a bubble blower taped onto them.

I should pen feel-good press releases for Vapoureyes. I told you they've just set up in Melbourne. Another way to put it? They've just been chased out of Adelaide by the law – the South Australian state government has banned businesses based there from selling vapes and juices online.

'My whole life is in boxes right now.' This Adelaidean on the run is yet to move these boxes, and his guitar, from the warehouse to the Airbnb where he's staying. 'How can I make plans? How can I make a future if I don't know what the fuck is going on?' At any given moment he could be shut down in Melbourne too.

None of the juices in the Dandenong warehouse contain nicotine. You'll need to squeeze and mix that in yourself, with nicotine delivered to you from Vapoureyes's New Zealand warehouse. Savvas tells me that back in South Australia this nicotine-free juice would be legal to sell if it was sold as food flavouring in Woolies, but it's illegal – run-out-of-town illegal – sold online as vape juice.

Head-scratchingly, vaping devices from Europe are required by law to declare 'This product contains nicotine which is a highly addictive substance'. Except they don't. They're merely metal and plastic contraptions. You can see why the public are bamboozled by the rules and regulations of the vape world.

Let's pause and ruminate over that label: 'This product contains nicotine which is a highly addictive substance'. Because God shines on Philip Morris, so much ends up serving their interest. How does this label serve Philip Morris? It frames the health battle as being against nicotine, not tobacco. Philip Morris pounces on this, declaring that the IQOS 'is not risk-free and delivers nicotine which is addictive'.

Let's go with a Hitler analogy here. I've tried mixing it up over the years, dabbling in Idi Amin, Augusto Pinochet and Slobodan Milošević, but nothing lands like Hitler. While true, Philip Morris's claim is a mind-fuck, gaslight, misdirection – it's like Hitler conceding, 'No, I'm not perfect, I've failed to pay many a parking fine.'

As with cigarettes, the nicotine in a HeatStick gets you hooked on deadly tobacco, without being deadly in and of itself. If the IQOS kills you it won't be because of the nicotine, it'll be because of the tobacco. Framing it as a war against nicotine, which is also in some vape juices, lets Philip Morris swerve around the salient point.

A forklift beeps by as Savvas shows off his wares. Not all vapers want to look like they're blowing a kazoo. For these folks there are mods – chunky contraptions so named because the original ones were modified torches, making use of their big fat batteries. This do-it-yourself subculture has only grown, producing tinkering hobbyists as passionate as those who restore old houses, knit jumpers, form rock bands or collect Scrabble dictionaries.

'This is their expression, the way they create,' Savvas says. 'There are entire communities of people who only exist within vaping, who only have friendship networks within vaping, who only wear clothing that's sold by vaping brands. For people who are socially isolated, that's an incredible thing. And then to be told, "We're going to take that away from you now." How would you feel about it? If your community was taken away from you?'

The answer is you'd have to prise my Scrabble dictionary from my cold dead hands. I can understand the passion.

We move deeper into the warehouse. Now evil clowns and demons and skeletons sneer down at us. This is the iconography of the heavy-metal album covers that bewitched me in primary school. Savvas plucks a bottle from the shelf called Killer Kustard. He says these zany flavours and madcap labels appeal to adults, helping wean them off the taste of tobacco.

Yet he concedes, 'There's another part of me that looks at all this and goes, if I were a kid . . . I mean, Candy King?' He points at a bottle of that. 'You think of Candy Crush, the online kids game. Immediately, your mind goes there, right? There is a problem here. Something is fucked here.'

Despite something being fucked here, Savvas says his hands are tied. 'If I go into a politician's office and say, "Hey, you should fix this," it just goes too far. It becomes, well, now we're going to ban all flavours.'

So *are* they trying to appeal to kids? I think about cigarette magazine ads from the forties and fifties. Those appealed to the part of the reader's mind that wanted to be more adult; dapper business suits, hunting trips and golf at country clubs.

Seems to me the shelves at Vapoureyes are filled with the imagery of ghouls and bubble gum not because they're targeting kids but because, unlike in the forties and fifties, no one grows up anymore.

I think I'll start wearing a suit.

The market

Behind his office desk, Savvas speeds through a Rubik's Cube, randomly coloured squares forming into solids blocks of white, red and green. It's not always the Greek prayer beads – sometimes it's this cube that occupies his fluttering fingers.

Savvas is not the only staff member vaping all day. I have to pluck percentages out of thin air to make this point, but the nicotine rushing through people's bloodstream makes this place 8 per cent zippier, 4 per cent jitterier and 7 per cent more off-kilter than a standard place of business; a sense of uncanny valley runs through the workforce, in the offices above the warehouse floor. I have evidence for this observation: listening back to our chats on my audio recorder, some workers are talking so fast I'm compelled to double-check I haven't hit the button that speeds up the playback.

Savvas, cube now solved, places it down. On the steps of parliament he groused about Philip Morris trying to destroy his industry through lobbying. He now reveals he too has sat in politicians' offices, pushing back against Philip Morris.

'To be frank with you, I have tried to deploy their tactics against them, in the sense that I am doing my best to muddy the waters. That's simply the pragmatic reality of lobbying. You've got to choose your message very carefully. And so, if there's a way for me to poison IQOS as much as I possibly can, I will always take that opportunity.'

'Why go so hard on IQOS?'

'IQOS represents a major threat to vaping. Because if it becomes the default way that people vape, that's the end of the industry.'

Savvas says Philip Morris are set to win this war. 'It already has all of the relationships it needs. It already is in every single

supermarket.' He means Coles and Woolies already peddle cigarettes, raking in billions, so Philip Morris stacking IQOS in their
delivery van next to the cartons of Marlboros and getting retailers
to stock it will be no sweat at all. 'The buyers in all those companies
already have personal relationships with the sellers in Philip Morris.'

The scales fall from my eyes. Something I thought was true, so
true I haven't stopped to question it for one second, is not true at all.

I've been assuming Philip Morris are pariahs. But no, they're not.
Of course they're not. No one's more mainstream than Woolworths
and Coles.

Take Woolies. They're the second-largest company in Australia,
and according to the Brand Institute of Australia in the top ten most
trusted. If you're accepted by Woolies, clearly you're not an outcast.

There are lepers in the business world – you can't buy pornog-
raphy at Woolies – but Philip Morris isn't one of them. They are
faux-pariahs. They're not pariahs, they're just very naughty boys. This
is both a revelation and a *duh*.

Add it to the list of why the killer is still on the loose. Smokers
were booted out of pubs and restaurants years ago, but the world of
business is yet to kick Philip Morris into the cold.

The invisible Marlboro Man

It has occurred to me that if you don't smoke cigarettes, you think
they've disappeared.

Cigarettes are hidden in cabinets behind the counter at supermarkets and convenience stores, with branding forbidden on those
cabinets. Also disappeared: Marlboro cardboard displays at the
newsagency, girls in bikinis smiling on 'Fresh is Alpine' billboards

across the city, Peter Stuyvesant glossy magazine advertisements and the Benson & Hedges World Series Cup.

1976: Cigarette radio and television advertising is banned in Australia.

1990: Newspapers and magazines advertising is banned.

1996: Billboard advertising is banned.

2012: Point-of-sale displays in shops are banned.

Between that and smoking bans in public, it's no wonder so many people have been left with the impression hardly anyone smokes anymore. The truth is that around three million Australians smoke, nearly 12 per cent of the population.

I went to a television producer's Christmas party in Brighton, an affluent beachside suburb in Melbourne. As I sat by the swimming pool, a man pointed out that there was lots of drinking going on, but no one was smoking. I looked around – he was right.

A day later I wandered down Fitzroy Street in St Kilda, passing the Gatwick Hotel, which not long ago was a boarding home. Channel Nine bought it in 2017 for *The Block* and the residents were moved on. Some settled elsewhere, but a homeless city of rugs and cardboard grew nearby, former residents of the Gatwick and new arrivals. I did not spot a mouth without a dart planted in it.

THE MARLBORO KID

Spool back your mind until the tape runs off the reel – find your earliest memory. I'm plucking a cigarette from my mother's pack of Marlboros on her bedside table.

I spent a lot of time, during my pipsqueak years, exploring my parents' drawers. Rolling jewellery between my fingers, rubbing the monogram on my father's handkerchief. Putting a mothball from the sock drawer to my lips. Running the edge of a condom wrapper between my fingernail and quick. But on this day, I slide a cigarette from my mother's pack. I know it was Marlboro because I remember that red and white box.

Now I'm in the backyard, shaded by the largest tree. Near the pile of wood where we found the family cat dead and rotting. I push the Marlboro into my mouth and chew. Then I'm gasping, dry retching, spitting out tobacco. I must remember this – what must be my first memory – because of the sensory overload.

So my earliest memory is of a Marlboro. I wonder if this explains my addiction to them – not cigarettes but Philip Morris.

Roll forward to either cubs or scouts. Around a campfire, a boy with a cigarette lighter heats a rope, coated in plastic, dripping atomic bombs onto ants. Another boy pulls out a cigarette and it's passed around. This next bit will make me sound like an idiot. I take the cigarette and, after a couple of puffs, tap it on my exposed thigh, like I'd seen people tap cigarettes on windowsills in movies. I clench my teeth to suppress a whimper of pain.

Age nineteen, I buy my first pack. A reaction to my first heart-crushing break-up, it flows in with other strange acts: cleaning not only my room but the whole family home, wiping down the microwave and mirrors, circling the lawn for hours with the mower. I choose Peter Stuyvesant, for the gold crest and classic font, but mainly for the soft pack. Arthouse films showed soft packs. I don't recall buying a second pack but, you know, it was years ago.

During my twenties and thirties, my party years, cigarettes are like bongos. If someone passes me a bongo at a party, sure, I'll give it go, but I'm over it pretty soon and I'm sure not going to a music store to buy my own bongo. This whole stretch of time, from cubs to nightclubs, I fail to draw smoke past my throat. People try to teach me, but it won't go through.

I'm guessing that's why now I'm feeling a rush through the veins in my arms, suckling the vape as Savvas drives me home. Before we left, Savvas offered me a kazoo, for research purposes. (Yes, I've decided a vape is a kazoo, not be confused with an IQOS, which I've decided is a doohickey.)

I asked for one infused with nicotine, from his personal stash, and now nicotine is hitting my bloodstream for the very first time. The vapour is making it past my throat in a way smoke never has.

I cough.

There's a little pulsation in my left eye. I like this.

I cough.

A migraine hits. Nothing big.

This vape tastes like a Big Boss Cigar or a Fag, the musk lollies I chewed on as a kid, which themselves mimicked cigars and cigarettes. Everything comes full circle. It's life imitating lolly dart.

Savvas questioned himself about that back at the warehouse. Is it right to sell vape juice labels styled on kids games?

Savvas wonders again about his role in this world, reflecting on an afternoon he spent with Dr Colin Mendelsohn, a pro-vaping campaigner. 'We were just out driving, taking him some place. I asked him, what if we're wrong? I spend my whole life advocating for these products because I really genuinely believe in them. What if I'm wrong? What if fifty years from now it turns out vaping is deadly?'

Dr Mendelsohn had an answer. 'He made the point that all the epidemiological studies, all of the statistical analysis – there's just physically no way that it's more dangerous than smoking. The one thing that we can say with no doubt whatsoever is it's safer than tobacco. And I think that's enough for me to say whatever it is we're doing, it's for the greater good.'

I've read that the best CEOs are psychopaths, because they don't doubt what they're doing. Savvas has now expressed doubt two times, so he's not a psychopath. That's good news for me, locked in a moving car with him.

By the time Savvas drops me home, it occurs to me I've been huffing for the whole forty-five minute trip. An hour later I have to, reluctantly, relinquish the device to the wall socket, a touch agitated that I now need to wait for it to recharge. I have a box of cigarillos in a drawer in my bedroom, next to a jar of foreign coins and my dad's old binoculars. I peel off the cellophane and rack my brains – do I have matches in the house?

VAPING ESCALATING

I'm not Mahmood Fazal's imam, so I don't mind that he drinks, but why must he have such bank-balance-thinning taste?

'Where are we going to go for our shisha?' I ask him, as we split the bill at a wine bar in the city. I could have bought a house by now if I hadn't gone out drinking with Mahmood over the years.

'Yeah. I've got a few hectic brothers. They've opened up a shisha lounge I'll take you to. Don't worry.'

'I'm on board,' I say. 'I mean, I've done way worse than shisha, so I'm not shy at all.'

'Very hectic Lebanese crime family,' he says, finishing his thought.

We don't end up at the shisha lounge of the crime family but rather one in inner-city Brunswick, a 15-minute Uber ride from the wine bar. So manage your expectations, this scene doesn't culminate in a shootout.

The walls are empty, save for a big television on which a man is plucking an oud. The lounge is empty too, bar two women in niqabs scuttling to a VIP area through doors behind the counter.

'This is the part of Sydney Road where I went shopping with Musa Cerantonio,' I tell Mahmood, of the colourful Melbourne identity from my last book, 'and bought books that explained how scientists are losers, because the Qur'an worked out everything about the sun and the Earth beforehand.'

'They're not that far off, man,' Mahmood says. 'Syria was the birthplace of the scientific revolution, baby. Every Muslim will tell you that proudly.'

The woman behind the counter wanders over, passes us mouthpieces sealed in plastic wrapping. We'll attach these to the hose of these hookah pipes, which are made of ornamental glass, gold-plated and about the size of a small child. They sit on the tiles by the couch we've sunk into. She places a little brick of shisha – flavoured tobacco – on the tray that rests atop the contraption.

'We're smoking, what's the flavour?'

'Apple mint,' Mahmood says.

'Apple mint. This is pretty much vaping. How's this not vaping?'

'It isn't vaping, man.'

I cough.

Where's Mahmood? His head has been swallowed by a giant cloud of shisha.

'It's heating up an ingredient and you're sucking in the vapour,' I say. 'It's vaping.'

'I like this, it's very – It's like Buddhism,' I hear Mahmood say. 'You're meditating, breathing. I don't pay as much attention to my breathing as I do when I'm smoking this.'

I tell Mahmood that the NSW Department of Health has released a television commercial addressing shisha. He's not a fan.

'You can't go into a different culture and tell them what they're doing is fucked up because it fits your scientific paradigm,' he argues. 'Like, maybe in different cultures, you can do things that aren't exactly good for your health, but it's a cultural practice, right?'

'The Lebanese Muslim Association have their logo on it.'

'I hate to break your eggshell view of our community, but just because some Lebanese association gives you the tick of approval —'

I pull out my phone.

'Let's go, let's watch it.'

We open on a family backyard barbecue. The grey-bearded patriarch flips meat, greeting his handsome nephew and hijabi niece.

The Department of Health helpfully subtitles the Arabic.

'Ahlan wa sahlan.' [Welcome.]

'How are you, Amou [uncle]?'

'Good to see you, Amou [uncle], it's been a while. How's work?'

'Yeah, not bad, Alhamdullah [thank God].'

Mahmood has his thoughts. 'From the start, I'm going to say this looks like no ethnic person or no ethnic barbecue that I've been to.'

'The ad shows a barbecue to show that Muslims are just like non-Muslims. They have barbecues.'

The advertisement continues. Now the grey-bearded patriarch waves barbecue tongs at his son, Mahlik, who's kicking a ball in the backyard with friends.

'What do you reckon guys, eh? Time for a shisha? Mahlik!'

'Yeah, Dad?'

'Get us the Argileh [shisha pipe], mate . . .'

'I'm playing soccer. Get someone else to do it, Dad!'

Mahmood interrupts. 'The narcs in our community, if they were to have a barbecue, this is what it would look like. The rats.'

The advertisement continues. The daughter, Iman, is lounging in a chair, lost in her smartphone.

'Iman!'

'Dad, I'm uploading something.'

Mahmood grouses, 'I've been in environments where there's shisha smokers and non-smokers. And I've never in my life heard someone be like, "Oi, I'm trying to scroll my Instagram feed over here." Fuck off.'

In the advertisement the shisha pipe has finally been retrieved and the grey-bearded patriarch prepares to offer it around. He makes eye contact with a young man.

'Shisha, Tahir?'

Melodramatic music booms. From Tahir's perspective we catch a special effect, cigarettes circling the top of the shisha pipe. We zoom into Tahir's worried face. Will he do it? Won't he do it?

He finally speaks. 'No thanks . . .'

Words punch onto the screen: *45 minutes on a shisha pipe equals 100 cigarettes.* Then the snappy slogan: *SHISHA, NO THANKS!*

'Okay. So, what did you think of the shisha ad by the New South Wales Department of Health?'

'It was very, uh, condescending and patronising to my people.'

ANTI-SHISHA AD, NO THANKS!

Mahmood continues huffing. He doesn't reckon forty-five minutes on a shisha pipe equals one hundred cigarettes.

'I don't actually know,' he adds. 'Don't fact-check that.'

'I like how when you think you might have got something wrong, it's not "fact-check that", it's *"don't* fact-check that".'

'Don't fact-check me, fact-check the government. I'm not an institution of power that you should be keeping in check. I'm just a lowly Afghan boy on Sydney Road trying to smoke shisha.'

LIFE MOVES ON

It's been a week since Savvas dropped me home from the Vapoureyes warehouse. It occurs to me that I stopped vaping days ago. So that didn't last – the addiction didn't take. The vape's probably buried beneath the mess of papers on my desk, or maybe on the floor of my car.

I did burn through the box of cigarillos. I sit on my balcony, twiddling the last one in my fingers, thinking about my upcoming meeting with Savvas Dimitriou's devil, Simon Chapman.

The World Health Organization awarded Simon a medal for his service in the war against tobacco, while Savvas has pinned 'turd' and 'fucking arsehole' on him for his attack on vaping. Savvas lamented 'what credibility do I have?', while Simon has spilled alphabet soup all over his business card: AO PhD FASSA Hon FFPH(UK). That's an Order of Australia and public health diplomas from respectable universities.

What do I want to learn from Simon? For decades, he has cast his eye over the public and their hate affair with Big Tobacco.

Maybe he can tell me: Why isn't Philip Morris's brand-new hustle rousing people up, like, say, climate change? Don't Philip Morris, too, pollute humans and kill them, only faster?

I meet Simon at his home in Stanmore, in Sydney's inner west. The world's most expensive fish, koi, glide through his backyard pond. Simon tells me he scored them for a bargain and I shouldn't assume he's one of those rich fish guys. I didn't know there were rich fish guys.

Simon became a health education officer largely because his mother cut out a job ad from the newspaper and that was the job. He helped addicts in juvenile detention and educated teachers on how to teach kids about the dangers of drugs.

He and a few workmates decided they were 'pissing in the wind' and needed to get to one of the roots of the problem: kids are groomed to take drugs by the media. In the late seventies they formed the Movement Opposed to the Promotion of Unhealthy Products, which, like all clunkily named protest groups, comes together in the acronym – in their case MOP-UP. Their first target was Paul Hogan, the comedian who'd go on to become Crocodile Dundee; Rothmans paid him to be a spokesman and poster boy for their Winfield cigarettes.

'There was a clause in the advertising self-regulatory code which said that no one should be used in tobacco advertising who had major appeal for children,' Simon says, as we wave bye to the koi and head to his lounge. 'And Hogan had major appeal for children through his variety show.' I remember not remembering that show; it ran the same night as cub and scout night, so I had to hear the skits second-hand at primary school the next day. MOP-UP took

Rothmans to the advertising tribunal. The arbitrator sided with MOP-UP, and Rothmans had to fire Paul Hogan.

What did Aussies think of this? That MOP-UP were wowsers or, worse, wankers? Maybe this attitude helps Philip Morris – only a prude, a tosser, a wanker would hassle a bloke relaxing with a ciggie and a beer. It could be that finger-wagging goes against the Aussie spirit.

Former prime minister John Howard says the chief Australian value is mateship. Social justice group Welcome Australia says it's our welcoming spirit. However, the only distinctly Australian value I've noticed, time and again, is 'don't be a wanker'.

A wanker, according the dictionary, is someone 'annoyingly pretentious'. You don't have to do much to get branded as a wanker in Australia. Don't tell people you look up words in the dictionary, for one.

A stranger on social media once called me a wanker because he saw me on the street, wearing a red scarf. 'Get over yourself, you're just eating a kebab like the rest of us,' he scolded me.

On assignment, hanging out with white nationalists and anarchists on the streets of Australia, it was striking how much time was invested trying to pin 'wanker' on the enemy. Over, say, 'dangerous' or 'violent'. At one rally the anarchists chanted, 'You are a racist!' across police lines, aiming it at Blair Cottrell, the leader of a far-right gang. Blair didn't give a faaark and just continued Hitlering into the microphone. But when the anarchists switched to 'You are a wanker!', Blair blushed and fumbled his lines.

Do white Australians know that this debilitating anti-wankerism is exclusive to their culture? It's no mystery that all those primary school kids in China can play Schubert. When they pick up the violin for the first time, no one's calling them a wanker.

So given all that, I'm not surprised to learn from Simon that anti-wankerism loomed over the seventies' smoking wars.

In one advertisement Paul Hogan, in a beret, chisels away at a sculpture. *Art.* Not just that, the worst type: art-gallery art. Don't tell us Hoges has become a wanker?! After chatting up some bird in the gallery (she's hot, but French, so a wanker), the camera pulls out to reveal he's not chiselling some Michelangelo-style sculpture like a poofter but rather the Winfield slogan. Phew, he's not a wanker after all. In another advertisement he interrupts an orchestra to yarn about Winnie Reds, then instructs the stuck-up conductor to play the Winfield jingle.

MOP-UP instinctively knew what flies in Australia. They formed a mateship with a group called Billboard Utilising Graffitists Against Unhealthy Promotions, or BUGA-UP. With buckets of paint they struck Winfield billboards across the nation. *Anyhow Have a Winfield* became *Anyhow Have a Wank, It's Healthier.* The press covered it, Australians loved the larrikin humour, and they won out, undermining any accusation they were the wankers by pinning wanker on Winfield.

GENERATION X

To time-travel a turn of phrase, back then being a wanker got you cancelled. That was the seventies and eighties – these days the tentacles of the culture wars stretch out and tickle different itches. What do people care about today? And does that help or hinder Philip Morris?

BUGA-UP feel like my forefathers, my bloodline. Corporations are the bad guys. Out of all the forces messing with our lives, they're number one. That's a social justice starting point. And renegades fight the power, rage against the machine. BUGA-UP destroyed billboards, I write my book.

But an uneasy feeling has fallen over me in the past few months. Viewing corporations this way might be very Generation X. We're the generation squeezed between the Baby Boomers and the Millennials, and life has moved on. Maybe for whatever the Millennial version of me is, corporations aren't, intuitively, bad guys. Or for Zoomers, if that zippy term for the generation following Millennials sticks.

For Generation X, corporations were our central villain. Our Christ Nailed to the Cross was Nirvana's Kurt Cobain – when he made it onto the cover of *Rolling Stone*, he scribbled on his t-shirt in black marker: 'corporate magazines still suck'. You didn't have to be Exxon drilling for oil or Lockheed Martin building bombs. Kurt was thinking what his fans would be thinking: corporations can never be trusted.

At university we all read, or pretended we had read, Naomi Klein's *No Logo*. That book mocks brands, like Nike, for co-opting social justice activism to sell products made in sweatshops. Or at least I think it does – I never read it. Corporations had hitherto co-opted safe, mainstream values like patriotism and motherhood, but, come the nineties, Nike and others were pilfering from radical movements like feminism and Black empowerment.

In one ad, shot like a gritty music video at a time when almost all ads were squeaky clean, Black and white girls tell the camera that, if you let them play sports, they'll grow in confidence and be more likely to leave a man who beats them. Cut to Nike logo.

The woke weren't called the woke then, but the kinda sorta nineties version of them weren't buying it. *Time* magazine, reporting on the 1999 protests against the World Trade Organization, confirms my memories. The largest demonstrations in America since the Vietnam War, they describe '. . . outright furies about the global economy collected on the streets of downtown Seattle and crashed through the windows of NikeTown'. 'Special attention' was paid to Nike, the representative villain for these worldwide protests.

And it wasn't just the readers and the pretending-they-were-readers of *No Logo*. On their top-five album *Apocalypse 91 . . .*

The Enemy Strikes Black, Public Enemy slams Nike for their faux-Black activism, rapper Chuck D telling Nike they're 'gonna shut 'em down'.

But Chuck D is an old man now. As am I – Shmuck Me. What's the lay of the land these days?

Colin Kaepernick, quarterback for the San Francisco 49ers, enrages Trump types by refusing to stand for the national anthem at football games. And each time a microphone is pushed into his face, he foregoes talking sport in order to blast America about police brutality. He becomes a leading voice in the Black Lives Matter movement.

That's when Nike swooshes in. They announce their new campaign, plastering Kaepernick everywhere. *Believe in something, even if it means sacrificing everything. Just Do It.* I titter reading this. Boy, Nike are about to be pummelled by the social justice wokes! Imagine co-opting Black Lives Matter to sell sweatshop sneakers and thinking that's going to fly! Haven't they learned anything from Chuck D?

But the pummelling never happens. Not from social justice types, at least. It comes from the other side – a bunch of Trump supporters burn their Nikes to protest the company's support of Kaepernick. This only seems to strengthen the idea that Nike is on the side of the progressive resistance.

Finally, I find the needle in the haystack. A prominent activist tweeting what I thought everyone would be tweeting. Rosa Clemente is '1st Black Puerto Rican/Afro-Latina to run for Vice-President, Green Party. Bronx. Organizer, Lecturer, Independent Journalist'. And, I note, Generation X. She writes: 'Nike is not our friend. I still admire what Colin Kaepernick has done. I just don't get how activists and organizers now support NIKE? How can people now uplift a billion $$$ corporation that we know exploits workers. So much cognitive dissonance these days.'

Corporations

I want a second opinion that I'm not misremembering that corporations were public enemy number-one for activists in the nineties. That I'm not misreading the shifting landscape: corporations have been knocked down the list of villains. Which might help explain why Philip Morris's IQOS plot is going unnoticed.

Leslie Moliere-Batichon screams down the phone at me from Florida. 'She was a self-absorbed idiot who walked around acting like her world was terrible because she became a princess!' Leslie loves the British Royal Family, but not Princess Diana. 'I have three favourite royals, with a special mention.' Those are Prince Charles, Camilla Parker Bowles and Prince Philip. The special mention goes to Princess Margaret.

I tell Leslie that I think the Royals have a complicated legacy, what with the centuries of British colonialism.

'As a Black woman who's the descendants of slaves, I still say shut up.'

Leslie met 'me' two decades ago on MySpace, after one of my TV shows ran in America. She and 'I' became long-term online friends. Here's the thing – I never had a MySpace page. She was talking to someone pretending to be me.

Then our relationship moved to Facebook. That was the real me. It took me a while to get my bearings as to what had happened, but I've never told her the truth. We've had our heated moments over the years, and she clearly prefers MySpace me.

Her bio reads, 'I'm a Gen X'er, 53, married to a millennial, 37. I have a podcast with a Gen Z, 19, co-host and producer.'

I want her take on all this. 'How come in the nineties, Nike was considered – if you were the nineties version of a social justic—'

'Yeah, all of those of us who were in the know, we knew all their labour was from China. And I wouldn't buy a pair of Nikes.'

'And part of the reason they were considered the worst of the worst is because they were trying to get away with being whatever the nineties version of woke was.'

'They were trying to be the next United Colors of Benetton while using sweatshop labour. I don't care if Michael Jordan is on your goddamn shoe, I'm not buying it.'

I move the conversation from the nineties to today.

'So why don't people on Twitter, who get offended by everything – why didn't they attack Colin Kaepernick and Nike for co-opting Black Lives Matter?'

'Because right now they're killing us.' By 'they', Leslie means the cops. 'And we can't fight both those battles.'

The other battle is sweatshops in China. At the same time they were putting up the Kaepernick billboards, Nike was lobbying US Congress to reject a bill banning imports made with forced labour by Uyghurs, a persecuted Muslim minority in China. Nike don't deny this, although they say it wasn't lobbying, they were 'constructive discussions'.

'How does the whole people-in-China-in-sweatshops thing factor into it? Does Colin Kaepernick owe them anything?'

'He should, but he's not thinking about that right now. He's thinking about his own. We can't fight everybody's battles. And to expect us to is a white-privileged, white-supremacist notion. I'll give you one example. I said it to a woman who was going off about veganism. That's a fucking privileged fucking stance to take, because there are places in the world where eating killed game is their only source of fucking food.'

'Yeah, I know. I ate a hedgehog in West Africa,' I say, centring myself.

Growing up, I noticed it was taboo for grunge bands to take brand deals, while rap artists flaunted theirs. Pearl Jam refused to sell their concert tickets through corporate behemoth Ticketmaster, while in the music video for *Walk This Way* Run DMC showed close-ups of their Adidas. Why was that?

'That's not our issue,' says Leslie. 'Black people as a whole don't have anything. So if we want something, we've got to get it from white people. Most white people are problematic in some way, shape or form. So are you telling me that I can't get money from white people because white people are problematic? So I can't get mine because you are problematic? Not taking corporate money is a white privilege. Luxury.'

New world order

I began this book assuming people would be enraged by Philip Morris. Now I fear not only do people shrug their shoulders at them, they shrug at corporations in general. People have more immediate battles to fight.

The word 'corporations' once took top spot, explaining what was responsible for the ills of the world. It carried a weight, a feeling of menace. But, using my Twitter feed and left-leaning news outlets as a barometer, the word 'whiteness' has substituted in for 'corporations'. Philip Morris, the lucky buggers, are the beneficiaries of a cultural shift. Judging eyes have drifted away from corporations, the very same moment they're sending the IQOS into the world.

Corporate rap sucks

I'm not beating myself up for only making sense of this now – easy mistake to make. The concept of selling out to corporations weighed heavily on Gen X, including me, rapper in RMIT's Battle of the Bands winner Raspberry Cordial. One night I had dinner with Lachlan and Sarah Murdoch and the staff of Murdoch's *Australian Style*. They were launching a new issue and those, like me, who featured in the magazine were invited to a beautiful restaurant. Guilt ridden, this inspired me to later pen the rhyme: 'I'm more than a sell-out/I'm Murdoch's man-bitch/stuck in a Lachlan and Sarah sandwich.'

Landmines

The cultural landmines today include: race, trans rights, climate change, #metoo and animal abuse. Frustratingly, complicity in killing 8 million people a year doesn't make the cut.

To bring down Philip Morris, there's no point flapping around x-rays of cancer-riddled lungs. What I need is to find an Instagram photo of a Philip Morris executive with a rifle slung over their shoulder, grinning widely, crouching next to a slain lion.

FREE CHOICE

Yes, imagine the slaughter on social media if any Philip Morris executive was photographed with a hunting trophy. A head might roll. But those same executives can be complicit in millions of dead people with no fear of guillotine.

A friend tells me this observation is not as clever as I think it is. The difference is that people choose to smoke but the lion didn't choose to take a bullet. My friend explains this is why people don't get worked up by Philip Morris as much as African Safaris, Black Lives Matter, #metoo or the other issues on my list: free choice.

Okay, I'll sit on that reality for a while. That free choice makes the difference when ranking What to Give a Hoot About. Surely it's not that simple, that you choose to smoke. When it comes to smoking, two concepts overshadow all others – one is free choice, but the other is addiction.

What does that word, 'addiction', mean? Six Theodore Dalrymple books sit on my shelf, so I clearly like his writing. He's a former prison psychiatrist and physician, and we might as well take his definition of 'addiction'.

Down the line from London, Dalrymple tells me he doesn't get as many interview requests as I, a fanboy with six of his books, might expect.

'I'm very disappointed I've never been deplatformed,' he says. His Queen's English is better than the Queen's. 'But you have to be platformed before you can be deplatformed.'

'So, what's addiction?' I ask, sounding like a convict.

'It's a physiological state in which people become habituated to a drug, where they will require more of the drug to produce the same effect. And where stopping the drug would have withdrawal effects.'

So it's not just 'a state of mind', or something woolly like that, as people might think. Addiction is a measurable biological truth.

'There's a psychological aspect of it, but there's also a physiological aspect of it. That is to say, you can produce addiction in animals, in rats and so on. So it's a real physiological phenomenon.'

The two big considerations used to draw conclusions about smokers, free choice and addiction, bash against each other. Smokers have free choice. But, if you're addicted, your free choice is stripped away. Or at the very least, it gets messy.

Where the bodies are hidden

A tickle in my pocket. I pluck out my phone. It's the first text I've had from an ex in a while – Michelle Bennett, a girlfriend from a lifetime ago.

'My dad has cancer. We've been treating him but it's spread too rapidly now. Have just moved him into palliative care.'

'That is so awful. What type of cancer?'

'Lungs/face. From smoking. Started with an awful tumour on his face. Huge surgery. Many other surgeries. And emergency surgeries. But it had already spread. Sorry to just spring that. Just wanted you to know for some reason. I'm ok. I've had to research funeral plans and Fawkner Cemetery comes up all the time. Henry, Hector and I often bike ride there. I always think about your incredible family there.'

Yes, a mother, auntie, cousin and grandmother all lie beneath the dirt in Fawkner Cemetery.

'Let me know if you need any help with anything,' I type.

Another tickle, only three days later.

'Dad passed away yesterday morning.'

'I'm so sorry, please tell me where the funeral is.'

'It will just be a memorial, Tuesday, 11.30 am. Crick Chapel, Fawkner Cemetery. It won't be huge, I don't think. Dad was a funny thing. He's being cremated today. I'll get his ashes next week.'

I tell my father about Michelle's dad's upcoming memorial and he pulls out a card from his wallet. It reads *Fawkner Cemetery Tea Rooms. Coffee Loyalty Card. Buy 9 coffees and get your 10th one free!* The card has been hole-punched twice. Only seven more of his friends have to die. I tell him the memorial is catered so I won't be swinging by the tea rooms to get another punch on his card.

Biting my lip behind the steering wheel on the tangled roads in the cemetery, I follow the yellow line leading to Crick Chapel. Lines of other colours guide you to other chapels. Christian privilege! There's no line to guide you to the Jewish temple here. In the past, I've driven around in circles, panicky and lost, arriving in the nick of time.

In the chapel, I huddle in the back pew with a couple of Michelle's friends from community radio. Ten minutes in, word gets to our ears that Michelle wants us to join her near the front. I don't like that walking there makes us look like we've arrived late.

'Grief is not a series of steps. It is messy, ragged and random, and it inflicts its pain on each person differently,' the man conducting the service begins. 'It is as individual as a fingerprint.'

We hear about Michelle's father, one of this year's 8 million. The man who 'started with an awful tumour on his face' thanks to Philip Morris.

He was born in 1945, the son of a factory worker and bookie, from a long line of Collingwood supporters. 'One of his mum's greatest disappointments was when Paul chose to support Geelong over Collingwood.'

Age twenty-three, he married Mary, and they had three children together. 'Every Saturday he would have the record player on, and it was a tradition that when Neil Diamond's *Hot August Night* was played, all the kids would go crazy, dancing around in the living room and jumping on each other with cushions.'

A family tragedy struck in 1984. 'Paul was a very committed father to Damien. He was devastated by the car accident that impaired Damien for the rest of his life. Even though things weren't always easy, right up to the end Paul had a strong sense of standing by his son.'

The solemnity in the chapel is broken by the squeaks of babies. 'A great joy in Paul's life were his grandchildren Oscar, Lily, Rex, Henry and Hector. The Saturday before Paul died, Oscar wrote "Pop" on his wrist and dedicated his basketball grand-final to him.

After they had won, he took his medal in to show Paul. Paul appeared to know he was there, but we will never know how aware he really was.'

Children and grandchildren follow on with beautiful eulogies. The memorial wraps up with the Geelong Football Club anthem. I realise that the aphorism is true; one death is a tragedy, a million deaths is a statistic. Filing out, it occurs to me that Paul's killer, cigarettes, didn't rate a mention.

Silence

A few weeks later, Michelle and I lounge on a long, squeaky couch. Two people rendered tiny in a grand, Victorian-era hotel bar in the CBD with more waitstaff than patrons, chandelier light flattering us.

'At the memorial – I just feel if your dad had been shot in a massacre, it would have hung over proceedings, been in our heads, even if it was never mentioned. "He died because of the psycho-path who went on the shooting rampage." But because it's cigarettes, I don't think it's floating around in anyone's head.'

'No, I don't think it was,' she says. 'Telling his sister or my cousins, we didn't go, "Oh, Dad's passed away – smoking." It was "Dad's passed away – *cancer*." Yes, you're right. It should be "cancer because he smoked". On my dad's death certificate, it should say "Because he smoked."'

Philip Morris never loses. Not mentioned, rendered invisible, even at the death of one of their customers. On the gravestones in the cemetery, you'll wander by *Died in This or That War*, but Philip Morris get off the hook. Michelle agrees, but she points out that it's noble to die in war. This eases the conversation into uncomfortable territory. Society thinks smokers, and people addicted to other drugs, have died a less noble death. They've had a hand in their own death. They were complicit. Mourners won't mention cigarettes because they know it takes two to tango.

'It's like the Mafia on TV shows,' I tell Michelle. '"You can't squeal on me because you'll be squealing on yourself. You were also at the crime." Philip Morris have this thing where people aren't going to squeal on them at the memorial —'

'Or in the death notice. I think that's completely right.' Michelle thinks it's part of a wider subconscious agreement to not speak that uncomfortableness out loud. 'It would not have even crossed my mind to say at the memorial that Dad was a smoker for fifty years.'

The precise word chosen changes everything. By pinning a death on 'cancer' instead of 'cigarettes', the guy in the coffin gets off the hook, but so does Philip Morris. Another reason Philip Morris can soldier on.

'Addiction is such a strange area,' I say. 'Because it's a person doing something of their own free will, but they're doing something not of their own free will at exactly the same time.'

'It implies a weakness in somebody's character. I think that's how the tobacco companies or alcohol companies get away with it. You can have a couple of drinks, but if you become an alcoholic, it's because you're a bit weak. Or if you become addicted to smoking, you're a bit weak.'

'So do you blame Philip Morris?'

'No. But I don't blame my dad either.'

TARGET MARKET

I dig through the Philip Morris archives. In-house documents reluctantly tabled during court cases. I come across this, from the nineties:

'Good morning. I'm Susan Black, Senior Vice President, Group Research Director on the Philip Morris business at Leo Burnett Advertising. And I'm here this morning to try and help answer the question WHAT IN THE WORLD CONNECTS WITH GENERATION X?!'

(OK, Boomer.)

'Pretty tall order. Particularly when members of today's young-adult population often answer this question by saying "You can't!" Baffled Baby Boomers have tried to come to grips with the idea that there really is a new "younger generation" out there, and that they really are nothing like us. Their anthem is "I don't want to be no target market!"'

(Petulant eyeball roll while chewing gum.)

'Today's young adults are the first truly technological generation. Fax, beepers, personal CDs, Virtual Reality are all commonplace ways to communicate in their world.'

(Fact check: virtual reality was not a commonplace way to communicate. I have a page of sales figures proving this. Give me your number and I'll fax it to you.)

'Born between 1968 and 1974, they are part of the group the US media have been calling Generation X, after a popular book by Douglas Coupland of the same name. The term has come to designate a sensibility that rejects mainstream culture and consumerism.

'SLIDE A: FASHIONS

'The first thing we see is more diversity in fashion than ever before. Young adult male smokers today have a whole spectrum of styles to choose from:

'1. Baggy, decorated jeans, a fashion favored by rap musicians.'

(Fact check: as a rap musician in Raspberry Cordial, my jeans were well-fitted and free of adornments.)

'2. "Kross Dressing". Named after the rap music group Kris Kross, Kross dressing means wearing your baggy clothes about 4 sizes too big, and putting everything on backwards.'

(Fact check: I read this and it commenced to make me jump. Kris Kross in fact had only one top-ten hit, in 1992. I don't recall this trend breaking out widely into the world.)

'3. Grunge. It's a slang word that means filth.'

(Hehe.)

'The Grunge look begins with worn jeans, flannel shirts, combat boots, and unwashed, uncombed shoulder length hair.'

(Unlike Kross dressing, this happened.)

'This is a generation that grew up feeling emotionally bruised. They are children of fractured families. Generation X knows that the Baby Boomers failed to realise their idealistic hopes.'

(Pretty funny how back then Generation X was ragging on Baby Boomers and, decades later, it's like we tagged in Millennials and they continued ragging on Baby Boomers. Why did the ragging skip a generation?)

'We are told that these young people are cynical and skeptical. At the same time we are told they are naïve and trusting.'

(Scarlett-Jae – born in 1987, so either Gen Y or a Millennial – is pouring a cup of tea in my kitchen. She says, 'That's you.')

'Far from being "slackers", they are adaptive.'

(Yes! Scarlett-Jae is right. This is me.)

'They live by their wits.'

(Yes!)

'They're not ambitious? They don't have a work ethic? Baloney!'

(Hmm. I'm late with my manuscript. I cannot in good faith 'yes!' this one).

'They are quick to reject any advertising they consider shallow, obvious, manipulative or poorly executed.'

(Yes! I can see through Philip Morris and their IQOS gambit.)

I'm glad I found this document in the archives. It has brought me clarity.

The maniacal Philip Morris is plotting to kill everyone in the city. This looks like a job not for Superman, but X-Man.

X-Man, with his Generation X powers of x-ray vision. He can see through corporate villains, in a way other generations may not care to. Born on a strange planet in the early seventies, brought up on drollness and cynicism, but not in a bad way.

From her lair in the Philip Morris building, his arch nemesis Bat-Chan plots his demise.

A reverse of Spiderman, you might find X-Man rolling around, overthinking everything, caught in a million webs he doesn't know how to get out of.

THE LOBBY

I put the call out on social media. 'If you work for a cigarette company, pipe up! Looking for smoking and vaping leads.'

A direct message pings in my pocket. A woman I'll call Mandy works in upper management at a vape giant, one of Savvas's competitors.

'I'm having a lunch with one of Philip Morris's external affairs managers on Tuesday and some other guy from there.' They called the meeting – she hasn't met these particular men before. 'If there are any questions you'd like me to subtly ask and report back on, I can try.'

Inside job

Tuesday comes and I'm two drinks in, at a wine bar in Ripponlea, one train stop up from mine. My arm brushes the wall of the bar. On the other side of this very wall is the restaurant where Mandy is having lunch with the two Philip Morris men.

I'm buzzing, a little from the alcohol, mainly from the thought: *Philip Morris, look what we have here.*

I have a mole on the inside.

I bide my time, tearing a serviette into a hundred little pieces.

Now I'm five drinks in and Mandy is sitting opposite me. I crane my neck to look out of the window, where I can see the Philip Morris men, tiny in the distance, climbing into an SUV.

'What was this meeting about?' I ask sloshily. Mandy says they were feeling her out, trying to get a vibe from her, while being furtive themselves.

'Several times now people from Philip Morris have tried to get me into situations where – my impression is, anyway – they're going to compromise me in some way. It seemed clear to me that what they wanted was a puppet. One of the guys even said it: "There are things that we can't say and people we can't meet, that you can meet and you can say."'

She means that Philip Morris are toxic – to politicians, to the media and to the public. No one wants to hear them talk about harm reduction, no one trusts that Philip Morris really cares about their health.

The two men acknowledged that Mandy's company and Philip Morris are competitors. She wants vapes to win, they want IQOS to win. Still, they hold a joint interest, and this is what they focused on over lunch. The government, through the Therapeutic Goods Administration, will soon pass regulations on vaping. These regulations could be helpful to both the vape industry and Philip Morris, or they could be devastating.

'They need a voice that they can't have. They've got their level of influence, but they need other voices to join the chorus in order for their strategy to work. I think that's what it was, ultimately. It was about figuring out whether or not I could be a useful idiot for them.'

Mandy says she won't work with them – she doesn't want to be a useful idiot – but appreciated the seventy-five dollar steak and potatoes cooked in Wagyu fat.

So, this must be that thing called lobbying. You hear so much about it, and I'm finally privy to it going down. Near Ripponlea train station, up the road from the confectionary store.

Mandy reckons she has gamed the system. She's taken their seventy-five dollar steak but won't give them anything in return. Can you do that, or are you kidding yourself? They've opened the door and, in a small way, you owe them something. I don't quite know what. But seventy-five dollars is one expensive steak.

Freebies

Leslie – my fake MySpace friend – also believes you can take a gift and remain true. She tells me about a friend of hers who worked in the arts and refused corporate money:

'She said, "If I don't take corporate sponsorships, then I'm not beholden to the corporations that gave me the money." And my response is, are you a weak piece of shit? Can you not say no? Just because someone hands me money doesn't mean I'm going to do what they tell me to do.

'I will give you a perfect example of this in my personal life. A quote unquote friend of mine, he gave me $300. I thanked him profusely. And we always kind of flirted online, but it was nothing. And he said something about sending me a dick pic.'

'Uh-oh.'

'And I said, please don't. He sent it anyway. I didn't say anything to him, I just quietly unfriended him. He came to me in DMs and he goes, "Did you unfriend me?" And I said, "Yeah." And he said, "What, $300 wasn't enough?" And I said, "No, it was not." And he said, "I hope you choke on the money." And then I blocked him.'

'Oh.'

'That's the way the world works. That's how our politicians work. "If this lobbyist gave me this money, then I got to do what this lobbyist says." What are you, a fucking child? Do you have no spine? Well, the answer is no, they don't. I want to do it differently. You will not break me. My father taught me to take a punch. Swing at me.'

Leslie makes a compelling case. I've been overdramatising this. Accepting a freebie is no biggie. I think.

Optics

I see the Philip Morris Annual Shareholders Meeting is approaching. They knocked me back for an interview, so that would be a rare chance to directly ask them what I want to know about the IQOS. Here's the rub: to ask questions, you need to be a shareholder.

I buy roughly $2000 worth of shares. But I don't do it through my own name, I do it through a company name, giving me the option to hide that I gave money to Philip Morris, if I decide the optics are bad.

SMOKE

Jeremy Weinstein places down WEASLE. Is he spelling that right or is it WEASEL? If I challenge his word, look it up in the Scrabble Dictionary, and discover he is correct, I'll lose my next turn. That's the rules.

I'll let it slide. I'm here to get Jeremy, a former smoker, to try out the IQOS I got from JapShop.

I've never seen a lifestyle pivot as dramatic as Jeremy's. He used to live in an apartment where the air was more cigarette smoke than air, the floor more pizza box than carpet. One visit, I peeled cheese off my shoe. Then his mother died and it seemed only five minutes later he was married and his home was sparkling clean and smoke free.

And we stopped fighting. We used to fight over so much. This one time, in Bethlehem, for instance . . . But I'm not going to take up space in a book about Philip Morris to litigate who was right and who was wrong.

'It's very cigarettey,' Jeremy reports, drawing in the HeatStick, seated before the Scrabble board, generations of Weinsteins staring down from the walls. 'It's a strange sensation. It smells and tastes like a cigarette, but I'm not feeling a head rush, or any nicotine reaction. I haven't had a cigarette in a while and if I would've had a regular cigarette, after about three or four drags, I would have some kind of head rush.'

A plume forms over Jeremy's head.

'Does that seem like smoke to you?' I ask.

'Totally,' Jeremy declares. 'So they are saying that there is some kind of discharge, but it's not smoke?'

I tell him Philip Morris insists it's aerosol.

'I am getting a bit of a head and nicotine rush now,' Jeremy says. 'Do I have to smoke the rest of it?'

'Yes, you do.'

'Oh God.'

My guinea pig takes another drag of what Philip Morris insists is not a cigarette. I probably should have dealt with this earlier, but while I'm playing Scrabble, what does the dictionary say a cigarette is?

Tobacco or other substances in a thin roll wrapped with paper, intended to be smoked.

The HeatStick ticks most of these boxes: 1) it's tobacco, 2) in a thin roll, 3) wrapped with paper. But is it *smoked*? This may sound like a silly question but perhaps according to the dictionary only smoke can be smoked and aerosol can't.

Indeed, one definition of smoke (verb): *To inhale and exhale tobacco smoke.*

So, no mention of aerosol. Dictionaries – from Oxford to Chambers, to Macquarie, to Scrabble – present similar variations of these definitions. But Philip Morris can pluck out the meanings that serve them best and argue that, if the plume exhaling from Jeremy's mouth is aerosol, not smoke, the HeatStick isn't smoked. And since it isn't smoked, it's not a cigarette. And since it's not a cigarette, the European Union can't include it in its upcoming ban on menthol cigarettes. Billions of dollars in sales and perhaps millions of lives (if the HeatStick proves deadly, like cigarettes) hang in the balance over these hair-splitting meanings of words.

Another grey wisp escapes Jeremy's lips and hits me in the face, along with this question: Why *isn't* this smoke? Philip Morris says it isn't smoke because it's aerosol. Which means I need to know: what is aerosol?

A colloidal suspension of particles dispersed in air or gas.

Ugh. What's 'colloidal'?

A homogeneous non-crystalline substance consisting of large molecules or ultramicroscopic particles of one substan—

Ugh! Let's not get bogged down in that. Here's the bombshell: the dictionary lists several examples of aerosol – and one is smoke! So even if a HeatStick emits aerosol, that aerosol might still be smoke.

Philip Morris has thought this through. A cigarette burns, so combusts, and it generates smoke as a result of this combustion. A HeatStick, on the other hand, never burns, so it doesn't combust, so they argue it doesn't generate smoke.

If the HeatStick doesn't combust, what *does* it do? Philip Morris explains (and this is true) that there is a stage before combustion called pyrolysis. This is where the tobacco leaf begins decomposing due to high temperatures but is not combusting. Pyrolysis, not combustion, is what is generating the aerosol Jeremy is blowing in my face.

But not so fast. Second bombshell. Philip Morris is relying on no one googling any of this, because an American Medical Association paper explains how a cigarette works and, contrary to Philip Morris's explanation, it is *not* combustion that activates the smoke in a cigarette. It's pyrolysis.

'The harmful components of tobacco cigarette smoke are products of incomplete combustion (pyrolysis).'

Philip Morris says the HeatStick is activated by pyrolysis.

I slow down so I can take this all in.

Smoke is activated by pyrolysis, before combustion. Therefore, the HeatStick could emit smoke, even though it doesn't combust.

It turns out, once again, Philip Morris are . . . what's the word I'm looking for? WEASELS. (Jeremy, I discover, spelled it wrong. But the board's packed up and I'm back home, so he's got away with his cheating/illiteracy this time.)

Actually

Listen, about that fight with Jeremy in Bethlehem – tell me I'm not right here.

We're on vacation in Israel. We're twenty-one, twenty-two? Something like that. One evening, we book lodging at a church in Bethlehem. A nun is telling us to park our rental car behind the church and, standing in a tight alleyway, motions Jeremy to drive through. It seems likely the car will scrape the walls, but the nun keeps waving us forward. Jeremy doesn't want to risk it, but the awkwardness of the situation – are we calling the nun stupid, or a liar? – pushes me to insist he give it a go.

Before returning the rental car, we paste mud onto its doors to hide the scrapes. Jeremy has no sense of humour about it, and he seethes for the remainder of the holiday. He claims my insistence he drive up the alleyway reflects a broader never-think-things-through impulsiveness. Now that I'm seeing this on the page, I'm concerned this is one of those stories where I'm assuming everyone will take my side but that's not the case.

Pyrolysis

Philip Morris keeps two sets of books, so to speak. On their website, they guide punters through the science of the IQOS. But they've also submitted reams of pages to the US Federal Drugs Administration, trying to convince them to legalise the IQOS. And two different stories are told.

The website informs readers that the IQOS heats tobacco 'without combustion', and this explains why the aerosol is not smoke. Yet buried deep in their FDA submission (Philip Morris is still waiting for a response), they concede something else produces smoke: 'Smoke is composed of airborne solid, liquid particulates and gases evolved when a material undergoes *pyrolysis* [emphasis mine – I've always wanted to do an emphasis mine] or combustion.'

So, Philip Morris and I no longer need to fight over this. They agree, pyrolysis activates smoke.

Here is their argument why the IQOS still does not produce smoke. It generates 'very limited pyrolysis' that does not 'have a relevant influence on the aerosol formed: less than 2% by weight of the aerosol components may derive from the pyrolysis [. . .] which would not be sufficient to characterize the aerosol as "smoke".'

Hang on, if neither combustion nor significant pyrolysis created the cloud that the Scrabble cheat blew into my face, what did?

Philip Morris say it's vaporisation, the heating of liquid into steam. But the HeatStick doesn't look like a liquid to me. Their explanation? The tobacco leaf used by HeatSticks is not the same as the tobacco leaf you'd find in a cigarette. Instead, it's processed with propylene glycol, the chemical compound found in vape juice. And that's what produces the cloud that Jeremy blew into my face.

Is the HeatStick, for better or worse, just a vape? Should it live or die based on whether vapes live or die?

Not so fast. I'm not ready to move on. Philip Morris acknowledges that, unlike vape juice, when using the IQOS you're inhaling not just propylene glycol but tobacco. And also unlike vaping, Philip Morris admits, there is pyrolysis as well as vaporisation. And Michelle Bennett's father died because he inhaled tobacco generated by pyrolysis.

Perhaps two things can happen at once: yes, the vaporisation in the IQOS produces vapour, but the pyrolysis produces smoke. And if there's smoke, it's a cigarette. And if it's a cigarette, the European Union shouldn't let Philip Morris sneak around its ban on menthol cigarettes.

More fundamentally, if it's smoke, the IQOS isn't a smoke-free device. The foundation holding up the whole Philip Morris edifice – that they're building a Smoke-Free Future – crumbles away.

The PMI-58

Let's take a breath.

Philip Morris has hired more than 400 scientists, engineers and technicians to develop the IQOS. Perhaps one is reading this and accusing *me* of being the weasel. John, they'll groan, didn't you read what we said? If the HeatStick produces 'smoke' through pyrolysis, that's outweighed by the fact that this 'smoke' weighs in at less than 2 per cent of the aerosol – the other 98 per cent or so is vapour.

First things first. Quite apart from everything else, we have to trust Philip Morris that this 'only 2 per cent' claim is true. And how am I meant to corroborate that? Set up mice, monkeys and Bunsen burners in my apartment? That's not feasible.

What *is* feasible is pointing out that Philip Morris has been very tricky with another scientific claim in their FDA submission. They looked into the 'harmful and potentially harmful constituents' in cigarette smoke and HeatStick aerosol, to compare the two. They labelled these constituents up for examination as the PMI-58, covering fifty-eight of them, from carbon monoxide to mercury.

In all fifty-eight cases, the HeatStick aerosol contained a lower level of the nasty constituent in question, sometimes significantly lower. So how could anyone not conclude that the HeatStick is safer than a cigarette?

Here's how. Here's Philip Morris's magician's trick, their misdirection, their sleight-of-hand.

There are more than fifty-eight 'harmful and potentially harmful constituents' found in cigarette smoke and HeatStick aerosol. The FDA lists dozens more. Philip Morris cherrypicked the ones that showed up lower in the HeatStick and ignored the ones that showed up higher. Sometimes I think the Marlboro cowboy should be riding a weasel instead of a horse.

Anyway, that's why I arch a cautious eyebrow at their 'less than 2 per cent' claim, or really any scientific claim they make. Regardless, because I can't afford the monkeys and mice, I'll go along with their reality that only around 2 per cent of the HeatStick aerosol is activated by pyrolysis and therefore only 2 per cent of the aerosol could be smoke.

Is that how science works? If only 2 per cent of an aerosol weighs in as 'smoke', is the aerosol not smoke? In this parallel HeatStick universe, does Michelle's dad not die?

Dr Ween

At the Royal Adelaide Hospital Lung Research Laboratory, Dr Miranda Ween is studying the health consequences of vaping.

I'm like an old-world travelling salesman these days, and when I go see Dr Ween my bag is again packed with samples of my wares: a traditional vape, a pack of cigarettes and the IQOS with HeatSticks. Then I pitch the features of the IQOS to Dr Ween, across the boardroom table at her Research Laboratory. I want to know how much smoke needs to be smoke for it to be smoke.

'When you put this question to me,' she says of my introductory email, 'I was like, is that something we've ever had to define before? And, you know, it's not something we've ever really discussed, in respiratory science at any rate. But perhaps this is where it's going to come from – these alternative products, like IQOS, and having to put a limit on what the definition is. For me, it's physical burning – there'd be carbon particles, physical matter, being released into the smoker. That is what most of us would consider smoke. But what percentage? There's no definition yet that I've heard of.'

The HeatStick has raised a question that hasn't needed to be posed before, let alone answered. There has never before been a motive to fudge whether smoke is smoke. It's always been clean-cut. When someone screams down the phone that smoke is coming from a building, the firefighters don't sit around and ponder, 'Yes, but what *is* smoke?'

Sohal mate

I'm not mad after all. Either that or both Dr Sukhwinder Singh Sohal and I are mad.

It's credible to dismiss me. I'm a – whatever I am. Author? Comedian? Something to do with the arts, the discipline most densely populated with loons. But scan Dr Sohal's CV. He's got the credentials, including a PhD in Respiratory Immunopathology, and he's currently a Senior Lecturer and Head of the Respiratory Translational Research Group at the University of Tasmania. He's not thumbing through the Scrabble dictionary for the definition of smoke; he's no doubt got some leather-bound medical encyclopedia on his shelf in a lab. I'm picturing a skeleton and microscope too.

There is apparently one other human on planet Earth who has picked up that Philip Morris is trying some chicanery with this whole HeatStick gambit. This smoke-isn't-smoke situation. And I can't believe my luck – he doesn't work in Brussels, Beijing or

Cape Canaveral, he sits at a desk a dirt-cheap flight away, across Bass Strait.

Philip Morris never loses. Dead kids in America – dead from vaping – means the fear has gone mainstream. There are many scientists studying vaping, but next to no one is examining the IQOS as a distinct device. Dr Sohal is the rare specimen who is; he's one of the scientists behind the paper 'IQOS exposure impairs human airway cell homeostasis: direct comparison with traditional cigarette and e-cigarette'.

A taxi drops me off at the university in Launceston. I trot up the staircase of a glass and brick building, turn up a quiet hallway and find Dr Sohal's room. Two young scientists are hovering around Dr Sohal. I see the good doctor does have leather-bound medical books on his shelf.

'A roast chook will smoke if you cook it too long,' one of the young scientists offers up as the bleeding obvious – something bleeding obvious that hadn't occurred to me. Smoke without fire.

What does the man himself have to say? Dr Sohal is examining the photo of the sickly woman on the warning label of the pack of HeatSticks I've brought along. Outside the window, gumtree branches sway in the wind.

'When you are heating up solid tobacco, that's generating smoke,' Dr Sohal declares. 'It's not a vapour or aerosol the way they've publicised it. It's smoke.'

Ha!

I've been poring through science papers in peer-reviewed medical journals. They always begin with an 'abstract', a summary. Let me bash out one of those.

ABSTRACT

Objective: John Safran has been suss on this whole Philip Morris Smoke-Free Future situation. He thinks that we're all being taken for fools. And we're all going to die! Or 8 million of us a year, at least. Philip Morris has killed more people than Idi Amin, Augusto Pinochet and Slobodan Milošević, and now they say they've got something that isn't a cigarette but it sure looks like one, and something that sure looks like smoke blew out from Jeremy's lips. Governments are banning cigarettes and Philip Morris are substituting these in. Yet he can't find anyone flapping their arms, sounding the alarm. No exposés in the press. No tweets. Why has no one noticed this? He's started thinking he's mad. Maybe he's mad. Maybe this isn't a thing.

Result: A scientist with a 'Doctor' before his name – and not one of those 'Doctor' titles that humanities students get for a dissertation on 'Starbucks Seating and Fifth Wave Feminism', but one where you needed to cut open frogs – has told him it is a thing. He was right and everyone else was wrong. What we have here is smoke.

From here on in the IQOS will no longer be referred to as a 'doohickey'. I retract that and now anoint it the Philip Morris Smoke Machine.

I walk from Dr Sohal's room with a spring in my step. I imagine the boffins in the Philip Morris laboratory reading this, furious, aerosol shooting out of their ears.

Boffins

As if my day couldn't get any better, I discover that while Philip Morris wants to hold their cards close to their tar-infected chest, they do submit studies to reputable science journals, including those published by Oxford University Press. OUP is promoted as 'the world's most trusted dictionary provider', while an Axios-Harris poll found Philip Morris was considered the second-least reputable company in America. Number one was the government, which was labelled a company for some reason. So publication in these sorts of journals gives a much-desired sheen of respectability to Philip Morris.

One study in OUP's *Nicotine and Tobacco Research* shows a 'Tobacco Heating System' and 'Tobacco Heat Stick' that look like the IQOS and HeatSticks. The Philip Morris science team explain that they are testing whether the Tobacco Heat Stick will be less harmful than a cigarette.

And, be still my beating heart (from joy, not cigarettes), here they describe the discharge from both as 'smoke'.

'Biomarkers of exposure to tobacco smoke toxicants which inform product risk assessment were significantly reduced with Tobacco Heating System use compared to the Combustible Cigarette . . .'

So, less smoke than a cigarette, but still smoke. This is the only place I've found Philip Morris describing the HeatStick discharge as smoke. My theory? The paper was published in July 2016, and presumably the research itself began much earlier – before Philip Morris decided they were going to bet the whole farm on this notion of a Smoke-Free Future. The scientists didn't know they shouldn't call it smoke.

This tracks with another rumour: that IQOS originally stood for I Quit Ordinary Smoking. That is, the name before they decided the absence of smoke was going to be their heat-shtick.

Regardless of why, Philip Morris, you're no longer only fighting Dr Sohal (and me) over whether this is smoke, now you're fighting your own boffins.

BOOK OF PROVERBS 16:18

Pride before the fall, John. 'Pride goeth before destruction, and a haughty spirit before a fall.' I don't need to swing by Father Bob's to grapple with the meaning of that Bible warning. I'm the haughty, arrogant spirit who's convinced I've outwitted Philip Morris. Is there something I've missed?

American author Naomi Wolf had her book about gay men on trial in Victorian England pulped. She assumed 'death recorded' on judges' verdicts meant the men had been executed. But, it turns out, it was some Ye Olde legalese for 'technically speaking, the law requires us to execute you, but we're actually going to let you off'. Wolf had built much of her book around what turned out to be a misconception. Is there something *I'm* missing, in my haughtiness?

You see, Philip Morris are the world leader in beside-the-point nitpicking, not shy to use Twitter to paint their critics as fools, even when relying on very thin gruel to do so. If at any point in this book I've used 'their' instead of 'there', Philip Morris will be tweeting:

'Mr Safran doesn't know the difference between *their/there/they're*. Can we really be sure his claim our Marlboros give you cancer isn't also a big blundering howler of a flub of a car crash of a train wreck of a housefire of an error?'

I'm convinced that their Chief Tweeting Officer has already caught something I wrote many pages ago and thinks they can get me for my 'mistake'. That I, the scoffer, am about to become the scoffee; their fingers are poised at the keyboard ready to strike. But I knew you'd catch that, Chief Tweeting Officer. I've been stringing you along for all these pages, playing you like a cat plays with a mouse.

Philip Morris's favourite beside-the-point nitpick is to draw a distinction between Philip Morris International and Philip Morris USA. It's true – on paper they are different companies. They're listed as different entities on the stock exchange, the latter under parent company, Altria. But, to be clear, Philip Morris USA flogs Marlboros in the USA, and Philip Morris International flogs Marlboros in other countries. Philip Morris International flogs the IQOS around the world, except for the USA, where, if approved by the FDA, Philip Morris USA's parent company Altria will flog it.

Under 'The Facts' on the Philip Morris International website they grouse that their enemies 'are spreading falsehoods in an effort to scare others . . . it's time to clear up the facts'. Philip Morris International's professed mission is that they want people to stop smoking cigarettes. If this is true, their enemies ask, why are they still marketing their cigarettes? Philip Morris International addresses this, stating that, in fact, 'We do not market our products in the USA.' This would seem to demonstrate that they are serious about winding up as a cigarette company and moving to smoke-free alternatives.

But while it's true that Philip Morris International don't market cigarettes in the USA, Philip Morris USA does! And Philip Morris International markets cigarettes outside the USA! Philip Morris are geniuses. They can somehow tell the truth but it's less truthful than when I tell a lie.

So yes, Chief Tweeting Officer, I'm aware that earlier, when I pointed out that Philip Morris tout gay-friendly credentials yet fund a politician who campaigns against gay rights, I conflated the two Philip Morrises. Philip Morris *International* touts their gay-friendly credentials, while Philip Morris *USA* paid the politician (through their parent company, Altria).

I know I sound paranoid and defensive. But if I hadn't clarified this, Philip Morris International would be tap-dancing, fancy-footworking like *Singin' in the Rain*, insisting *they* didn't pay the politician.

SURREAL

Let's take stock of what I've learned so far. The shadowland tactics Philip Morris harnesses to try to shift the universe to their favour.

Lean into the ambiguity of science. It'll take years before scientists can definitively rule on this new configuration – tobacco laced with propylene glycol, vapour laced with smoke. Make vague claims that can't yet be disproved. Philip Morris doesn't say the IQOS is safer or healthier, they say it's a *better* alternative. How can a scientist fight that bendy and unscientific word?

Arrive first and define the terms. If you're the first guy on earth who comes across a cow and calls it a cow, everyone starts calling it a cow, and good luck to anyone trying to get people to stop calling it a cow. Philip Morris appears out of nowhere and says 'this is a heated tobacco device', so not a cigarette, and even their critics are lulled into playing along. Articles in the *Guardian* and *Bloomberg* use the terminology Philip Morris made up – the term that exculpates this tobacco rolled in paper from being a cigarette.

Misdirection. The HeatStick looks, waddles and quacks like a cigarette. So distract the eye with the shiny and schmick IQOS heating device, which is in and of itself harmless.

Omission. You'll recall the PMI-58. Here, Philip Morris contrasted the chemicals in a HeatStick with that of a cigarette. They drew attention to the fifty-eight harmful chemicals that showed up in lower quantities in a HeatStick. But they omitted the dozens of harmful chemicals that showed up higher than in cigarettes.

In 2002, US Secretary of Defense Donald Rumsfeld said the 'unknown unknowns' are the true danger in a war. 'There are known knowns; there are things we know we know. There are known unknowns; that is to say, we know there are some things we do not know. But there are also unknown unknowns – the ones we don't know we don't know.'

Philip Morris's omissions are the unknown unknowns. How can you fight against what you don't know is there?

Lean into the ambiguity of the law. Tobacco advertising has been banned from newspapers for decades, yet to promote their new 'smoke-free' mission, Philip Morris took out full-page ads in newspapers. Is advertising the business plan for their new tobacco product the same as advertising their new tobacco product? Who knows? Philip Morris slithers through the many cracks left by 'who knows?'.

Above all else, dance around the meaning of words. An iconic 1929 painting by surrealist René Magritte shows a realistically rendered tobacco pipe; beneath, written in cursive script, *Ceci n'est pas une pipe*. 'This is not a pipe.' Magritte's joke is that language can be a snake in the grass, telling the truth at the same time as telling a lie – technically, it isn't a pipe, it's a painting of a pipe. Magritte's not lying, but he is.

It's eerie how closely the HeatStick gambit maps onto this work of surrealism. We can see it with our own eyes: tobacco rolled in paper with a filter at one end. Yet Philip Morris tells us, 'This is not a cigarette.' A modern remix of the famed painting.

Such a spot-on homage feels like the work of a hoaxster. Perhaps I'll sneak past the security guards at the Philip Morris building, slink up the hallway, burst into the CEO's office and find Banksy sitting behind the desk.

Hold up

I re-read the journal article where Philip Morris referred to the Heat Stick discharge as 'smoke'. Or did they? In fact, I now see, they refer to it as 'smoke *toxicants*' not simply 'smoke'. Does that make a difference? Are smoke toxicants different to smoke? Words, words, words, creepy crawly words. Has Philip Morris slithered through another crack?

We've been here before; Philip Morris telling us they're bringing out a healthier cigarette.

In a 2003 class action suit in Illinois, the judge awarded $10 billion in damages against Philip Morris, for deceiving smokers into thinking Marlboro Lights were safer than other cigarettes.

And that wasn't Marlboro's first rodeo.

The *Journal of the American Medical Association* began 1883. When issues were compiled and bound for libraries, the advertisements were sliced out. Who wants to read the ads?

In 2017, researchers from the Stanford University School of Medicine recovered the lost advertisements. They found a forgotten chapter of Philip Morris history: from the late thirties to the fifties, they were a major advertiser in the *Journal of the American Medical Association*.

A 1942 advertisement shows a doctor's prescription pad with an order of Philip Morris cigarettes.

'What! Prescribe Cigarettes?!?' the headline asks. 'Addressed to you not as a smoker but a doctor.'

Philip Morris explains. 'When smokers change to Philip Morris, substantially every case of throat irritation due to smoking cleared completely or definitely improved . . . Recognised laboratory tests have conclusively proved the advantage of Philip Morris over other cigarettes.'

Even back in 1942, they were there to heal the world and had the science to back them up.

PROFILE OF A GENERATION X MALE

I've found another in-house document from the caches reluctantly tabled in court cases. I kick my feet up on the coffee table. Here is Philip Morris building a profile of a Generation X male, in 1992, in aid of 'giving "the new age target" a cigarette to call their own.'

'Celebrity counterpart
- River Phoenix
- Keanu Reeves
- Brad Pitt
- Johnny Depp'

Yes, those men are me. This is Johnny Depp eleven years before *Pirates of the Caribbean*, Keanu Reeves seven years before *The Matrix*, Brad Pitt nine years before *Ocean's Eleven*. It's nice to see that besides, sadly, River Phoenix, all these Generation X archetypal men have not only survived but thrived. Actually, come to think of it, Johnny Depp hasn't quite.

'Celebrity dream date
- Winona Ryder
- Bridget Fonda
- Juliette Lewis
- Uma Thurman'

My girlfriend at university asked me to name my celebrity crush. I didn't want to get into that conversation because I sensed danger, but she insisted, telling me I was being silly, it was just a fun game. I said Winona Ryder. She snorted, telling me a girl in our film-theory class looked quite like Winona Ryder, so wasn't it interesting that out of all the celebrities in the worl—

What the hel—

What do we have here?

I find another Philip Morris in-house document. Another proposed campaign from the early nineties. Except this one isn't grappling with how to draw in Generation X. These advertisements are aimed at Baby Boomers, and Philip Morris are laying the boots into Generation X.

'Wouldn't you love to tell the next Gen-Xer to quit whining, lose the plaid, and work his way up like you did? You've got *Merit*. Lower tar. Great taste. For who you are today.'

'Don't you think grunge music is nothing more than whining set to recycled 60s rock? You've got *Merit*. Lower tar. Great taste. For who you are today.'

Playing both sides. I thought Philip Morris were there for us, but it turns out I was wrong. Like stage diving at Lollapalooza and no one catching you.

I lean back in my lounge-room chair, taking this all in. Out the window, grey clouds are rolling in. I slowly pull myself up.

I make my way down the hall to my bedroom, creak open the wardrobe and stare at my flannel shirt. I take it off the hanger and pull it on.

I am X-Man, my body vibrating like Bruce Banner's.

I head out the front door with renewed vigour.

VAPING AND THE
PLEASURE PRINCIPLE

3CR Community Radio, in inner city Melbourne, is lovingly worn-in – or some other euphemism for shabby. In reception there's wooden panels, peeling socialism stickers, a tape deck next to the kettle. Bouncing about are ex-Jehovah's Witnesses who are now proudly LGBTQ+, their t-shirts revealing this. While researching my last book, white nationalists burst in here, uninvited, seeking to throttle the guys who run the anarchist show.

I'm here for Nick Wallis, co-host of the show *Enpsychedelia*: 'Breathing reality into the myths, fabrications and distortions that exist around drugs.'

'What's the good thing about drugs?' I ask him.

'Very interesting,' he chuckles. His golden beard and hair form a lion's mane. 'That word "drugs" is such a loaded term. I'm sure most people who have had any kind of surgery would be very thankful for the fact that an anaesthesiologist can perform their witchcraft on your body and stop you from feeling pain.

That's amazing. That's drugs. It's incredible.'

Nick's point is that normie society is not anti-drugs. We have a community and a health system built around the reality that drugs are not only tolerable but can enhance people's quality of life. From my asthma puffer to your schizophrenia medication, we end up at a shared agreement: some drugs are anointed as good (morphine) and some are anointed as bad (heroin). That heroin is an opiate drug made from morphine shows how slippery the words 'good' and 'bad' are.

Society has ruled on those opiates, but what happens when a new drug rolls into town, in this case vaping? Who rules whether it's good or bad?

At the time of typing this sentence, federal health minister Greg Hunt and our Therapeutic Goods Administration are ruling that vaping is bad.

Savvas says nicotine vape juice has relieved both his physical and psychological pain. He reports he's no longer seedy and sluggish from smoke and he's over the moon in his mind. So why isn't his juice classed as a pain reliever by the medical establishment, like Panadol or the ones shot into you by an anaesthesiologist?

Politician Fiona Patten, who has worked with Nick Wallis on drug-reform policy, had her own thoughts when we spoke in her office/erotic art gallery. She said anti-vaping sentiment is an emotional one, stretching beyond science. Our moral betters (her term) in the community and those running public health can't stand the thought of people experiencing pleasure while healing themselves. *You can have this methadone, but you better not enjoy it.*

Vapers with their coloured kazoos, candy-pop flavours and big fat plumes, smoke signal to the world that what they're doing is pleasurable. The joke goes, *Why don't Baptists approve of premarital sex? Because it might lead to dancing*. Fiona said that something like that – that pleasure is sin – surrounds the debate over vaping.

Nick says that some people who consume 'bad' drugs fight for them to be pushed into the 'good' column. 'There's a renaissance of psychedelic discussion at the moment, the science going on behind it.'

Around the corner from this radio station, at St Vincent's Hospital, researchers are running trials that measure how the drug psilocybin (mushrooms) can lower anxiety. Nick appreciates this but, like Rabbi Gutnick, worries about subjecting everything in life to science's measuring stick.

'Lots of people have psychedelic experiences that they'll claim are a benefit to them, but you can't measure it. And I think it's the same with a lot of other drugs as well.'

'Totally,' I say. 'I write my best when I'm freaking out and I'll just have gin, gin, gin, gin, gin,' I flick my wrist and scull the air with each *gin*. 'How do you measure that?'

'Yeah, exactly. People will go, "But maybe your work would be better if you weren't having a drink".'

'Yea—' Hang on, is he having a go at my work?

'You can't *what if* these things,' he continues, 'because people do the things that they feel they need to do, and that's what helps them.'

I'm starting to form the opinion that the best argument for vaping is the one you can't make: it's a recreational drug that provides pleasure. We're not living in a time where that argument flies.

'Oh, hi, Health Minister Greg Hunt, I think you should legalise vaping because it gives me a pleasant buzz and I like the taste of unicorn custard.'

That the pleasure defence doesn't fly anymore is shown by Philip Morris. A couple of decades ago, the defence of their products circled around freedom and pleasure. Marlboro cowboys roaming the frontiers. But now they're hectoring us like Baptists, insisting they're here for our own good, not our pleasure.

Nick ponders the respectable drugs that can wean you off cigarettes. The nicotine patches, mouth sprays, lozenges and gums put out by pharmaceutical companies.

'We're so into controlling what people can access,' Nick says. 'And personally that, for me, is my tinfoil hat point. Because I wonder, for example, who's the one selling Nicorette and the Nicabate products? Because they're making a killing. There's heaps of people that will go onto those products. They're quite expensive. I'm making wild accusations here and have absolutely no proof, but are Quit Victoria and Cancer Council Victoria – are they getting money from Nicorette? Do they have a financial interest in maintaining a prohibition against anything that could compete with their product? I sort of wonder that sometimes. I think it's probably a bit far-fetched, but why are they so adamant?'

Follow the money!

Fact check

The square brown building of the Cancer Council Victoria is a Sex Pistols song and a half from my home. When the receptionist greets me, I mishear at first. 'Cancer Council' sounds so much like 'cancel culture'. Come to think of it, cancer is the ultimate case of this. God cancels you.

I sit across from Dr Sarah White, director of their Quit Victoria venture, in a grand high-ceilinged room where modern furnishings and flourishes are slowly taking over.

Dr White knows the power held by the cigarette giants. She had to clean up her uncle's home a couple of years ago, after his funeral. 'I've still got the photo of where the cigarettes were sitting on the Heart Foundation brochure, on his bedside table. But he was just so heavily addicted, he just couldn't help himself.'

After twenty minutes, rambling about adjacent matters so I can delay the awkwardness of accusing her of being a stooge for Big Pharma, I bite the bullet.

'Some vapers,' I mutter, 'like to build a story that Big Pharma is behind the push to prohibit vaping because they make too much money from Nicorette gum and patches and inhalers and everything like that.'

Bite the bullet? I flatter myself. More like nibbling the bullet, and it's a chocolate bullet.

'I've never seen any real evidence of that,' she says.

'So, they're not donors, or anything, to Quit or the Victoria Cancel Culture?'

'Definitely not,' she says. 'We have a policy where very clearly we do not accept any donations from pharmaceutical or biotech companies. We were approached to do a clinical trial last year and the principal investigator, a clinician at a major hospital, received funding from, I think, the Pfizer Foundation.'

Pfizer is the world's largest research-based pharmaceutical

company. The clinician wanted to reach smokers through Quit Victoria's Quitline.

'The clinician said "I'll pay you for that." And we said no, because we didn't want to be in any way, shape or form able to have that accusation made against us. That's it, I'm afraid. Non-story on that one.'

Southern Gothic spy story

I still carry warm memories of the free Quit Victoria showbags I got from the Royal Melbourne Show; flicking the frisbee with my dad in the backyard, chewing the biro in primary school until the ink leaked into my mouth.

So you could think I've been bought off by the anti-smoking lobby and their swag bags. To prove I'm incorruptible and independent, I offer you the tale of another anti-smoking organisation.

Complicity is out to get you, I learn, whatever your job. You can't avoid it just because you've decided to fight the good fight.

A woman I'll call . . . I stop typing, swivel my chair and scan the nearby bookshelf . . . a woman I'll call Flannery O'Connor meets me in a beer garden in the city on a sunny afternoon.

'I worked at the United Nations Development Program,' says Flannery. 'We were contracted by WHO's Framework Convention on Tobacco Control.'

This is the world's peak body fighting Philip Morris and Big Tobacco.

'They would send what we call "missions" of people to different countries. They'd talk to governments about tobacco taxation and ways economic policy could be levered to help public health outcomes.'

'What sort of countries?'

'I worked on Latin America and the Caribbean, so Nicaragua, Colombia, Jamaica, Brazil and Argentina.'

Flannery O'Connor's drink arrives. I'd like to say it's a mint julep, but it's a schooner of beer.

She begins discussing how these missions were funded. I'd never pondered how World Health Organization projects get their money.

'WHO knew they didn't have the funds – they didn't have the finance to deal with this particular thing – so they went to different governments. It was my understanding that our funding was coming from the Russian government.'

She waits for my reaction, but I don't have one. What's she getting at?

I learn that Russia, because they forked out the cash, got quite a big say in the specifics of the project. For one, they chose the Latin American and Caribbean countries that would be the focus of the mission.

'When we did a lateral analysis of why those countries were chosen, we noticed that there was a mining interest in those places for the Russian government.'

The sun is making me squint. I think I get what she's getting at. Even though this mission was about smoking, that wasn't why Russia chose to become involved.

'We went through a due diligence process, they were cleared, we took the money. But I can't say with a clear conscience there wasn't another motivation.'

Is my imagination running wild? I might as well ask her the question that has formed in my head.

'This was a way to place spies in these countries?'

'Yes. There was someone in our project directly reporting to the Kremlin.'

Jesus! I love this. How did this happen? Now we're in a spy novel.

'We knew that's what they wanted.'

So, she turned a blind eye to Russian espionage. For some reason I try to downplay this. I don't want her to feel bad.

'I guess Russia is not that controversial. It's not like turning a blind eye to North Korea. I mean, people don't like Russia because they support Trump or something, but besides that . . .' That's my razor-sharp geopolitical analysis. Hire me, *Four Corners*.

'Russia's pretty controversial.' Flannery begs to differ. She accuses them of election interference, helping put Trump in power. 'Everyone I worked with was okay with it, though. However, it's a bit murky.'

I'm sensing she's questioning if she did the right thing.

'I know you hate Donald Trump,' I say. 'And the Russian government supports Donald Trump.'

Is this the reason for her unease?

'You were helping the Russian government in your own little way. You were one of the cogs.'

She takes a moment.

'I joined the UN to work on issues like tobacco control, and I appreciated the opportunity to actually do that. And I think that we had a lot of impact because of that money. It's just the way international relations work, where you find you can disguise your intentions in a certain way and use the UN to do that.'

I don't mind that an anti-smoking group is providing a front for Russia spooks in exchange for filthy lucre. In fact, it sounds exciting. Maybe Sarah at Quit Victoria could liven up her workplace by getting involved in gun running.

Actually, hold up – let me mull this over. Flannery O'Connor told me the Russian spies were staking out a 'mining interest'. What was that all about? Neither the Kremlin nor the mining industry are known for their impeccable ethics, especially when it comes to human rights. So maybe there was a cost to her complicity she just doesn't know about.

A friend of Flannery's joins us at the outdoor table, vines strangling the fence dividing the bar from the laneway, and pulls out a lighter. Flannery O'Connor asks her for a cigarette. Now I'm sitting with two women smoking who say they don't smoke.

Her friend ribs her for this habit.

'So, your point is,' I say, in my best sarcastically accusatory *Four Corners* reporter voice, 'that she's worked in tobacco control and right now has a cigarette in her hand.'

'That's my point,' the friend says.

'And what's your answer to that point, woman in tobacco control?'

Flannery O'Connor breathes out a plume into the sunny afternoon.

'Life is for living,' she says, in not a Southern drawl.

COMPROMISED

What follows is a story I'm apprehensive to tell because it just sounds too convenient. But what am I meant to do? Lie and change the story so the truth sounds less like a lie?

I'm scratching my ear in synagogue, reading *The Godfather*, knowing that from Rabbi Gutnick's angle it looks like a prayer book. This old man floats over and sits next to me. He says he knows my dad, and knew my mum when she was alive. He inquires what I'm up to. I tell him I'm working on a book about Philip Morris and vaping, and he clucks his tongue.

He says something to the effect of, 'I was surprised Alex Wodak let Philip Morris pay for his trip. I'm old friends with him.'

I know that name. Where from, though? Oh, he's one of the scores of pro-vaping campaigners I've started following on Twitter. More than that, he was the doctor on the vaping panel that Fiona Patten ran in parliament.

This old man tells me there was an e-cigarette conference in

Poland and Philip Morris funded Alex's trip. A pro-vaping advocate taking money from Big Tobacco? How strange and serendipitous. What an obscure piece of information – useful to pretty much no one except me.

We chat for a long while about other matters, and then the man wanders away again. It's like God sent a spirit to whisper in my ear and help me on my path.

The dilemma

'Can I ask you a question?' I ask Scarlett-Jae.

You've met her before, but it was only one sentence, so why would you remember that? She was the one pouring a cup of tea in my kitchen, telling me I was an archetypal Gen Xer, as I read through Philip Morris's analysis of Generation X.

Her mother is a Bible-adhering Catholic. A little of that has passed on to Scarlett-Jae, a lot of it hasn't; she snorts a line of cocaine she has brought to my apartment.

I tell her I'm faced with a moral dilemma.

Savvas's company, Vapoureyes, are running a stall at the upcoming Vape Expo Oceania in New Zealand. His boss in New Zealand, a man called Morris Lazootin, has heard I'm flying over to be there – he has invited me to stay at an Airbnb mansion he has rented for international guests, including his US juice suppliers. On top of that, Lazootin is organising three days of fun, all expenses paid: white-water rafting, a winery trip and a tour of the Hobbiton movie set.

Scarlett-Jae wants to know why Lazootin is offering to be such a gracious host.

'He might think I'll be a good advocate for vaping. Not having to spend over a grand on accommodation for a week – that's pretty okay.'

'What's the moral dilemma?' Scarlett-Jae asks.

It's this: am I compromised by accepting free accommodation from the largest vaping empire in Australasia? Not to mention the Hobbits.

'Usually that wouldn't worry me, but . . .' I tell her my synagogue tale. Vaping advocates make a big hoopla about how they're not in bed with Philip Morris. But, if what the old man says is true, I've found the two of them holding hands.

'Can I call Alex Wodak out for the free flight – if he did take it – when I'm going to be taking free accommodation?' Will people go, if you're claiming you're defiled once you take a freebie from a corporation, why are taking a freebie?

'You're not espousing for vaping, you're just finding the story,' Scarlett-Jae says. 'So it doesn't really matter if you take their accommodation, because it's not like your morals really come into it at all.'

That makes no sense whatsoever, but she's saying what I want to hear.

'Done,' I conclude.

I message Lazootin. He says he'll pick me up from the airport.

The FDA-57

As much as I'm looking forward to frolicking among the toadstools, my agenda for hitting New Zealand is not related to Bilbo Baggins. It's because Savvas has told me Philip Morris have rented space at the expo. Philip Morris won't let me through their doors in

Melbourne, but what can they do to stop me wandering up to their stall?

The day before my flight, I pore over more material.

Philip Morris promote their PMI-58 as fifty-eight 'harmful and potentially harmful constituents' in cigarette smoke that show up at a lower rate, sometimes a much lower rate, in HeatStick aerosol. The implication? The IQOS is less harmful.

But, as we've discussed, Philip Morris have pulled a cheeky little trick in doing that. There are many more constituents in smoke and aerosol. They cherrypicked the fifty-eight that served their purpose.

Some boffins at the US Federal Drug Administration picked up on the ruse, and examined fifty-seven others, digging into Philip Morris's very own data. In all cases, *these* 'harmful and potentially harmful constituents' showed up as a *higher* rate in the HeatStick. So if we go by what I'd call the FDA-57, the IQOS is more harmful than cigarettes.

The FDA-57 is a tipped-over box of Scrabble.

1,2,3-Propanetriol, diacetate (diacetin) 1,2-Propanediol, 3-chloro 1,4-Dioxane, 2-ethyl-5-methyl 2,14-Labdadiene-7,8-diol, (8a,12E) 1 hour-Indene, 2,3-dihydro-1,1,5,6-tetramethyl 1-Hydroxy-2-butanone 1-Hydroxy-2-propanone(1,2-Propenediol) 2 (5H)-Furanone 2,3-Dihydro-5-hydroxy-6-methyl-4 hour-pyran-4-one 2,4-Dimethylcyclopent-4-ene-1,3-dione 2-Cyclopentene-1,4-dione 2-Formyl-1-methylpyrrole 2-Furancarboxaldehyde,5-methyl 2-Furanmethanol 2-Furanmethanol, 5-methyl 2 hour-Pyran-2-one, tetrahydro-5-hydroxy 2-Methylcyclobutane-1,3-dione

2-Propanone, 1-(acetyloxy) 3 (2H)-Furanone, dihydro-2-methyl
3-Methylvaleric acid 4(H)-Pyridine, N-acetyl 5-Methylfurfural
Anhydro linalool oxide Benzene, 1,2,3,4-tetramethyl-
4-(1-methylethenyl) Benzenemethanol, 4-hydroxy Benzoic acid,
2,5-dihydroxy-methyl Butylated hydroxytoluene Butyrolactone
Cis-sesquisabinene hydrate Cyclohexane, 1,2-dioxo
Cyclohexane-1,2-dione, 3-methyl Eicosane, 2-methyl
Ergosterol Ethyl 2,4-dioxohexanoate Ethyl dodecanoate
(ethyl laurate) Ethyl linoleate Ethyl linolenate Furfural
Glycerol Glycidol Heneicosane, 2-methyl Hexadecanoic acid,
ethyl ester Isolinderanolide Isoquinoline, 3-methyl
Labdane-8,15-diol, (13S) Lanost-8-en-3-ol, 24-methylene-,
(3beta) Maltoxazine Methyl furoate Phenylacetaldehyde
p-Menthan-3-ol Propylene glycol Pyranone Pyridoxin Stearate,
ethyl Tar Trans-4-hydroxymethyl-2-methyl-1,3-dioxolane.

Let's take just one ingredient, Phenylacetaldehyde, which is
'considered a hazardous substance' by the US Department of Labor
Occupational Safety and Health Administration. It shows up in a
HeatStick at a rate 167 per cent higher than in a cigarette.

Before my flight to New Zealand I print out the FDA-57, fold it
up and tuck it into my pocket.

PACIFIC ADVENTURE

In the echoey and near empty Auckland airport, past midnight, I catch sign of Lazootin. In that moment I realise I've subconsciously built an image of him in my head where he resembles seventies adventurer and *World Safari* documentary film-maker Alby Mangels: sinewy and leathery, shirtless and in thongs.

I have no idea why that was, because Lazootin looks nothing like that. He is twenty-eight but could pass for nineteen. Pale blue eyes and marshmallow coloured skin. A tall Christmas elf.

'It's the cheapest Tesla,' he says of his ride, as we dart down the freeway. 'It's the model three.'

In recent days, Tesla's CEO Elon Musk unveiled the prototype for a Cybertruck at a press conference that would have been a disaster for any company but his. To prove that the windows were bulletproof, one of Musk's assistants smashed a sledgehammer against one. It shattered.

Lazootin went to order one online and accidentally ordered two, although the deposits are only a couple of hundred bucks. He's pretty sure the prototype won't come to fruition, but he doesn't care, he's in it for the adventure.

Enticement

New Zealand is so good-looking, you can build a giant flat grey box and surround it with a carpark, and you'll still be knocked out by the greenery, trees and hills in all directions. That's what the show-grounds in Auckland's Cornwall Park are like.

'Youknowwhenyouhavelikeachocolatecoatedcoffeebean?' I ask Savvas, rejoining him after a wander through the giant hall. One booth was offering samples of nicotine toothpicks, designed to calm vapers on flights. I've had about fifteen. 'Whenyouhaveoneandit'sfine andsoyouhavemore?' I concentrate, slow down. 'You think it's like M&M's, and then it's twenty minutes later and you're shaking?'

We stroll past an ice-cream truck promoting ice-cream-flavoured vape juice and a booth staffed by promo girls dressed as nurses and promo boy dressed as doctors.

'One of the reasons why I love going to expo so much is just the swell of humanity that comes here,' Savvas says. 'I know that there's a stereotype about vapers, the douche flutes and fucking hipsters. But you look around and there are people from all walks of life. There are older people, there are younger people – not too young, obviously. There are people with mullets and there are people with different hair. It's beautiful to see, in a way.'

I'm hiccupping, somehow drunk on toothpicks.

A young woman who works with Savvas, Ren, joins our stroll. Before Vapoureyes took her on, she was a NSW axe and knife throwing champion. 'You can tell when someone makes juice because they are real chubs, usually. The better their juice, the chubbier they are.'

'Why are they so quote unquote chubs?' I ask.

'They've probably been eating artificial flavouring their whole life. They just know what flavours go together really well.'

At one booth an enormous poster hangs, showing an art director in China's perception of a sophisticated Caucasian: a silver-haired man in a turtleneck.

Another Vapoureyes employee wanders over. Known as the Vaping Bogan, he's a YouTube celebrity, with 169,000 subscribers who follow his vape reviews. 'What's your Nazi book?' he asks me.

Like most mean looking people, neck tattoos crawling towards his face, the Vaping Bogan is not mean at all. His wife has read my last book, on extremists. 'She was like, do you think that when they were sitting down with John they realised he was going to make them look like fucking Nazis?'

'Well, they were fucking Nazis,' I say.

The Vaping Bogan impersonates his wife, concerned about this very book you hold in your hands. '*He's lulling you into a sense of comfort and he's going to make you all look like idiots.*'

Savvas defends me. 'I think they lulled themselves into a sense of comfort.'

I continue roaming and clowning around. There's a common complaint I'm hearing, which is that the expo is different this year because Big Tobacco has joined the carnival. The makers of Camel are the straw that has broken a vape vendor's back. (Buzzing on toothpicks, my head spinning, I've lost my bearings on puns pushing their luck.)

'They've set up a racing simulator to promote their new vape. In a climate where we're all working really hard to address the teen vaping issue. The whole industry is under the gun because we're all being construed as appealing to minors. And then they come along and pull something like this?'

Philip Morris has secured the best patch of real estate. 'I'm really disappointed about that,' says one vape campaigner. 'You come in the door and it's Philip Morris IQOS. And I just spoke to an old man who came here a smoker – he came to get a vape. He didn't even get past them. He got an IQOS. I mean, I'm for whatever works to help people, but I'm still a little bit sad about that.'

THE BOOTH

I take the long way around to go to the bathroom – I don't want to stroll past the IQOS booth before I'm ready. I feel the FDA-57 folded in my pocket.

On the way back, I take a quick peek, and there it is in the distance. The IQOS booth.

Through the smudge on my glasses, from fingerprints and vapour, I see a man staring back at me. I approach.

The booth is expansive, with spaces for different sections. In one area a barista serves complimentary coffee in IQOS cups from behind a shiny silver coffee machine. The main section is manned by a sparkly looking young man and woman. They look freshly washed, making me self-conscious about the sleep in my eyes. The man looks like PewDiePie if you know what PewDiePie looks like. I will find out he is William Churchill, Manager External Affairs, and she is Rhenu Bhuller, Manager Scientific Affairs.

A third man is supervising a desktop metal contraption with

pistons that, if you want to take Philip Morris at their word, simulates puffing and shows how your lungs are stained by cigarette smoke but not HeatStick aerosol.

'Is that a cigarette?' I ask. Will anyone from Philip Morris admit it is?

'Yep,' Rhenu says.

That was easy.

She realises I'm pointing at the HeatStick. 'No. Which one? No, that's a tobacco stick.'

'But why? Because it looks like a cigarette. Cos I've seen it in —'

'That's the smoke smell from all the smoke residue,' the man operating the machine says, jumping to something else.

'Why is that not a cigarette though? It looks like a cigarette.'

'It looks like it. It's a HeatStick,' Rhenu affirms.

'So, the tobacco leaf is different?'

'It's the same tobacco leaf.'

She says the leaf is processed differently though, stirred into a slurry and pressed into sheets, then rolled into HeatSticks. Because of this method, she says, it can deliver the same amount of nicotine with less tobacco. Maybe. Another scientific claim that I don't have the monkeys, mice or Bunsen burners to corroborate.

'I've got an IQOS,' I say. 'And there's gunk left in it after you go through a few HeatSticks. Is that evidence HeatSticks produce tar?'

'No,' Rhenu says.

I'm not sure she's right, but what am I meant to do? Throw a tantrum?

I unfold the FDA-57 list from my pocket and point to 'Phenyl-acetaldehyde', the hazardous substance that shows up at a higher rate in a HeatStick than in traditional cigarettes.

She takes a moment, fingering the figures.

'There are a few chemicals which are higher in the IQOS, but if you look at the level of chemicals overall, ninety, ninety-five per cent of the constituents are lower in IQOS cigarettes.'

So she talked around that. What am I meant to do? Grab a Zippo and light the booth on fire?

William plucks the sheet of paper from Rhenu. 'Normally when a journo comes in, we're like, okay, what kind of stitch-up are we about to walk into?'

Like Rabbi Gutnick, he's concerned I'll be unfair to Philip Morris.

He says his colleagues have been chatting about me on a Philip Morris WhatsApp group. 'When people want to really talk about what we're trying to do, the company is really open. The biggest thing for us is, can we have a fair and honest discussion about what we're trying to do? That's where we just get burnt in a lot of instances.'

You might recall I bought Philip Morris shares, roughly $2000 worth. I've made $230 so far. I tell them this. (I don't tell them that I bought the shares to gain entry to the upcoming Annual Shareholders Meeting. Although, I've got to admit, a 10 per cent return is pretty sweet.)

Rhenu perks up, surprised. 'You'll have to disclose that in your writing,' she says. 'Someone would say, "Oh, but you're writing nice things because you have shares."'

Unbeknown to her, the nicest thing I've written about Philip Morris so far is that she and William are freshly washed.

Knowing I've bought in, they loosen up. William motions to an exhibit in the booth. A stack of paper, thousands of pages of science, representing so much research. A plaque explains that the application to the US Federal Drug Administration seeking approval for the IQOS 'is such a big document that if it was printed and stacked it would be as tall as a twenty-storey building. *IQOS simply amazing.*' If quantity counts for anything, this proves the IQOS is legitimate. The FDA are yet to return their ruling.

'I was a pack-a-day smoker,' William exclaims with passion. 'I would pinch darts when I was eighteen at parties.' Like Savvas, for years he was enslaved. 'And then I switched to IQOS. And I feel good for it. People who keep saying, "Oh, it's just as bad as smoking," are climate change deniers, they are flat-earthers. I find that really insulting. Our R&D cube in Switzerland has shown it's legit.' He twitches. 'Now I feel like I'm getting worked up.'

This is reminding me of something else.

'You know how I like to interview Scientologists and people in cults?'

'Yeah,' William says.

'So, I was wondering, like . . . are you in a cult?'

I point to the stack of papers submitted to the FDA.

'In that you have to abide by the religious scripture there.'

I tell him that when I talk to Scientologists, they're really nice. 'But then if you say something that goes against their scripture, or you start going, "Oh, is that really true?" then they get a bit twitchy. So how do you know you're not in a cult?'

'Yeah, I hear you. In Japan, when we launched the IQOS, that was the first moment, like, "Holy shit, this thing's actually successful. People want to switch." You do start getting a cult-like love for the product, that it's working and people are switching. And that pervasive enthusiasm for what we're doing is really infectious.'

Rhenu interrupts, having overheard William's earlier mention of this 'cube' in Switzerland. 'You should go check out the cube, it's amazing. It's *amazing*.'

Muslims make pilgrimage to an enormous black cube, the Ka'bah, in Mecca. I learn that Philip Morris disciples trek to a giant black and glass cube in Neuchâtel, Switzerland, where the company's boffins attend to their beakers and their brain trusts ponder. Both sets of worshippers make throaty sounds. The first because that's Arabic, the second, cancer of the oesophagus.

In the passing crowd, I spot vape campaigner Dr Alex Wodak. I tell William and Rhenu what the old man told me in synagogue. 'I heard Philip Morris paid for his plane trip to the Polish vape conference.'

'No,' Rhenu says. 'We've never paid for him.'

I look out again. Alex has disappeared.

'And if we did pay, it all has to be disclosed,' she says. 'Like, if we paid for you to go to the cube, you'd actually have to write that we paid for you to go to the cube. That's how strict our disclosure policy is.'

Dangle?

I duck outside. It's cloudy, but I've been in the hall all day so the sky is making me squint. Please tell me the recorder got that. Did they just – Was that – Did she just feel out if I'd accept a free flight to Switzerland? 'If we paid for you to go to the cube.' That's better than a seventy-five dollar steak. A lot better.

I sit down on the kerb, look out beyond the showgrounds carpark, to the rolling green hills and, too perfectly, a chimney stack. I ponder. *Did* Rhenu just dangle a free trip? To someone writing a book about Philip Morris?

I click the tiny plastic box open and pluck out the last nicotine toothpick. I gnaw at it and the head rush returns.

Compromised

I go to the bathroom and in the cubicle (not the cube) I place my recorder down on the floor, along with my shotgun mic and my headphones. *Kosovo Is Serbia* and *Fuck Scopje* is penned on the wall. What does that . . . Oh God, my urine has splashed onto the headphones. I'll have to wash that off.

Heading to the sink and I'm thinking, this is what I'm thinking: is this the universe telling me that I'm tainted? Because I took the Airbnb accommodation from Lazootin, and I bought the Philip Morris shares, and I'm going to Hobbiton tomorrow where Vapoureyes will pay for the Hobbit ticket? And Rhenu just floated a free trip (I think?) and, in my head, I've already said, *deal*.

Do you know what I mean? I'm tainted. I've pissed over myself. Does that make sense? Maybe you can never unpiss over yourself.

The lights are so bright.

Leaving the bathroom, dragging myself through the expo and my foot, it feels squishy. My sock is soaked and I . . . I don't know. It's like, is it sweat? Or did I also piss in my shoe? Am I walking around in my own piss? But it just shows how once you've been corrupted – you're walking around and you don't even know whether you've got piss in your shoe or not.

Nicotine Free Dry Particulate Matter

On a stage, a 10-metre-long ruler glows on a giant video screen, measuring how far contestants can blow a vape cloud.

I had asked Rhenu about the gunk left in the IQOS device. Is that evidence HeatSticks produce tar? She said 'no'. I pull out my phone and hit up Philip Morris International's dedicated science site to check what they have to say on this matter.

'Tar' – An outdated concept that can mislead consumers.

I see Philip Morris leverage not only language but punctuation, placing 'tar' in sneer quotes to signal it's not a real thing.

So what is 'tar'? It's simply the total weight of solid and liquid residue in cigarette smoke after the weight of nicotine and water has been subtracted. Expert scientists call it Nicotine Free Dry Particulate Matter (NFDPM).

Hmm. In fact, expert scientists at the FDA, for one, list the HeatStick residue not as NFDPM but as tar – no sneer quotes.

The cigarette giant is trying to retire the word 'tar', with its ugly connotations, and replace it with a more positive term (nicotine free!). Hey, don't stop there, Philip Morris. We need your expert wordsmithing for all stages of smoking, from go to woe.

No, you're not 'wheezing', you're what expert scientists call Human Slide-Whistling.

No, no, no, that's not a 'tumour', it's a Harmony Growth. Harmony Growths occur naturally in nature, for example in animals like the Tasmanian Devil.

No, your father isn't 'dead', he's what expert hearse drivers call Sustainably Non-Breathing.

Look, Rhenu was just doing her job, and quite well.

Dr Wodak

I nose around and find Dr Alex Wodak relaxing in the spacious Vapoureyes booth. There's a VIP area that hides behind a partition, where drinks and nicotine toothpicks are served. I sink in next to him on one of the buttock-pleasing couches.

Dr Wodak is a respected pioneer, campaigning for safe-sex programs during the AIDS crisis in the eighties. He now campaigns for a needle and syringe program for prisoners who take drugs. Vaping is a continuation of this work in harm reduction.

'E-cigarettes are a disruptive innovation,' Dr Wodak says. 'The digital camera was a disruptive innovation of the analogue camera, and Kodak fell over because of that.' (Mental note: if I fall into a battle rap with him, rhyme Wodak with Kodak.)

'Philip Morris are beyond reprehensible, what they have done,' he says. 'I mean, they're responsible for a hundred million deaths around the world in the twentieth century. And they will be responsible for a billion deaths in the remainder of this century, from smoking.' Still, he believes the IQOS plays it part, as does vaping. 'Much as I hate Big Tobacco and would gladly waterboard them – all of them – I have to say on the other hand, on this issue, they're right. This will save many, many lives. If we let it happen. And so far, we're not letting it happen.'

I gulp, knowing what I have to bring up now.

'I heard – it was the weirdest thing. I'm sitting there in synagogue and this guy comes up to me . . .' I fumble it all out, that a man said he took funding from Philip Morris to attend an e-cigarette conference in Warsaw.

'Yeah,' Dr Wodak says. 'It's a very dirty game. I was in Canberra last week with Colin Mendelsohn, going around, seeing politicians.' Dr Mendelsohn is a fellow vaping campaigner.

Dr Wodak says one politician with whom they had a meeting scheduled – he won't tell me who – was suddenly too busy and couldn't make time for them. But this politician's staffer told them that senior public health officials had swung by and pretty much threatened the politician. 'They said, if you come out publicly supporting vaping, there will be serious consequences for you and your party.' So that explained the cancelled meeting.

'That's why your friend said that to you in synagogue. It's a dirty, dirty game.'

Hang on, let me get this straight. Big We Hate Tobacco got wind that I was working on a book, so they sent an agent to my synagogue to plant a rumour about him?

'So it's not true?' I ask.

'Did I go to Warsaw? Yes, I did. I've been there three or four times. Did I get paid by Big Tobacco to go? No. Big Tobacco's never given me a cent.'

'Not even a ticket or a plane flight?'

'Not a ticket or a plane flight. The organisers of the conference, who I've worked with for twenty-five years, gave me some money towards my flight. They didn't pay for my expenses but they helped me, which I appreciated.'

Dr Wodak wants to point something out else. 'But listen. All these people who are paid by Bloomberg on the other side . . .'

He pauses, which leads me to fill the silence with a yarn of my own and, listening back to the recording, makes me want to punch myself in the face. Because Dr Wodak never circles back to the matter of Bloomberg.

The best I can do now is provide the take on Michael Bloomberg held by many campaigners for vaping.

The billionaire businessman and former mayor of New York City funds Bloomberg Philanthropies, which in 2019 launched a $160 million program to 'end the youth e-cigarette epidemic'.

Those in favour of vaping say the people who accept money from Bloomberg are compromised. They've pissed in their shoes. They can never admit that vaping serves as a harm reduction tool, no matter what the science proves, because Bloomberg would cut off their funding.

Dr Wodak and I continue to chat, and I shut up this time.

'We've got to sit down with the tobacco companies and give them an honourable peace. When Kennedy met Khrushchev, the advice that was given to him was not to humiliate the enemy. To give him an honourable escape route.' He thinks the escape route for Philip Morris is letting them transition from traditional cigarettes to their 'smoke-free' alternatives. 'Kennedy took that advice, and he was right to take that advice.'

I thank him and head off for a stroll, swiping a nicotine tooth-pick on the way out of the Vapoureyes VIP area.

Warsaw

What was this Warsaw conference anyway? The one Dr Wodak attended – his flight, according to him, subsidised by the organisers. Later, back at home in Melbourne, I poke around.

The Global Forum on Nicotine is an annual event. In 2019, it took place in Warsaw. This forum is run by something called Knowledge-Action-Change Limited, a private organisation. That organisation is funded by the Foundation for a Smoke-Free World, who, in turn, are funded by Philip Morris International.

THE SHAPESHIFTING JEW

Philip Morris is disappearing words and what they signify. 'Cigarette' becomes 'HeatStick', 'smoke' turns to 'aerosol'. Why am I feeling something here – something big – that others are not? I suspect it's because I'm keenly aware of the consequence of these slippery and insidious word games.

Parallel to the Philip Morris gambit, I've caught wind of another one. Scrubbing out the word 'Jew' and substituting in the word 'white'.

Neil Erikson, a far-right campaigner, had just wrapped up a twelve-month supervised community correction order. A magistrate had found him guilty of stalking Rabbi Gutnick. Yes, the one you've met in this book!

Now, Neil Erikson was helping to organise a rally against multi-culturalism in the Melbourne CBD, a two-minute walk from Rabbi Gutnick's synagogue.

I turned up to the counter-rally, organised to protest the neo-Nazis and their fellow travellers.

I started shooting zingers on social media. 'I'm here at the rally this morning. If you see me come over and say heil.'

I stood at the counter-rally and was flummoxed to learn my presence was a problem. Not for the neo-Nazis, but for some on this side. A young man, who now writes about racism for Australia's multicultural broadcaster, made it clear I was not welcome in the Melbourne CBD that morning. Why on earth not?

He wrote of me on social media: *Anti-racism doesn't need any more white people to speak on its behalf.*

'Fuck off we're full' seems like a weird message to send to a Jew at a rally against neo-Nazis. But that morning, I learned, for the first time, that we are no longer 'Jews' – a word that affords us a specific history, one entwined with antisemitism, and so a place at the counter-rally. We are now 'white people', a word that affords us 'ugh, white people'.

I went on to discover this wasn't some glitch in the system, some one-off aberration. Academics had spent a decade pushing for this word substitution, in a discipline called Critical Race Theory.

In California, the state legislators considered a bill. High-school students would be required to take a course examining bigotry and racism. The law was passed, and the state's leading academics were now tasked with writing a syllabus for this course. In 2019 they returned one. It covered bigotry against Black, Asian, Native American, Latino and Muslim Americans.

Where were the Jews? They'd made it to the other side of the ledger. Millions of high-school students would learn that Jews had become white – part of the privileged overlords.

Here comes the dark comedy punchline. Two and a half weeks before this syllabus was submitted, also in California, a white supremacist wandered into a synagogue with a semi-automatic, killing a sixty-year old woman, wounding an eight-year-old girl and blowing off the rabbi's fingers. We hadn't become white to the gunman. We were definitely Jews.

(Jewish groups fought back against this proposed syllabus and, at the time of writing this sentence in May 2021, a final draft is yet to be released.)

After a flattering *New York Times* piece about Louis Farrakhan, the head of The Nation of Islam, who has called Jews 'termites' and 'devils', the termites complained. The writer of the article responded that 'people who have become white' don't get to complain.

Following a different American synagogue shooting to the one mentioned above, and the massacre at a mosque in Christchurch, our national broadcaster wanted to host a panel on the neo-Nazi problem today. I was invited, then uninvited, after it was decided that only Muslims and people of colour should be part of this discussion, not white people.

These academics, these woke *Volk*, have achieved what neo-Nazis never could. Creating a reality where Jews are unwelcome to rock up to the Melbourne CBD anytime they wish. Slam poets with Critical Race Theory degrees pulling off what ISIS never could. A no-go Zone for Jews would otherwise be laughed out of town. *Back off, white man, this is a space for people of colour* gets the caliphate done without all the mess.

Do you understand now why I'm attuned to the power of a word switcheroo?

With this word substitution, 'white people' for 'Jews', history is erased. Eight days old, the knife uncuts my penis. I unlive at my grandparent's home, grandmother mentally ill, the guilt of fleeing Poland while her family were murdered. The gas unswirls, back into the pipes. And further back it goes. The rock reverses back into David's slingshot.

Philip Morris places 'tar' in scare quotes to signal it's a thing that doesn't actually exist, that we've moved on. If you want to submit to their edicts, where cigarettes, smoke and tar no longer exist, I can't stop you.

But I'm not submitting to the critical race theorists dancing around the meaning of words.

I am a Jew, not a 'Jew'.

Swing at me.

LATE-STAGE CAPITALISM

Ren, the former knife and axe throwing champion who now works at Vapoureyes, is describing Lazootin's place. 'It's kind of like this clearing on the top of a hill where there's just this big fuck-off mansion with huge solar panels on it. And the whole house wraps around itself, a hexagon of timber and iron. And you have a view of the entire bay. And you just know that someone with a lot of money lives here and they're looking down on everybody else.'

'Why are you so much better at describing things than me?' I ask Ren. I've been spluttering into my recorder, trying to set the scene at the Lazootin homestead in Tangoio, five hours' drive south-east of Auckland.

Morris Lazootin, the only man above Savvas in the Vapoureyes empire. The Not-Philip-Morris Morris.

Ren tells me that the bit about Lazootin looking down on everyone is sarcastic. 'Vapoureyes is the most left-wing place that you could work. Morris actually pays his employees properly.

There are a lot of vape companies out there that aren't even on the books.' She says Lazootin finds people on welfare with untapped skills. 'He finds little lost puppies and makes them great.'

From the hill, we look down to a forest. A gong hangs from a pine tree in the distance. People are taking turns firing a rifle to ding the metal plate. Back in the house, partygoers from the expo are huffing a Volcano Vaporizer, a bag filled with I'm not saying what. I don't want to get anyone in trouble.

After countless bullets, I achieve one ding and go out on this high. I retrieve a bottle of gin from the kitchen and lie on the grass next to Savvas. The sun is setting and I'm sure Ren could say that better.

'Dad's a gambler, is the best way I can describe him,' Savvas says. 'Mum does pastoral care at the women's prison in Adelaide.' They split when he was six. 'Dad moved to Australia from Greece when he was in his twenties. He doesn't speak the language very well at all. So he can't communicate with anybody other than people within the Greek community.' Well, at least he has them. 'He doesn't associate with the Greek community,' Savvas continues.

He has tried to ease his dad over to vaping. 'He feels like he would die if he quit smoking. He said the doctor told him that. Now, that didn't happen,' says sceptical Savvas. He explains that if his dad didn't smoke, he would have nothing to do. 'Quite literally. He just sits around the house smoking all day and playing with his dog.'

So Savvas didn't pick up his business acumen from his home life. 'Nobody sat me down and said, this is how you run a business or this is what you need to think about when making plans.'

A roly-poly American, a juice maker, comes out of the house, complaining that there's no toilet paper in the bathroom. A very similar looking American, his Tweedledum, announces, 'I won't need toilet paper because I'm going to take a shit so big and wipe it with my hand and flush my hand down the toilet.'

The hand flusher is a former drug addict. He asked me earlier, 'You're Jewish?' He then told me that when he was a kid he was jumped by Black people. 'So I got the swastika tattooed on my hand and, within twenty-four hours, I thought – because I had sobered up – that I made a bad decision. And so I got it covered up with a black tattoo. I figured if I ever got a job and there was a Jewish guy that was going to be signing my cheques, I'm definitely not going to have the job.'

'It's a broken industry, full of broken people,' Savvas says. 'And I think we like it that way. It makes it what it is.'

He waves away a tray of brownies doing the rounds.

'I mean, can you imagine half the people that you've met here working in any other industry? A huge percentage of them are former drug addicts and current drug addicts, in and out of jail, can't find steady employment anywhere else. They might outwardly seem to be just a fucking loser, but they have plenty to offer. But who's gonna let them offer it?'

'Anything informal, like the vape industry, people are uncomfortable with that,' I say. 'And are like, "We've got to pin this down."'

'Order always gets introduced to chaos because order is the most efficient way to make money.'

I like the chaos.

'The other thing about the vape industry,' I say. 'It's not like – hey, we'll give broken people the bare minimum. Not only can they earn a basic living doing this, they can thrive.'

The swastika-hand-flusher's former job was wiping windows at a car wash. He told me: 'My company started off with a borrowed $50 from a friend. Made some bottles of juice and drove around town selling them to people. We're having our time now where we're blowing up really well, doing really good.'

'They can only thrive for as long as it takes for the normal people to notice,' Savvas says. 'Inevitably, the normal people come in. They have their lives together a bit more. And because they don't have to battle addiction, or the consequences of having been addicted, it's easy for them to introduce that structure. To turn it into a more rigid system, with its own rules and regulations and defined boundaries. And then those broken people just get pushed to the side again.'

A woman sits down next to us, taking in the beach. She's lost in a loose hoodie, her glasses serving as a hairband, pushing back her brown hair. We're so high up on a hill, we can see beyond the pine trees, to the sea. Before Vapoureyes took her on, she was a buyer for a big tobacconist chain.

'You go to China, they have these gift shows, and there's huge halls the size of football fields,' Redacted says. (She told me to name her that, so that meta's not on me.) 'So you trawl and trawl and trawl, up and down. You do it for six days straight. And the object is to find something you like and say, I want it, put it in this box, and I want it changed a bit.'

She sips her beer.

'And so, I got them to make two shipping containers full of ashtrays that look like skeletons having sex.' She tossed up calling them Boney Maronis but settled on Sexy Skellies.

The night she returned home from China, she held an empty milk carton over the sink, ready to rinse it and toss it in the recycling bin, when her girlfriend spotted a Sexy Skellies sample on the kitchen table.

'What the fuck is that?' her girlfriend snapped.

'It's a bonking-skeleton ashtray,' Redacted said. 'I just made 54 cubic metres of them come to Australia. I just made 54 cubic metres of landfill.'

Redacted says she thought to herself, 'Don't bother rinsing the fucking milk carton. The milk carton doesn't make up for what I did at work today.'

'You can't help but be both grist for the mill and the mill itself,' Savvas broods. 'You can't help but be one of the cogs that grinds other cogs. I'm struggling with that a lot lately.' He waves his vape. 'Devices like this, ultimately someone's slaved away to make it. If it's not the device manufacturer, it's the child slave that dug up the minerals that made the lithium that made the battery. I mean, on some level you're just fucking someone. And you cannot escape it.'

I want to make them feel better. I tell Savvas and Redacted that I heard a right-winger on a podcast say capitalism has lifted China out of poverty.

No one looks consoled. I have another go.

'That guy who's digging up the lithium in Nigeria? He was back at his little hut and you know what? He punched his sister in the nose.'

'Fuck him,' Savvas says. 'I'm going to buy another vape just so he has to dig up more lithium.'

The all-seeing eye

I can't lift my head from the ground, from all the gin. Redacted left hours ago, or at least I think she did – I can't lift my arm to check my watch. Wind is whistling around my arms and head.

'Do you think they have secret rituals?' Savvas asks. The black sky fills up all the available space, and it's all available, skyscrapers and cities far away. He goes on. 'Human sacrifices and things.'

Savvas is rolling this around his mind: to embolden and de-sensitise themselves for the task of killing millions through cigarettes, Philip Morris executives might conduct mystical blood rites and pray to idols.

Savvas is speaking to the collective unconscious. That we just know there are secret societies out there. The elite performing esoteric rituals behind locked doors. We grow up hearing whispers about the Illuminati.

I realise he's hit upon why I'm so drawn to Philip Morris. My urge to scale their walls and peek behind the curtains. It's because corporations like Philip Morris are the true secret societies. Their office headquarters as impenetrable as the castle in Bavaria where the Illuminati meet. Their paperwork with their true plans as closely guarded as that of the Catholic secret order Opus Dei. Those logos – the Nike swoosh, the Shell petroleum shell – draw us in and ward us off, hypnotic and pulsating like the Masonic All Seeing Eye. The white of the Marlboro logo, a pyramid, the Philip Morris crest at its apex.

To me, Philip Morris International is L Ron Hubbard's top-secret naval vessel. It is the gold-domed temple on financier Jeffrey Epstein's private island. And I'd jump in the ocean and madly try to swim out to either of those, swallowing mouthfuls of salt water, just to get a closer look. Adventurers are drawn to the unknown unknowns. And by definition – unknown – they don't exactly know what it is they are seeking.

HOBBITING AND LOBBYING

Is this strenuous? Am I so hung over from last night that a walking tour designed for all ages, and 'chubs' Americans, is taking such a toll on me?

Eighty-nine dollars. That's the cost of a Hobbiton ticket. Which I'm not footing, because Vapoureyes is paying. And it's actually more than eighty-nine dollars all up, since I'll also be getting the meal at the Hobbiton Green Dragon Inn. Plus mead.

There's no hiding from the sun. Not even Peter Jackson, the mastermind behind this tightly controlled reality, could dim that.

Savvas, Lazootin, Tweedledee and Tweedledum, and a carnival of others, stroll past lakes and knolls that were either always here or not. Everything is messing with my head. Is that fake moss or real moss on the post box outside that Hobbit hole? Over there is a clothes line with an elf outfit swaying in the wind.

A real tree then a fibreglass tree.

A Hobbit!

'The sign at the start said no smoking,' I tell the Hobbit. 'What about vaping?'

'I don't know!' says the Hobbit in a springy Scottish brogue. He frolics off.

We wander over a bridge and take snaps of an abandoned cart stacked with barrels of mead. Savvas wonders what creature hauled this cart. I read the book on the tram in Year 7 but can't remember anything.

We catch up to the Hobbit again. I ask about the plumes puffing out the chimneys of the Hobbit homes, built into the hills.

'Is that smoke or steam?'

'I don't know!' says the Hobbit and again frolics away.

Savvas pulls me aside, telling me the Hobbit doesn't work here, he's just a person who has dressed up to go on the tour.

We see the Hobbit disappear behind a turn in the distance.

Eighty-nine New Zealand dollars. That's more than a seventy-five dollar steak too. But it's not that – I'm learning that lobbying presents a pickle, but a different one than what I'd expected. It's not that you're getting paid off, it's that you're forming friendships.

Can I slam my friends, the biggest vape empire in Australasia, after this?

I don't know.

I frolic off. Slowly, hungover, limping.

TIKI TIMEBOMB

When I left Australia, bushfires were burning. Bushfires smoke. A volcano has just erupted in New Zealand. Volcanos vape. Thank you, Mother Nature, for staying on theme.

But something other than lava is burbling on these islands. 'Free West Papua' posters hang behind Ricardo Menéndez March in his office at Auckland Action Against Poverty. It makes me feel like I'm back at uni. 'Decolonise' pamphlets on his desk, a crammed-up bookshelf. I hope Naomi Klein's *No Logo* is tucked in there somewhere.

'Philip Morris had contracted a PR company called Silver Eye,' says young, handsome, bespectacled Ricardo. (He's Mexican but fair skinned; I'll leave it to the critical race theorists to measure his skull.) 'And they had reached out to us, trying to arrange a meeting.'

Auckland Action Against Poverty works with Māori communities. Nearly 30 per cent of Māori people smoke – more than three times the rest of New Zealand's population.

Silver Eye told Ricardo, 'We want a Smoke-Free New Zealand. We want to particularly target Pasifika women.'

Ricardo twigged this wasn't a conventional public health campaign.

'We declined the meeting. And then we got a follow-up email insisting to meet up, which I thought was slightly aggressive.'

Philip Morris wouldn't be dissuaded. 'I found out that they had been trying to reach out to local marae.' These are carved structures, sacred spaces, where tribes meet. 'The PR tactics that I've seen from Philip Morris – obviously it's happening at a very high level, but also at a very on the ground, community level.'

Ricardo rebuffed them.

This granular campaigning is audacious. I find it giddying. They've crossed the rubric, sidling in on holy spaces.

I shouldn't be as shocked as I am. On my first television assignment, in 1997, I investigated voodooism in Ivory Coast. One morning, between the mud huts, I spotted a four-wheel drive freshly painted in a Marlboro livery. I tried to film this Philip Morris push into a far-flung village and the surly driver leaped out of his vehicle demanding I turn off my camera.

The dark arts

Leaving Ricardo's office, I fall into conversation with a man in the reception area named Lliam Jordum. He tells me that Ricardo may have rebuffed Philip Morris, but a Māori woman, Dr Marewa Glover, a public health researcher, did not.

Lliam is seated on a lounge chair like he's seated on a throne, but children are crawling around on the floor. I take the couch across from him.

'How do you know of Dr Glover?'

'She came under a bit of strife for receiving funding from Philip Morris,' he says, with stately enunciation. 'You could follow *any* money. And it goes through so many rotten hands. When do you consider it valid?'

Lliam's point is that other public health researchers are funded by the New Zealand government. Considering the bloody history of colonisation, a Māori might think government money is as tainted, in the same way a Gen Xer thinks corporate money is.

'It's dirty through and through,' he says.

So, who's this Dr Glover?

'There's a lot of jealousy around,' he says. 'They all came out of the bloody woodwork. But I stood up for her. I said, I'm a traditional Māori holistic practitioner and I wouldn't have any qualms at all about receiving a million, $10 million, $20 million from Philip Morris. Not at all. Roll it on.'

I wonder how much Dr Glover received.

Lliam explains Māori people were trade kings, but other cultures stole their words in the course of this trading. 'All that Kiwi fruit you sold, you used the mana of my language, of my culture, by which to sell it to the world.' Considering this dubious business practice, he thinks it's a bit rich for white people to tell Māori people like Dr Glover how to do business.

I tell him people are dark on Philip Morris skulking into Māori communities. 'They think that it's exploitative and stuff like that.'

'Of course, they would, wouldn't they?' he says. There's no need for him to roll his eyes, his tone of voice does it all. 'There's always some convenient argument about "exploiting the natives". Actually, we've been fucking exploited enough and we'd be happily exploited by Philip Morris. Happily! Why not? We get something for it. All the blind people in this country. They just want us to be the beaten housewife and shut up, cook the feed, sit in the corner.'

I remember Leslie Moliere-Batichon telling me, down the line from Florida, that rejecting money from corporations was a luxury – white privilege.

He says Dr Marewa Glover's research will bring an important perspective to the public-health debate over cigarettes.

'The Māori way is divining. Marewa realises that she isn't just a Western scientist, she's got some other inherent qualities that come out, that inspire that divining.' Divining is intuition, magical insight. How does Lliam know Dr Glover can divine?

'I belong to a line of shamans, dark arts witches, the best of the black you could possibly imagine. And I am their descendant. I am all of those things. I am this utter darkness and I am this utter light.'

He has my attention. The midday sun through the window lights up his eyes. I spot his bag next to his throne. A concoction in a glass jar peeps out. I learn he has had a brush with Philip Morris himself.

'I met a manager from Philip Morris, just bumped into him. Which is what happens when you're a Māori holistic practitioner. You talk about stuff and it happens. He got all excited. We talked about the customary usage of plants and herbs.' Perhaps, they both agreed, there was something in that for a new Philip Morris product. 'I was a little bit annoyed because he said, come back and see me in one week.'

One week later, as agreed, Lliam returned to the tobacconist where they had met. 'He wasn't there. And I said, well, he's just wasted a whole week of my time. How dare he. The bugger.'

The one who prepares it

Walking out from the reception, stepping over a baby, into the hot afternoon, I mull over something Lliam said about potions. 'The part that Westerners really have to get through their thick heads is that it's not the contents. It's the carrier. It's the one who prepares it.'

His sister imbibed a potion, hoping it would rejuvenate her. Instead she was poisoned. But he doesn't hold the ingredients responsible. It was that the person who prepared the potion had committed too much evil. They were cursed, so the curse passed through to the potion.

Yes! This speaks to me. I'm not obsessed with e-cigarettes as such. Rather, I'm obsessed with the diabolical Philip Morris, the 'carrier'. Philip Morris are the ones who prepare the IQOS. I have validation from a Māori shaman. The most important aspect of a concoction is 'the one who prepares it'.

Putting science aside, have Philip Morris killed too many millions of people and now they're . . . I know you're not going to like this word . . . but are they cursed?

Tasmanians might understand, maybe. Martin Bryant (יִמַּח שְׁמוֹ, may his name be erased) massacred men and women and children at Port Arthur. Something remains in the air and dirt there. Murder doesn't evaporate. A heaviness hangs over the landscape. I've been there, you can feel it while strolling across the grass.

So why wouldn't a shadow, a curse, hang over Philip Morris and everything they touch?

'She got what she deserved,' Lliam said of his poisoned sister, who didn't listen to his warning. 'And she realised, Oh, this thing is true.'

Centre for Research Excellence

That Philip Morris is funding one Māori academic is underselling the matter. Through their Foundation for a Smoke-Free World, Philip Morris are the sole funder of an entire indigenous health organisation.

No one likes a coloniser these days. Statues of such men are being bloodied with red paint by protesters across the world. The health organisation in question, the Centre for Research Excellence: Indigenous Sovereignty and Smoking, provides Philip Morris with a story to fit these times. One of their reports concludes, 'To punish indigenous people for not obeying Western public health demands to immediately stop smoking, carries on the colonising mindset. It is up to all sovereign peoples to work out for themselves what solutions they would choose to reduce the harms smoking is doing to their people's health.'

I'm trying to figure out if that makes sense. Philip Morris products disproportionately kill indigenous people, captain cooking their lungs and colon(cancer)ising their rectums.

Dr Glover, the centre's director, wrote that report.

A long Uber ride takes me to the centre, which is in Torbay, on Auckland's North Shore. The shops here are the type enjoyed by people who don't have to worry about money. The centre itself is less than eighteen months old and smells of freshly unboxed Macs. Expansive windows draw sunlight (the best disinfectant) into this shopfront building, formerly a doctor's surgery.

Dr Glover, a behavioural scientist with nearly three decades of experience working in public health, moves quietly and gently. She has a soft olive face and long black hair. She leads me to a boardroom and lifts a cardboard box onto the table. It's full of nicotine and tobacco curios from her travels around the globe. Snus from Sweden, tobacco-filled pouches that rest in your cheek; tobacco bullets from Denmark, which you chew; a Juul knock-off from South Korea. She says there is an IQOS knock-off in South Korea too.

'One of the things I try to do is fight that Eurocentrism in public health.' Eurocentrism means you view everything from a white European perspective, in case you didn't grow up with Public Enemy albums or find out about it some other way. 'Public health is dominated by white Western academics and medical doctors, and they think everybody around the world is exactly like them and that their ideas should be applied everywhere. And isn't that what colonisation was?'

Dr Glover packs the trinkets back into the box.

She says her research is 'looking at the link between that loss of sovereignty, for indigenous people, which you have at a national level, and that loss of autonomy at a personal level'.

She's making a connection between white people telling indigenous people what to do with their land and their culture and white people telling them what to do with their cigarettes.

'Not having control over your own life – that's a driver of smoking.'

I'm uncomfortable talking about money, but I'm busting to find out how much Philip Morris paid her, through The Foundation for a Smoke-Free World.

'And, um, so, so how many years of funding has the foundation committed to the centre?'

'I have a commitment of five years.'

'Oh, wow. That's good to know. And are you allowed to say how much you get?'

Dr Glover thinks about it. There is a pause so long a bird squawk fills the silence.

'It's been made public,' she finally says. 'It was on Jean-François Etter's slide at the e-cig summit.' I find out he's another pro-vaping academic. She's jogging her memory, trying to recall the figure on this slide. 'I think he said . . . I think it comes to $9.8 million.'

Philip Morris must really value this venture.

'Oh yeah, that's good.'

What do I mean by this vague declaration? It escaped my lips without any rumination. It's good because it's a worthy project? It's good for her to be fleecing $10 million from a corporation that deserves to be fleeced? Good for me because it's killer information? I reckon a lot of number two, and a bit of number three.

We make our way out of the office. Dr Glover says it's such a nice day, we should try the park, but the slope down the street is so steep that I'm already thinking I'm not going to enjoy the walk back.

Beyond Māori people, she says, marginalised groups – poor people, LGBTQ+ people, those with mental health issues – smoke more than others. She says laws against smoking may seem compassionate, but if you dig into the substance of those laws it becomes clear they're not.

'There's no compassion anymore. We've got laws against discriminating on the basis of sexuality, ethnicity, health. "Oh, this person's got schizophrenia, I'm not renting to them." Legally, you can't do that. But it's alright, because you can discriminate against people who smoke, and that's the same people. So I think it's become a proxy for those forms of discrimination that have been outlawed.'

This line of thinking led her to campaign against taxes on cigarettes, which disproportionately hit the hip pockets of the poor. Her fellow academics, researchers in public health, were stunned. 'That's when I fell out of favour, because they can't have a dissenting voice. They won't get their punishing, stigmatising policies championed across the board. And so they began excluding me, way back before I got foundation funding.'

I float in and out of going along with her reality . . . Yes, on the one hand, governments are colonisers, but, on the other hand, then why aren't corporations colonisers too? But, on the third hand, even if they are, Lliam said he'd happily take Philip Morris money. Happily!

The park is drawing closer. Both the sun and the 50+ sunscreen are stinging my eyes. I can't wait to collapse under the shade of a tree.

Dr Glover says the foundation's funding is 'no strings attached'.

One of her research missions sent her to Fiji, meeting with the indigenous iTaukei people. One of their sacred practices is sipping kava, a local plant brewed, which brings on both sedation and euphoria. Dr Glover's centre's report back explained:

'Smoking tobacco has become integrated into customs over the hundred plus years that iTaukei have been smoking. It became common to expect visitors to present gifts of tobacco to iTaukei shrines. Communal smoking also became an ordinary part of gatherings of a political and social nature, such as village meetings, and when drinking alcohol and taking part in kava drinking . . . iTaukei use of tobacco cannot be understood without considering how smoking and kava are used together. In modern times, smoking a cigarette or suki is closely linked to kava drinking.'

I recall Father Bob and I riffing that a prison rollie – a page torn from the Bible used as cigarette paper – was a holy item. Little did we know that across the ocean Dr Glover *had* sanctified the cigarette, decreeing smoking a Philip Morris a sacred act alongside sipping kava.

Finally we arrive at the park. Trees everywhere. Beautiful, shady trees. Not for me, though. Dr Glover continues strolling through the sunshine.

She's not just a researcher, or an everyday campaigner, she's a lobbyist. In 2019 the Filipino government proposed regulating vapes and heat-not-burn devices like the IQOS. Dr Glover argued to their inquiry that it is 'important that the acceptability of the products is not undermined by unnecessary restrictions', even recommending that 'retail vouchers, prize draws and gift packs could all be used to incentivise quitting or switching to the risk-reduced alternatives'. In effect, by funding work like Dr Glover's, Philip Morris gets to advocate for laws that will help their IQOS push, without needing to put their name to it. The disclosure statement in Dr Glover's submission mentions the Foundation for a Smoke-Free World, but that's it. Sneaky!

I'm trying to use mind power to get her to stop walking and sit in the shade, but I am no diviner. The sun sniggers.

In 2020, Dr Glover pushed back against a New Zealand smoking and vaping bill. She attacked what she thinks is the central tactic of campaigns against smoking: 'denormalising'. That is, public health campaigns that demonise the act of smoking.

'Denormalisation is deliberately dehumanising and seeks to strip people of their dignity,' she argued in her submission. 'The punitive tone of the Amendment is inconsistent with a kaupapa Māori perspective drawing on Māori knowledge, beliefs and values . . . Denormalisation has been a key strategy of colonising nations and is still being used in New Zealand to stigmatise and marginalise Māori.'

Other Māori people see this a different way. Māori public health group Hāpai Te Hauora has cut ties with Dr Glover. 'By serving the interests of Philip Morris International, the foundation is complicit in commercial tobacco use and the associated absolute and dispro-portionate tobacco-related harms to Indigenous peoples.'

I can't take it anymore.

'Can we sit under a tree?'

'Of course.'

I wipe my face with my t-shirt.

'Are you allowed to criticise Philip Morris?'

'I can criticise anybody.'

She takes a moment.

'Am I being pragmatic? What could I criticise them for? For existing? Yeah. Okay. Is that going to make any difference? No. They're going to sell their products. I've seen it for thirty years. We can go blah, blah, blah. It doesn't make any difference to them.'

I'm settling into the shade. The joy of no sun and no walking. I look back up the steep hill and my back starts to tighten.

Dr Glover tells me cultures see things differently. 'There's a huge, big world out there. I was in Sweden, went to learn about the Sami people, the indigenous people up there. And I'm walking around Stockholm and in the windows, on one of their famous fashion streets, there was this jacket and this handbag. And it's the same colour – the olive colour – of the plain packaging on cigarette packs in Australia. In Australia, it scored as the most offensive colour. That's why it was chosen for cigarette packs. But in Sweden, it was the "in" colour. And that's one of the things that I've always been trying to educate people about – how culturally bound things are.'

I'm trying to figure out if that makes sense. After all, a banana looks good yellow, but I'd never pick up a pair of yellow pants from Just Jeans. But she's right that cultures are diverse, and what I'm learning is that Philip Morris will adapt to them all. They judge you by the content of your wallet not the colour of your skin.

I like Dr Glover a lot. Can't knock the hustle.

Lazootin drives me to the airport. Before I leave, he places a greenstone Māori necklace on me for protection.

WORDS, WORDS, WORDS, CREEPY CRAWLY WORDS

The North American Scrabble Players Association (NASPA) is purging racial and ethnic slurs from the Scrabble dictionary. Everything from that n-word to slurs against white people like 'redneck'. This is their response to the Black Lives Matter movement.

The Scrabble dictionary hoovers up the words that make it into mainstream dictionaries. It's not like the NASPA board members go undercover at skateparks to pick up lingo from the kids. So the strongest case for allowing Scrabble players to lay down words like 'wog' and 'cocksucker' is the same as the case for allowing those words to appear in the Oxford, Merriam-Webster, Collins and Macquarie dictionaries. Which is that it's vital to have a record of words that are circulating, or have circulated in the past, so we can better understand the world.

Scrabble players understand this is the context for these words' inclusion in the game, so laying down 'blowjob' or 'yid' on a triple-word score is less heated than it appears to non-Scrabblers.

Scrabble players are made of harder stuff than those in the Hungry Hippos community.

Offensive words are a poor barometer for measuring what's offensive. Politicians draft laws that start wars and throw people in detention centres without a single 'fuck'. Meanwhile those same politicians berated an Aboriginal person, Tarneen Onus Williams, for screaming 'Fuck Australia!' at an Invasion Day protest. And indeed, measuring offence by words used, Onus Williams is bad and the Minister for Home Affairs is good.

Onus Williams followed up 'Fuck Australia!' with 'Hope it burns to the ground.' They didn't have to go on an apology tour, exactly, but a You Need to Dig Beneath the Surface When It Comes to Words tour.

Scrabble dictionary open, I read that two long-serving 'Scrabble Consultants', Darryl Francis and David Sutton, have tendered their resignation from the Scrabble dictionary editorial committee in protest of the word cull.

Darryl Francis writes: 'There will be bad publicity when people look at the list that Mattel has chosen and realise that children can still play "fuck", "cunt", "slut", "milf", "felch" and "prossie".'

NO SUCH THING AS A FREE LUNG

William Churchill, the freshly washed man from the IQOS booth in New Zealand, has left me a voicemail. I missed the call, busy rifling through drawers in my kitchen looking for a black marker.

I read an article about wine mums and it said that if you drink half a bottle of wine a day, that's the equivalent to smoking five cigarettes. I'm not sure how that translates to gin, but I imagine it must. Anyway, with this in mind, I've decided to start writing on the gin bottle the date I'm opening it and then, when it's empty, a closing date. I want to track if I'm going through them too fast.

'Accept my apologies, please, for piss farting around getting back to you.' William says after phone tag. 'A colleague of mine called Simon Dowding, he's keen to meet, if you're still interested in going to the cube.'

The cube, the black cube! Philip Morris's version of the Ka'bah in Mecca. Where they worship the Holy Profit, Wheeze Be Upon Him.

'Simon used to manage a lot of that stuff. So he can help. He can basically make it happen if that's something you're still keen to do. I don't know what your plans are, but what I thought I'd do is put you guys in touch to go out for lunch.'

I wonder if I read Rhenu right, back at the IQOS booth. That they might dangle a junket. 'If we pay for you to go to the cube . . .' I checked Webjet – a round trip to Neuchâtel, Switzerland, is nearly four grand. Regardless of whether that's in play, I'm nearly sure they'll pay for this lunch.

THE MINIONS

My upcoming lunch makes me wonder about the people who work at Philip Morris. As does something I dig up from their archives.

Corporations need to file a report each year with the US Securities and Exchange Commission, declaring the risks of investing in them. Serious stuff. Play games here, get taken to court later. One frank admission in Philip Morris's 2015 report grabs the eye. 'We may be unable to attract and retain the best talent due to the impact of decreasing social acceptance of tobacco usage.'

How hurtful for the Philip Morris lawyer who had to draft that, knowing Philip Morris settled for them, unable to attract a better lawyer.

So, their 'unsmoke the world' story is not just for customers. They need to change their image in the eyes of potential employees, too.

Companies create advertising campaigns to attract the best staff, and big corporations like Philip Morris hire an external 'employment branding' agency. Anne has worked in this industry for close to a decade.

'We've worked with Philip Morris,' Anne says. I didn't need to hunt her down – I've bumped into her at a friend's house, cuddling my friend's cavoodle on the couch.

She holds a different view to the one Philip Morris declared in that SEC report. Or at least, she thinks life has moved on since 2015. 'They're one of the best in talent acquisition, and you can understand why, because it's come out of necessity. You've got a brand that isn't sexy. No one wants to work for cancer sticks.'

I've been babbling to her about the New Zealand vape expo.

'Just like you're saying that they've changed the brand in terms of smoking, they did that ten years ago from a talent perspective.'

She says Philip Morris's pitch to potential staff is to not listen to what people are saying. 'We're not who you think we are. We're actually spending all this money to make the world a better place. And be part of that journey. Come work with us to make us better. So they owned their poor reputation. And it's why the people who work for them are evangelical, because they have to drink the Kool Aid.'

In the IQOS booth at the expo, William was overcome with fervour, a true believer, and he didn't deny it.

It's brilliant. 'Unsmoke the world.' Unlike their competitors – British American Tobacco and Imperial Brands – Philip Morris workers can say they're not working for a cigarette company, they're working for a company that's trying to end cigarettes. In fact, they can go a step further. The IQOS houses a computer chip, so they can say what Marian Salzman said at an 'innovations festival' in Vilnius, Lithuania, in 2019: 'I am Senior Vice President of Communications at the science and tech start-up called Philip Morris International.' No need to mention cigarettes at all.

And then there is that other matter.

'They pay crazy money,' Anne says.

Goody gumdrops. I'm glad she's brought this up. It's considered poor taste to ask someone how much they're paid, which must be why there's a thrill in finding out.

'A friend of mine, out of the blue, has just asked me if he should take a job with Philip Morris, who are offering $300,000 for a policy advisor role. It's a public-facing lobbying role.'

Woah. I wonder if William's on that much? He had nice shoes. I could tell they were expensive even though I don't know anything about shoes.

Mo' money

I want to know if they look after everyone.

Alan worked in the now closed Philip Morris factory in Moorabbin, in south-east Melbourne. A job agency initially found him a casual position that involved freezing, heating and drying tobacco.

'I remember my first pay,' he says. 'I thought they'd made a mistake, because it was incredible money. I contacted the agency and said, "I think there's been a mistake in my payroll." And they said, let's check it. But they said no, there hadn't been a mistake.'

He won't cough up exact figures. Baddy gumdrops. But this morning he pulled up on a Harley he bought for $30,000 in 2005, when he was still working for Philip Morris.

Alan spent seventeen years on the factory floor, until 2013, just before the factory shut for good. Philip Morris now sources their tobacco from overseas.

We meet in Mordialloc, a Melbourne beachside suburb. He's sipping coffee, our table outside the deli attracting a couple of seagulls.

'Were there any conversations about how, "Oh man, we're working in a cigarette company, that's not too good"?'

'It was a funny thing. I think we all did sometimes – had a moral conviction of what was going on. And then you'd have the thought, we're not forcing them down people's throats, we're not handing them out, we haven't got a store at a schoolyard.'

Another seagull, noting I'm enthralled by Alan's story, joins us to see what's up.

'I'd walk out of the meetings when they were trying to shove propaganda down your throat.'

'Like what?'

'Stuff about how we're very generous in regards to our giving. They'd have marathons and they'd raise money. I'd think, it's a bit hypocritical here, just quietly. Okay, you raised ten grand, but you probably caused about $50 million worth of damage to about twenty million people. But anyway, good onya, well done.'

'Hehe.'

Following high school, I worked at an advertising agency for a couple of years. I may have written brochures for Mazda (carbon emissions) and a jingle for Sea World (dolphin captivity), but every three months I hopped on a bus to the blood bank the agency booked. For all I know, my A-negative blood (quite rare) went into a sickly child. Surely that balanced out the ledger.

'They'd show so and so manager, probably hasn't run a mile in his frigging life, wearing a little thingo – you know the lycra, on the pushbikes? I was thinking, you're not riding that bike, you're just there for the photoshoot, you fat fuck. Yeah, there was a lot of propaganda.'

I tell him what William told me at the IQOS booth. That there's a new generation of Philip Morris staffers, and they're not like the previous generation – his – because they're here to unsmoke the world.

He says he read an article in the newspaper, an interview with a Philip Morris executive. 'That's what they were waffling about. We're a new generation. We're a new planet, just about. We're a new race of people that are bringing you this incredible new way of doing things. It was a spun-out article.'

He says the executive was championing the cause as if the Smoke-Free Future was the Polish Revolution of 1989, when communism fell.

'To take what Lech Wałęsa did and what the Polish Solidarity movement did, and Philip Morris putting themselves in that – that they're as proud as that – I thought that was just disgraceful. How dare you. How dare you. You wouldn't understand a revolution if it fucking fell over you.'

A new race

I meet with Mike Daube, former Director General of Health, Western Australia. He began battling Big Tobacco back in the seventies. He has his own views of what Alan snarked is the 'new race' of Philip Morris employees.

'They did some pretty bad things,' he says of the previous generation. 'But they were still people who'd come into tobacco before the evidence was absolute. Whereas now, you work for the tobacco industry, you know exactly what you're doing. So anybody working for the industry now is tougher, nastier, more cynical, than they were generations ago.'

Simon Chapman, whom you've met – Savvas's public enemy number-one – concurred when I spoke to him.

'If you came out of Harvard Business School and you thought, wow, who am I going to work for? Am I going to work for the IT industry, the aeronautical industry, the renewable energy industry or the tobacco industry? *I think I'll go work for the renewable industry.*' He says the type of people who self-select to go into the tobacco industry are typically cold-blooded. 'The usual taunt I see on social media is, "How do you sleep at night?" They sleep fine.'

Mike Daube cuts slack to workers who joined the company before the science was settled, branding only the new generation as diabolical. But William has flipped it around. The old generation were diabolical for selling cigarettes. He's the IQOS generation – he's here to kill the cigarette trade. And in his book, the sins of the father do not pass on to the child.

Heroed

I feel delightfully subversive hearing stories from those who were on the inside. A recent Philip Morris office worker whom I'll call Amy contacts me to talk about her experience.

Philip Morris really do have a brand problem; when she went for the job, the recruitment agency wouldn't tell Amy who her prospective employer was until she agreed, in principle, to meet with them.

'When they told me that it was Philip Morris, I was like, "Okay, shit." I spoke to my dad, who's also in marketing, and he said to me, "Look, I wouldn't do it."'

She wavered, but 'the whole IQOS side of things just made it easier for me to justify working for a company like that'.

So their employment branding strategy – that they're here to unsmoke the world – worked. But only to a certain point.

'When people asked me what I did, I would always answer "marketing". And then if they were like, "For who?" Then it would come. Philip Morris.'

She worked at one of their branches in Europe. You could smoke HeatSticks around the office.

'But you had to go outside to smoke your Marlboro?'

'You could smoke those in the kitchen.'

I think about those poor Teddy Bear biscuits.

Staff around the coffee pot were believers. 'If you smoked cigarettes, everyone looked down on you. It was like, "Ergh, that's so gross. Do you not know what we're trying to do with IQOS?"'

These don't sound like the 'tougher, nastier, more cynical' people Mike Daube described.

'I enjoyed it, I really did,' says Amy. 'It was an awesome brand to work for. The people there haven't been dropped on their heads, either. They're all very sharp.'

I learn more. The cigarette vending machine parked next to the toilet in the pub is yesteryear – Amy excitedly asks if I've visited an IQOS retail store.

'They're beautiful. The products are heroed beautifully. It's all very sleek. I had friends from Australia come to visit me. We were walking past and they were like, holy shit. They thought it was an Apple Store. It literally looks like Apple.'

I realise you don't need words, you can also tell a story about yourself through furnishings and fittings. This is the science and tech start-up Mariam Salzman said she worked for.

Amy offers me a sneak peek at what might be coming next.

'We tested this one thing. You could invite your friends, your smoking friends obviously, over to your home and have a . . . a Tupperware party, I guess. An IQOS coach would come over and have a chat to you about IQOS.'

Oh my God. If this goes ahead, the first ten readers to send proof of purchase of *Puff Piece* to PO Box 196, Balaclava VIC 3183, will join me in my lounge room for a Philip Morris Pufferware party.

When Amy left Philip Morris and returned to Australia, her dad told her, 'Let's get something where you can be proud of the product.'

'Or I could go a step further,' she says.

'Work for the weapons industry.'

'Exactly.' She chuckles. 'With smoking, at least you have a choice. With weapons we just drop them on your head. Yeah. That's next. Watch out!'

Slave drivers

It sounds like everyone at Philip Morris, from factory workers to boardroom fat cats, is remunerated more than fairly. But let's wind back to see if it was always that way.

Philip Morris was a flesh and blood man. There are five sentences about him on Wikipedia. (Raspberry Cordial gets twelve.) So not a lot to work from there.

But it's not just Wikipedia. The most the man gets anywhere is a couple of lines, including on the Philip Morris International website. As usual, I have to do everything around here. I burrow into ancestry.co.uk and find out even those couple of lines are inaccurate; Philip Morris has flubbed the facts.

Philip Morris the man is born 1835 in Middlesex, England. According to the Philip Morris International website: 'Mr Philip Morris opens a shop on London's Bond Street, selling tobacco and ready-made cigarettes in 1847.' Which would have made him twelve at the time. Adorable.

In fact it's his father, a German migrant, Barnard Morris, who opens that shop. This might be the first time Philip Morris International has misled people and it hasn't been calculated.

Philip Morris dies in 1873, Barnard seven years later, and relatives take over the business. In 1919 a firm owned by US stockholders acquires the company, later relocating it to Richmond, Virginia.

That state holds a special place in the story of tobacco.

Roll even further back, to the early 1600s. Spain controls the lucrative tobacco trade. Englishman John Rolfe wants to break their monopoly and, with seeds from Trinidad or Venezuela, depending on who tells the story, he sails to the first colony in America: Jamestown, Virginia. Rolfe harvests his first crop in 1612. By the 1680s America is producing tens of millions of pounds of tobacco per year, to sell back in Europe.

Something else, very important, must be sewn into this story.

Roll forward to 1997. A Black American woman, Tziona Nelson, sends a letter to Philip Morris Chairman Geoffrey Bible (what a name!). It's about the tobacco industry and its workers.

'I am writing to you requesting restitution for the free labor of our forebears who were forced to toil the tobacco fields of these United States without pay for hundreds of years under the worst circumstances known to mankind.'

The tobacco trade was built on slavery.

'Planters rejected emancipation because of the most lucrative significance of having slaves in the tobacco fields,' Nelson goes on. 'Slavery spread throughout the Southern Colonies, and as a result of the tremendous wealth manifested from tobacco growth and export, the colony, Jamestown, became the state of Virginia. From that time to this present day, growing tobacco and manufacturing its products have been one of the leading industries of the Americas.'

The 'zion' embedded in the name Tziona isn't coincidental. She is writing on behalf of a religious sect, The LawKeepers.

'We do not want restitution for selfish reasons. We have decided to relocate to Jordan where we can be close to God's Holy City, Jerusalem.' They need funding for houses, a school and a hospital. 'We would also like to establish a Museum to emphasize our history from Biblical times, the African Slave Trade, and, of course, our exile in Africa and the world. We will build our own place of worship. Perhaps there is a Tobacco Fund already organized to compensate the descendants of slaves for the free labor of our ancestors who established the tobacco industry as an economic giant. We anxiously await your response.'

Having been knocked back by Philip Morris myself, I'm not feeling good about where this is going.

Dear Tziona Nelson,

I'm writing in response to your letter to Mr. Geoffrey C. Bible requesting participation in your program. Although we appreciate your thinking of Philip Morris, we respectfully decline to participate. We wish you well in your endeavours.

Cordially,

John Barlow

Senior Consumer Specialist

Consumer Affairs

There is no denying that Philip Morris benefitted from the legacy of tobacco plantation slavery, built up from the 1600s on. Philip Morris mark their beginnings at the Bond Street 'Tobacconist and Importer' in 1847, fourteen years before slavery wound down in America. So it adds up that Philip Morris imported the popular Virginia crop of tobacco, and from other slave states. On the off-chance they didn't, this doesn't pivot to a feel-good story. If they imported tobacco from Turkey, for instance? The Ottoman Empire's slave story is as dark as Alabama's. There were no woke tobacco plantations.

Philip Morris see their American history through a different lens than Tziona Nelson. They tout they were the first tobacco company to hire Black salesmen. 'In the 1950s, the White Citizens' Council in the South called for a boycott of Philip Morris USA products because of the company's support of equal employment and civil rights policies, cutting sales in half, but Philip Morris USA stood firm.'

I suspect any warm and fuzzies you're feeling towards the company are about to be de-fuzzed, because slavery came up again in 2016, when the British government introduced plain packaging laws for cigarettes. Philip Morris took the government to court, demanding compensation for the predicted decline in cigarette sales. What possible precedent was there for this sort of compensation? Well, Philip Morris were relying on the Slavery Abolition Act of 1883, which compensated slave owners for the loss of earnings from freeing slaves.

The judges rejected the argument.

Any maniacal company can exploit slaves. To exploit the Slavery Abolition Act (in 2016!), *that* takes Philip Morris.

You might think slavery, as bad as it was, is in the company's past. But in fact, in 2010, following a Human Rights Watch report, Philip Morris admitted that children as young as ten were working on their tobacco farms in Kazakhstan. The children and their families, mainly from neighbouring Kyrgyzstan, had their passports confiscated by the farm owners, and often had to work without pay.

These workers weren't pulling up on the side of the road on $30,000 Harleys.

PHILIP MORRIS, CHANGE YOUR PASSWORD

Philip Morris, change your password. This is on you, not me. I am no hacker. All I did was google 'PMI' and 'employees' and ended up at what I assume is meant to be a restricted website. This in-house site is replete with Philip Morris concept art and ideas for how to attract new employees.

Click.

We see video of employees in the cube in Switzerland. People smiling with clipboards and beakers. I could be there soon.

A headline fades in. 'The PMI EVP: The story of our Employer Brand.'

What does EVP mean?

Click.

They helpfully explain. 'EVP = Employee Value Proposition. What Makes PMI an employer of choice.'

Click.

'WE CANNOT EASILY ESCAPE "BIG TOBACCO".

We need an Employer Brand that will overcome perceptions of the "tobacco industry".'

They're unhappy they're perceived as Big Tobacco. What will they do?

Click.

'OUR NEW VISUAL IDENTITY'

Get on with it!

Click.

'MOVEMENTS CAN CHANGE HISTORY'

This page is peppered with photos from political rallies and close-ups of protest signs.

A Black fist and the Black Panthers' slogan 'All Power to the People' features on one placard.

A young woman in a Che Guevara t-shirt stands before soft-focused red and black flags, the Antifa colours.

'None of us can predict the future,' the Philip Morris copy begins. 'But we can all learn from the past. There have been many simple movements that have changed society, far beyond their original intention.'

Surely they're not comparing their IQOS launch to historical uprisings?

'The fall of the Berlin wall; women campaigning for equal rights; the LGBTQ campaign shifting from protest to celebration; taking a knee on the football pitch, breaking down walls, mental barriers and glass ceilings.'

They *are* comparing the IQOS launch to the end of the Cold War and women's suffrage.

I think of Alan brooding about the executive talking up Philip Morris's transformation like it was the Polish Solidarity revolution of 1989.

Next: '#UNSMOKE Millions of consumers, millions of lives will be positively affected. It's no exaggeration to say that it is a generation-defining moment.'

Now we see photos of Gandhi and Malala Yousafzai, the Pakistani human rights campaigner who was shot by the Taliban.

'Time will prove this is something that future generations can talk about with similar feelings. Whatever role you do at Philip Morris International, you are going to be part of that momentous change. It's exciting today, but the rewards for "a job well done" will last a lifetime. Join us.'

Now comes a photo from a 2019 climate change protest (I used Google's reverse image search feature to place it), but one of the protester's placards has been photoshopped. Unbeknown to the protester who turned up that day to save the Earth, they are now marching while holding up the Philip Morris International logo.

Finally, in big block letters:

'HISTORY WILL BE OUR JUDGE.'

Reputational scars

Philip Morris needs to go down this path. People don't want others to think they're a bad person. One afternoon, a woman on the train, Chloe, tells me her friend was offered a job at Philip Morris.

Her friend, a Hindu, thought it was a bit of a dilemma. She was concerned taking the job would screw with her karma, and she wanted guidance. Chloe felt she wasn't just worried about Ganesh's judgement but what her friendship circle would think.

'I can't tell you what to do, you know yourself best,' she advised her friend. 'But what can you live with? What's a decision that will allow you to go to sleep at night?'

Her friend decided to have her cake and eat it. She'd take the Philip Morris job, but only for a short time. She'd pocket a fat chunk of cash and then skedaddle.

'This was 2007,' Chloe tells me. 'She's still with them. She's relocated to London.'

Our train is pulling up to the station.

'What do you think of her? That she did take the cigarette job?'

'If you were to ask me to name every person I ever knew in my life, who's on a good list or a bad list, like Santa, I would put her on the good list.'

Last week I drove up the lane behind my apartment block and spotted a baby crawling in a driveway. I thought that, if I had squashed that baby beneath my tyre, I would be the Squashed Baby Guy forever. That would be my scarlet letter, my mark of Cain.

Once I would have thought that taking a job with Philip Morris might be a person's Squashed Baby. A reputational scar. But I'm learning that's not the case.

I'm cool with this, just tabling it as one more reason Philip Morris gallops on.

BRAND ENHANCER

'I'm going to lunch with a cigarette company,' I tell Father Bob, who's once again sitting there and decaying. 'Should I let them pay for lunch?'

'Well, I'm Scottish. Of course you let people pay for lunch, you know what I mean?'

I'm across the stereotype he's referring to.

He scratches his face and I'm worried his cheek will fall off and plop onto the carpet here in his boardroom.

'What? You're saying the morality of it?'

'Yes.'

I have an image of me chasing around his big black poodle, trying to retrieve a piece of Father Bob from her fangs.

'If you allow them to pay for your lunch, it's precarious. Because, in fact, you might become their vassal, V-A-S-S-A-L. They might keep their eye on you and say, hello, Safran may be a brand enhancer for us – if we give him a free lunch.'

I'm surprised Bob has such a straightforward, normie view on all this.

But I speak too soon. He ponders scripture and finds another perspective.

'There's a famous thing in Luke something-or-other. "Zacchaeus, come down out of the tree!" Because Zacchaeus the businessman was up the tree . . .'

Bob takes me through the long and short of this biblical parable from the Book of Luke. (In fact, it mentions Zacchaeus is 'short in stature' – he has climbed the tree to see Jesus over the crowd.) In this passage, Jesus accepts the hospitality of Zacchaeus even though he is a dubious businessman, and despite the crowd grumbling, 'Jesus has gone to stay at the house of a sinner.' In Father's Bob analogy, Simon Dowding, my Philip Morris lunch date, is Zacchaeus. You, dear reader, are the grumbling crowd. I am Jesus Christ.

Bob concludes that Jesus wants me to take the free lunch. He pulls the parable in question from his wallet and unfolds it. He started carrying it around after people grumbled about the fact that he had blessed Crown Casino. Why, they ask, didn't he shun this questionable business run by the super-rich?

'When somebody says, "What are you hanging around with these people for?" I say, one moment, please. And I produce the text. I say, "Darling, that's the answer from the founder of the firm.'

Bob says that beyond merely allowing it, the God of the Torah – my God – demands that I accept the free feed. 'You're a desert tribe man. The desert tribe says, if you're invited in, you accept the hospitality of the tent.'

'In the case of Philip Morris, perhaps the oxygen tent,' I zing.

'Exactly. Thank you.'

'Because your lungs have collapsed from smoking Marlboros.'

'Thank you. Go to lunch, go to lunch.'

REFLECTION ON NEW ZEALAND: VAPE CAMPAIGNERS

I learned in New Zealand that vape campaigners like Dr Marewa Glover are accepting financial assistance from Philip Morris, through the Foundation for a Smoke-Free World. That's easy to denounce but, on the other side of the coin, what exactly is wrong with that? Why wouldn't a vaping campaigner accept a hand from Philip Morris, with their moneybags? Their enemy, who wants to strike them down, the government, has moneybags.

Plus, they have to consider what happens when you go it alone. Vincent van Heerden is an example of that.

'I'm on my way back from picking up my son from school,' he tells me down the line from Perth.

I ask him what type of car he's driving, just as a little colour for the book, but he's cagey about answering. It turns out he has good reason to be careful about disclosing that.

Vincent tells me he began smoking darts aged thirteen. After a night on the piss in 2009, he woke up to find his e-cigarette had gone missing. Annoying. Even more frustrating was the fact that none were available from shops in Perth – few people had even heard of the thingamabobs back then. That's when Vincent decided to set up an online e-cigarette store for Australians, the first in the country.

'And then one day, just out of the blue, these three black SUVs come piling up onto my lawn at my house.' It was the Western Australian Department of Health. This was 2011. 'They came in with black plastic bags and just started going through everything. They had a search and seizure warrant. Said I was breaching section 106A of the Tobacco Products Control Act.'

Let me help you out. That section reads: 'A person must not sell any food, toy or other product that is not a tobacco product but is designed to resemble a tobacco product.'

What an oddly worded law. What's going on there?

'The purpose of the law was to block those lolly cigarettes, you know, those Fags. Do you remember them? When we were kids?'

The Department of Health decided, regardless of the law's original intent, that these new gizmos – e-cigarettes – could fall under this language.

The case against Vincent begins in late 2013. The magistrate feels the e-cigarette in question resembles a ballpoint pen or a laser pointer, not a tobacco product. Vincent is found innocent.

'And they have to give me my stuff back. It's rusted, like they stored it in the back of a car. It's been almost two years. I can't sell any of it. My business had been shut down for all that time.'

Despite the setback, he breathed a sigh of relief. At least he was innocent of breaking the law.

'Twenty-one days later – and it was just the last possible day – I get a letter in the mail saying that they've decided to appeal the magistrate's ruling. I've got to go back to court. And at this point, my legal fees are thirty grand or something like that.'

I whistle down the line.

'I've got this GoFundMe fundraising campaign. It ends up raising a hundred and something thousand dollars. All the costs get spent on legal fees for when we go and argue the case in the Supreme Court.'

'How'd that go?'

'Judge finds me guilty. And, in doing so, she completely changes the ruling. She says that any object that has a hand to mouth action, that results in the exhalation of vapour, in her opinion resembles a cigarette.'

By now we've rolled into 2014. Vincent's lawyers convince him to have another go, at the Court of Appeal, later that year. He agrees. He loses.

'Then the lawyers said, if we appeal to the High Court, we're very confident you'll win, but you'll need another $150,000.'

A knot in my back is tightening just listening to this story, I can't imagine what it'd be like to be the guy.

Actually, maybe I can. I can't believe I'd forgotten about this until now. *I* was once dragged through the courts, accused of a nicotine-related crime. Cricketer Shane Warne had signed a lucrative deal with Nicorette gum, conditioned on him quitting cigarettes. In 1999, desperately needing content for a television show, I planted a cigarette between the beak of a stuffed seagull, stuck it atop a remote control car, and sent it out onto the ground at the MCG while Warnie was playing. The idea was it would induce him to smoke and break his contract. The cops arrested me for pitch invasion.

At my hearing, the court was packed with journalists – I assumed a serial killer case was scheduled after mine. I was found not guilty (which on reflection is weird, because I was guilty) and, leaving the court, all the journos chased me down the street. Very stressful.

A crucial difference to Vincent's situation is Channel Seven footed my legal bill. So it's probably a bit much to say I know what it's like to be in his shoes. He was being asked to spend $150,000 to continue fighting his case.

'That's when the show stopped. I had already spent every cent. To this day, I still owe the health department approximately $75,000.'

I find out that the original fine was $1750 dollars – the other $73,250 are court costs. I have to bite my tongue to not say, maybe this wasn't the cause to be Nelson Mandela over.

'Have they come after you for it?'

'Every few years they take me to court and ask me to do a means test. I have to show them the last years of my bank statements, every single purchase, and demonstrate that I'm still poor. And they're charging interest at 6.5 per cent, which means that even if I was to pay them let's say $5000 a year, my debt would still go up every year. It's impossible to pay off.'

'This health department doesn't care about your health.'

'Certainly not my mental health. It's ruined my relationship. I'm now separated. My daughter lives with my ex. Yeah, life has been challenging.'

Why did they go after him so hard?

'I was being used to try to create law out of a bullshit precedent.'

Vincent doesn't think this precedent was in aid of community health.

'It's designed to protect the people who get all the money today. The pharmaceuticals want to keep selling their shitty pharmaceutical products.' He means nicotine patches and gum. 'The government wants to keep getting the same $17 billion in excise a year.' That's the tax on cigarettes, the fourth-largest single tax collected by the government. (They *spend* $7 billion on smoking-related healthcare.) 'How do you replace $17 billion in our economy? That's a large amount of money.'

$75,000 is a large amount too. With the interest Vincent's being charged, it's probably gone up since he started telling me this story.

He brings up a matter that was top of my mind for me, although I didn't bring it up myself.

'Anyway, I was on the radio, and the guy asked me a question that I'd never expected. He said if a tobacco company like Philip Morris was to offer to fund my fight against the health department, would I accept the money? And I said I don't know. It's such a ridiculous thought that I've never genuinely considered it. But my answer would have been, ultimately, yes. I would have taken the money. Because it would have still been for the greater good of the community. If it pays to make sure that we can do what we should be able to do, I don't care.'

One of my rap cassettes shows KRS-One holding a gun beneath the album title, *By All Means Necessary*, a quote from political activist Malcolm X. I haven't met a vaping campaigner yet who comes across as insincere. They truly believe vaping will save lives. More so, that millions of people will die if vaping is suppressed. So why wouldn't they pursue that by all means necessary, even if that means dancing in the grey.

Vincent pulls up to his house in Ellenbrook. I hear the brake crunch down the line.

'And what kind of car do you have?'

'Um,' he hesitates. 'I drive a late-model sedan.'

'Okay, sure.'

'The lowest. I'm not allowed to have a car worth more than $8000, or I might have it taken by the health department.'

He thinks about what could have been.

'I was the first. I should've made a good amount of coin out of it. Instead, they kind of destroyed my life.'

Tap tap tap

I text Michelle, whose father's memorial I attended not long ago.

'Should I let Philip Morris pay for my lunch?'

'I think he's dead, but sure,' she replies.

'Philip Morris International! Is it ethical to let the COMPANY pay for my lunch?'

'Yes. If you write about it.'

I slide my phone into my pocket.

Another buzz. 'But also, thanks for taking money from the people who killed my dad.'

PHILIP MORRIS BEING LITTLE SHIITES

I thought by finding out that Philip Morris are getting involved in indigenous issues I had stumbled upon a juicy, sensitive matter that could explode in their face. But get this: Philip Morris tried to reinterpret the Qur'an.

'Don't throw yourself into danger by your own hands,' Allah commands in his top-selling book.

Since the early 1600s, there have been mullahs issuing fatwas on tobacco, citing the above passage in the Qur'an (4.35 stars out of 5 on Goodreads).

In 1984, a Pakistani newspaper calls a jihad against smoking.

Tobacco industry documents, uncovered by *The American Journal of Public Health*, reveal Philip Morris was worried by such news.

At a 1985 meeting, they decide they need to prepare for 'the possibility that religious fundamentalism will have an impact on our profitable Gulf markets'.

Philip Morris's solution? Paint Muslims against smoking as dangerous radicals. One tobacco lobbyist, Martin Haley, tells the cigarette giant, 'A Moslem who attacks smoking generally speaking would be a threat to existing government as a "fundamentalist".'

Haley tells them to compare these calls to quit to other 'extremist demands for prohibition under strict interpretation of Sharia', citing movies, TV, art depicting humans, electronic amplification of muezzins and the education of women.

Tobacco Observer, the industry journal, also alarmed by these fatwas, say they have seen this all before. 'In the early days of tobacco in the Old World, sadism went hand in hand with opposition to smoking, as smokers encountered persecution as brutal as anything meted out to religious dissidents and witches.'

Witches!

In 1988 Abdullah Borek, a Middle East tobacco lobbyist, and who my shisha-smoking friend Mahmood Fazel would no doubt call a narc, infiltrates the first Arab Anti-Smoking Symposium, held in Jordan. He promises Philip Morris 'to monitor and undermine the work of public health officials in the Middle East'.

Snitches!

Brashly, explosively, Philip Morris decides they need to tell Muslims what the passages in their Qur'an mean.

'Our invisible defense must be the individualism which Islam allows its believers,' Martin Haley tells Philip Morris in 1985. A Corporate Affairs memo from 1987 states they will 'develop a system' to 'identify Islamic religious leaders who oppose interpretations of the Qur'an which would ban the use of tobacco and encourage support for these leaders'.

A spokesman for the Canadian Tobacco Manufacturers Council, Jacques LaRiviere, 'agreed to make exploratory contact with the Islamic Studies Department at McGill University'.

In 1987, a lobbyist tells Philip Morris to hire Islamic scholars to produce 'articles, books and television cassettes' that interpret the Qur'an to be cigarette friendly.

It's impossible to find out, and measure, the impact of all this subterfuge. But we do know smoking statistics. In Jordan today, where Abdullah 'The Narc' Borek honed his snitching, 70 per cent of men light up, smoking 23 cigarettes per day, on average, in minarets and on the steps of ziggurats.

So what do we learn from all this? *They'll go there.* While other corporations sidle into primary schools, old people's homes and hospitals, Philip Morris know no boundaries. They'll push Mohammad to one side, look Allah square in the eye and tell Him what's up with His Qur'an. ('Lot easier to read than the Bible. It's also a lot shorter,' raves Tim in his five-star review on Goodreads.)

As audacious as this is, I discover that Philip Morris is also encroaching into *my* faith.

Looking through old documents, I'm startled. There it is, a 1986 cross-promotion. A woman holding a cigarette, a man thumbing through a dictionary over a boardgame. 'She likes Scrabble. He's at a loss for words,' reads the headline. 'But there's one taste they agree on. Benson and Hedges.'

A fatwa on Philip Morris! ('Fatwa' is nice. Fifteen points. And forty-five on a Triple Word, if F hits the Double Letter square.)

THE LUNCH

The restaurant Half Acre is hidden among panel beaters, in inner-city South Melbourne. Simon Dowding, my Philip Morris lunch date, has chosen the place. From outside it looks quite swanky. A triangular glass and corrugated iron roof announces *Bet you didn't think roofs could be glass and corrugated iron. That's because you don't read coffee table books, you bogan.*

A bouncer guards the door, a tiny golden Freemason badge pinned to his lapel. I'm already floundering.

This will be a delicate operation: gaining Simon's trust so I can gain access to the cube in Switzerland. I have my Pelican case but have decided, tactically, that it would be too aggressive to snap it open and pull out my recorder and shotgun mic. Even scribbling notes is out. This is a getting-to-know-you lunch. A friendly lunch. I'll just have to remember everything.

The Freemason lets me through the archway; a host is there to greet me, against a backdrop of expensive marble. (I think it was marble. At the very least, after the fact, searching my memory, it feels like marble. It's my truth.)

She shows me to a table. Simon is yet to arrive. I tap my foot on the wooden floorboard. (Unlike with the marble, I'm backing myself that it was definitely a wooden floor.)

Simon strides in, smiling. I concentrate on coming across as normal.

He takes a seat at the small round table.

I want to say he's in his early fifties? Very well kept.

'Very well kept'?

I'm saying he isn't fat.

A waiter pours us water and Simon opens with his origin story, jokingly telling me his career has been an escalation of evil. He started in government, moved to mining, and now here he is, Communications Manager for Philip Morris.

I like him, he's funny.

I wrote a profile piece on Musa Cerantonio for *Good Weekend*. I found him funny. Soon after, he was jailed for attempting to escape Australia to fight for ISIS. I'm not saying Simon is anything like that – I'm just saying I have to keep my guard up.

Simon has a chequered blue jacket and a pink shirt. And brown leather shoes. And he has a tan. The glass roof allows me to make out every strand of his salt and pepper hair. He is classically handsome.

Except for his nose.

Which I'm not saying isn't handsome, just not classically so.

Look, I'm not against his nose. My nose is crooked, my nose is off-kilter. I'm just saying Brad Pitt doesn't have his nose.

Simon tells me he's worked at Philip Morris for five years.

I'm frank with him. I don't make out like I'm on their side, but I don't make a song and dance that I'm not on their side, either. I tell him their Smoke-Free Future campaign is super interesting to me, which is true.

Because of Philip Morris's rock-bottom reputation, the media is strict in denying them a platform. Creationists hit the same sort of wall, although for them the platform they are denied is the science classroom. Educators tell them their theory lacks scientific validity. So Creationists came up with a clever piece of rhetoric to try to get their theory into the classroom: 'teach the controversy'.

Left with few other options, this is a Philip Morris strategy too. It's unfortunate for Philip Morris that they've ended up with me being the guy, but I'm the only one in this town willing to teach the controversy. So I am of use to them. How strange. With this book, I am launching the IQOS in Australia. You hadn't heard about any of this before. I am their spokesman. 'Bad for them' is still the best that they can get.

Simply Amazing.

Simon browses the menu and orders the wood-fired half chicken, seasonal mushrooms, herbs and jus. I'm drawn to the grass-fed porterhouse (300 g) but that's more expensive than Simon's order, so I ask for the half chicken too. (Come on, you know he's going to pay. I'm going to reach for my wallet when the bill comes, but, come on. As this is the case, something feels awkward about ordering a more expensive dish.)

The waiter takes our menus. I reckon I got it wrong. Mirroring his order is just as awkward. It's not quite like this, but it's a bit like us walking down the street in matching tracksuits. I matched his wine, too. And his side of pumpkin.

I ask Simon if they're doing Cannes Lions International Festival of Creativity this year. Last year they set up a marquee on the beach along the French Riviera, and actor Rose McGowan discussed their Smoke-Free Future on a stage: 'Begin the conversation. Acknowledge that it might be a little difficult. But that's no reason to shy away from it. We have to embrace that which is difficult and lean into it and not be scared.' In other words: teach the controversy.

Simon says they're not off to France this year.

Our matching half chickens arrive.

I wish he'd start eating so I can start eating.

Instead, he has more to say. He tells me Philip Morris have been closed off to outsiders in the past and they now realise that was a mistake. Part of their new plan is to let people in and have honest conversations.

He asks, a little furtively, whether I'm still interested in heading to the cube.

I look down at my Pelican case. I'm happy with my decision to leave the recorder in there. I don't think we would have gotten to this point with a shotgun mic held to his face.

I tell him, yes, it would be great to get to the cube.

He says he'll be able to sort it out and puts down his glass of red.

He tells a story about Philip Morris sponsoring a motorcycle event and inviting journalists to see the bikes at the cube, which eases him into asking whether I'd like them to cover my trip.

Oh boy.

It's happening. It's actually happening.

I'm writing a book about Philip Morris and how they use their money to try to bend the story their way, like their funding of Dr Marewa Glover, and now they're doing it to me.

I've now proven that they'll lavish a junket on people like me, who should surely be independent. Not a third-hand or second-hand story. Something I see and hear with my own eyes and ears.

I tell him yes, it would be cool if they covered the trip.

It occurs to me that I'm not as clever as I think.

I've also proven that I'll say yes to a junket.

I'm in cahoots with Big Tobacco.

Simon asks whether they'll be able to look over the manuscript before it's published.

I tell him no, but I'm such a weasel I put it on Penguin Random House and say that they would never allow it.

Finally, he begins to eat, which means I, with my matching-tracksuit chicken, can begin to eat. I'm enjoying my pumpkin crowned with blood orange when I see him pull at his lapel.

Something else occurs to me.

Is he recording this?

I scan the table.

Where's his phone?

I haven't seen his phone the whole time we've been here. Everyone's always pulling out their phone. Is it tucked in his jacket pocket?

I head to the bathroom, passing the marble, or at least the emotionally true marble. As I'm returning, he is swiping his credit card. I didn't even get the chance to reach for my wallet.

Outside, I wait by the Freemason for my Uber, thinking about the mountains of memos, transcripts and miscellany in the unearthed Philip Morris archives.

Why wouldn't he have been recording me?

THE CIGARETTE

The FDA must have finally finished reading Philip Morris's application seeking approval for the IQOS. No small task. Printed and stacked, it would be as tall as a twenty-storey building, at least according to the plaque in the IQOS booth in New Zealand.

The FDA's verdict? They are permitting the sale of IQOS across America.

Why is this passing unnoticed? In so much as it's being reported at all, no one is connecting the dots. Philip Morris have now successfully laid the groundwork. When, inevitably, someplace in America bans cigarettes, Philip Morris can substitute in HeatSticks. And no one sees what I see: the HeatStick is a cigarette! Unless it isn't. I admit it *does* seem suspicious that I'm the only one who's suspicious.

It doesn't help that the FDA's ruling is confusing. They've drawn two seemingly contradictory conclusions.

First, they agree with Philip Morris that switching from

cigarettes to the IQOS 'significantly reduces your body's exposure to harmful or potentially harmful chemicals'.

But they disagree with Philip Morris's claim that these 'reductions in exposure are reasonably likely to translate to a measurable and substantial reduction in morbidity and/or mortality'. So, no lowering of the likelihood of disease or death compared to a cigarette.

I'm trying to reconcile the two and this is what I've come up with: maybe some chemicals are deadly regardless of the quantity. Four chomps of an asbestos board isn't healthier than five, just because it's fewer chomps.

I read on. The FDA are explicit. They reject Philip Morris's claim that switching 'to IQOS presents less risk of harm than continuing to smoke'.

Philip Morris's only win is that the IQOS 'significantly reduces your body's exposure to harmful or potentially harmful chemicals'.

But I know from all my amateur research that's the only win they need. That and the simple fact that the IQOS has been permitted for sale – that's more than enough for their marketing team to work with. Consumers won't get any of the nuance, they'll just see a big tick of approval.

For example, you'll recall JapShop, the young man who sold me an IQOS from the boot of his Subaru in the dead of night. I catch up with him again to get more HeatSticks.

(I've huffed half the box (so ten) over a couple of months, and used up the others on guinea pig friends. They're minty and, as with vapes, the discharge makes it down my throat in a way cigarette smoke doesn't. But unlike when I vape, I feel the effects of the IQOS during my jog the next day. (Let me be clear – vapes might be harmful, I'm just telling you I don't feel them on my jog the next day.))

JapShop is an IQOS user himself, and when I meet him a second time he reassures me the IQOS is safe because it has 'FDA approval'.

I continue trudging through the FDA papers . . . It's hard to stay focused . . . I wonder if I left my water bottle on the train —

Well, well, well.

You were hoping no one would find this, Philip Morris, weren't you? Buried deep in the fat wad of documents.

Here we go.

Drum roll.

To get the IQOS through the FDA, Philip Morris had to concede that it's a cigarette!

It's a cigarette! The HeatStick is a cigarette!

The FDA writes, 'While these non-combusted cigarettes may be referred to as "heat-not-burn" or "heated" tobacco products, they meet the definition of a cigarette in the Federal Food, Drug and Cosmetic Act.'

The honeymoon is over. From here on in, the IQOS will no longer be referred to as a doohickey or Smoke Machine. Your doohickey pass has been revoked. What we have here is a cigarette.

Womp

I bathe in the blood of my enemy by sipping tea with Mike Daube, whom you'll remember as the former Director General of Health, Western Australia, in a hotel lobby in Melbourne's CBD. A silver-haired, softly spoken man, he started campaigning against cigarette giants in the early seventies in the UK, moving here in the mid-eighties.

'They tried to bribe me to work for them,' he says.

'Oh really?'

Do I tell him about my free lunch? And the Hobbit mead?

'I started doing things like asking questions at their Annual Shareholders Meetings. Innocuous questions. Like, how many deaths were the company's profits responsible for in the last year? And nobody had done that before.'

That got the attention of Rothmans, who were then the makers of Dunhill and Winfield. 'The chairman of Rothmans, Lord Pritchard, met me and he very generously offered me generous funding to work in any campaign of my choice, other than tobacco.'

Mike declined.

I move on to the FDA decision. 'It's funny to me because their whole marketing was 'this isn't a cigarette', but then to get it accepted in America, they had to concede it's a cigarette.'

'The situation in the US is complex. Sometimes it's implied their product has been approved by the FDA, but it hasn't been.'

He's right. It has been *permitted* by the FDA, not approved. Something can be reluctantly permitted.

'Is part of the reason the FDA permitted it that there wasn't an immediate reason not to, because they already permit cigarettes?'

'My very simplistic summary? Yes. It's because they're treated as cigarettes. They have no option, under certain circumstances, but to permit this, that and the other.'

The little shapeshifter. An e-cigarette when it needs to be, a regular cigarette when it needs to be that.

This section of the book carries an air of victory. *Got 'em.* Philip Morris has been insisting the HeatStick isn't a cigarette and I've caught them out.

There's just one problem. The smoking gun appears in a document that greenlights Philip Morris to sell the IQOS, and open IQOS stores, across America.

There's been a victory here alright. Theirs.

I had drum rolls before I revealed my bombshell, but now I need a trombone.

Womp womp.

'It's just like the cigarette it isn't'

So that's the state of play in America. What's happening in Australia?

Here Philip Morris is being even wilier with their little shapeshifter. They apply to the Therapeutic Goods Administration to permit the sale of the IQOS. Philip Morris holds up the HeatStick, arguing it's so *similar* to a cigarette – which is legal – it's hypocritical not to allow it, while not crossing the threshold and conceding it *is* a cigarette. It's both the closest thing to, and the furthest thing from, a cigarette.

The TGA rejects Philip Morris's application to change the Poisons Schedules to allow heated tobacco.

Murder

Andrew Gregson served as Head of Corporate and Legal Affairs for Imperial Brands, who are one of Big Tobacco's big three, along with British American Tobacco and Philip Morris. (Interestingly, the Chinese government outproduces them all, through their nationalised tobacco corporation.) Imperial Brands manufactures John Player Special, Kool and the choice of romantics who grew up watching foreign arthouse films, Gauloises. Andrew left in 2018 to run the Tasmanian Tonic Company with his wife, out of their gorgeous home in the Hobart beachside suburb of Sandy Bay. The boutique tonic-water syrup, for mixing with gin, is prepared in vats in his garage.

We sit under a pergola, sun peeping through the leaves, and drink fine wine while eating cheese, meats and breads from charcuterie boards. It's basically the aforementioned foreign arthouse film minus the Gauloises.

I put down my brie and pick up a HeatStick.

'Is this a cigarette?'

'It's an issue of semantics, nomenclature.'

'Nomenclature', from the French (like Gauloises), is a word that means 'devising or choosing names for things'. For instance, deciding if the item I hold in my fingers is a cigarette or something else.

'Do I think it's a cigarette?' Andrew continues. 'Yes. But who cares what I think?'

I do. Particularly because he reveals Philip Morris are bending language for another reason that hadn't occurred to me before.

Tax.

Cigarettes are hit with a brutal excise tax.

'One of the motivators for Philip Morris is to say, no, these are not cigarettes, therefore they fall into a different excise category. Excise is, and always will be, one of the key drivers inside a tobacco company. There's hundreds of billions of dollars, pounds and yen, globally, that are caught up in tobacco excise. When you have to pay that and how you have to pay that can make a major difference to the bottom lines of the global tobacco players. So don't discount some of that nomenclature being driven by excise policy.'

If Philip Morris gets to define the HeatStick as *not* a cigarette, they can renegotiate that brutal excise.

The UK Treasury grappled with the HeatStick in 2018. Philip Morris won that word war, too. For excise tax purposes, the UK Treasury does not consider them 'cigarettes' but rather 'tobacco for heating'.

A cigarette for FDA approval, but not for UK tax. The shape-shifting IQOS just keeps on giving.

Here are the spoils of war. In the UK, tax on cigarettes is determined by the weight of the whole thing. Not only the tobacco, but also the paper and the filter. The more the cigarette weighs, the higher the tax.

But for HeatSticks, tax is determined by the weight of the tobacco alone. It doesn't consider the paper and the filter. So on a stick-by-stick basis, Philip Morris has come out ahead.

Before the papers and filters are attached, Philip Morris is taxed per kilogram of tobacco used to produce . . . what's the collective noun for HeatSticks? Let's go with the one used for crows. Philip Morris is taxed per kilogram of tobacco used to produce a murder of HeatSticks.

STROKE

Thanks to their FDA green tick, by mid-2019 Philip Morris can start hawking the IQOS in the United States.

At the same moment, vaping has by now killed sixty Americans, and sent over 2000 to hospital. This is a big news story. The vape crisis, on the surface, should spell disaster for Philip Morris; the most well-known brand of vapes is Juul, and they hold a stake in that company.

How does Philip Morris respond to the crisis? They tweet this, for one: 'Just to be clear: Philip Morris International doesn't in any way have a stake in Juul.'

Hmmm. Philip Morris *International* doesn't. But Philip Morris *USA*'s parent company, Altria, holds a 35 per cent stake.

Even without that slithering dodge, Philip Morris is such a diversified behemoth, in the overall scheme of things, they can ride out this Juul crisis. Their priority is to keep the IQOS protected from this mess. They tweet diagrams of both devices, explaining how 'heated tobacco and e-cigarettes are not the same'.

Shapeshifter. Can I remind you that after the UK's NHS endorsed e-cigarettes, Philip Morris cleverly soaked up the glory, even though by 'e-cigarettes' the NHS meant vapes and not the IQOS.

But now here's Jacek Olczak, Philip Morris International COO, on Bloomberg News, saying that 'if a vape user is getting scared' they should explore 'the alternative, which is IQOS'.

God shines on Philip Morris. With good fortune like this, they don't need any conspiracy. Thanks to an unimaginable stroke of luck, the vape crisis means the press is looking the other way when they open their first IQOS store in Atlanta, Georgia. There's no examination of the potential dangers of the IQOS; instead, reams of paper and hours of broadcast time are spent on the dangers of vapes.

Philip Morris never loses.

The vape crisis

Two versions of why people are ending up in hospitals and morgues are flying about. The WHO and others say this crisis is evidence that vaping is deadly and the industry needs to be shut down. Savvas and others in the vaping industry suspect the deaths are the result of black-market juice laced with THC, and that legal and well-regulated vaping will save lives.

Savvas turns out to be right, or at least he is about the killer.

The Centers for Disease Control and Prevention, the US government's health agency, puts out a statement:

'National and state data from patient reports and product sample testing show tetrahydrocannabinol (THC)-containing e-cigarette, or vaping, products, particularly from informal sources, are linked to most cases and play a major role in the outbreak.'

EVERYWHERE

Philip Morris CEO André Calantzopoulos has just been asked if his company will venture into marijuana, now that those laws are loosening around the world.

'It is not an innocuous product, no matter how you look at it,' André says. He explains that he's not 'comfortable' with the science behind cannabis and thinks more research needs to be done. He's concerned about the health consequences of consuming marijuana.

Andre must be the world's most selective health nut considering that whole situation with the product he does sell. You know – rhymes with prancer, dancer, necromancer.

Beyond health concerns, André frets that selling marijuana could present a 'reputational risk' to Philip Morris. Reputational risk? You run Philip Morris. Forget marijuana, if your company moved out of cigarettes and into snuff films, people's estimation would go up.

'There is nothing today that makes me say this category is something we should be looking at,' he declares.

Can't be more definite than that. But, as usual, there's a bit of fancy footwork and shoe shuffling (or at least paper shuffling) needed for this Philip Morris claim to be entirely true.

Philip Morris *International* doesn't deal dope, but again, Philip Morris *USA*'s parent company does. Altria hold a 45 per cent stake in Canadian medicinal marijuana giant Cronos Group.

Marijuana is controversial. It's tempting to pull out the machete and hack into the tangles of Philip Morris becoming involved in what has been a long-time illicit drug. But for me, that's heading up the wrong path. With their foray into medicinal marijuana, 'medicinal' is the sensational bit, not 'marijuana'.

Let me explain.

Philip Morris is blacklisted by the health sector, as demanded by the WHO, Quit Victoria and pretty much every other public health body.

And not just them. Before working for Philip Morris, Rhenu, from the IQOS booth at the vape expo, worked for Roche, the largest pharmaceutical company in the world.

'I had presented at so many conferences,' she told me. 'And then last month, when I was going to an addiction conference and I registered as Philip Morris, I get a call saying, "Oh, you can't come."'

So, Philip Morris is shunned by the pharmaceutical industry too. Or so it seems.

Medicinal marijuana is a pharmaceutical product, requiring a prescription. And so through this product, Philip Morris is now part of the legitimate health sector. And once again, it appears no one has noticed.

Doobies

That Philip Morris USA–affiliated marijuana company, Cronos Group, is now reaching across the Pacific. They have joined with a Melbourne private equity firm to form Cronos Australia.

'What happened with the float?' I ask Rodney Cocks, CEO of Cronos Australia. The tram outside my apartment took me to this Italian restaurant in Hawthorn, a few suburbs up.

A former soldier who was awarded the Conspicuous Service Medal, Rodney previously worked counter-narcotics with the British government in the Middle East. This involved destroying illicit crops, including the very crop that is now central to his business.

'Yesterday we floated,' he says. 'Rang the bell at the ASX.'

'Literally rang the bell?'

'Yeah,' he says, enthused. He pulls out his phone and shows me a photo of the clang at the Australian Stock Exchange. 'We raised $20 million in capital.'

I realise there's another consequence to Philip Morris sidling into the world of marijuana. It's a scene that has, for decades, been delightfully illicit and countercultural. Will this ruin that? As Kurt Cobain might texta on a bong, does corporate pot suck?

'Is there a feeling amongst the medicinal marijuana industry that the people out front should look as little like Rastafarians as possible?'

'Yes,' Rodney says, sharply dressed himself. 'The people leading these companies and driving the industry are investment bankers, consultants, lawyers, private-equity venture capitalists. It's definitely the antithesis of the person you were describing.'

The plus side of this? Firmed-up regulation. You can trace a dodgy bottle of cannabis oil back to an accountable company, who can rectify the problem. Or, at the very least, you can sue them.

The negative? What's lost. I saw in New Zealand the joyful, ambiguously regulated vape industry, which is a welcoming place for misfits.

'We get people approaching us for jobs all the time,' Rodney says. 'They have twenty years' experience in the cannabis industry. Legally, we can't employ them.' These people, having been in the industry before it went legit, find black marks against their names. A criminal conviction, or just the lack of formal qualifications. You don't need a science or medical degree to mix Skitzo Green Apples vape juice, but this casualness doesn't cut it once a drug trade turns legit. Philip Morris is elbowing in and bouncing out the oddballs.

'Do you think there are investors who'll see you as a version of the cigarette industry, perceive you as Big Tobacco?'

'No, I don't think so. We think about our product range and we think, "Who are our end users?" They're people who are suffering from some of the worst diseases and conditions, and we are relieving pain and suffering.'

This isn't just theoretical for Rodney – his wife is battling breast cancer. Cronos isn't available in Australia yet, so she drips one drop of a competitor's cannabis oil beneath her tongue twice a day.

Rodney served in a United Nations unit clearing land mines in Iraq. For him, running a medicinal marijuana company is a further humanitarian mission.

He makes convincing points. Cronos is in the business of medicinal, not recreational marijuana. And cannabis oil involves no smoking. Besides, what's so wrong with recreational marijuana, particularly in a country that abides alcohol?

But these solid arguments don't address the big question in my head. I remember Lliam, the Māori shaman, telling me that it's not the contents of a concoction that curses it, it's the carrier, the one who prepares it.

I better not express it that way to Rodney. I can't be blathering about curses. Simulate a normal person.

'If there's medicinal marijuana and big business is involved, cool,' I say. 'But when it specifically comes to Philip Morris, have they done too many bad things to be given a seat at the table? Like the corporation version of Harvey Weinstein.'

Rodney chuckles. 'I think that's not for me to judge. I'm not trying to avoid the question.'

We drink and exchange stories of our travel adventures. He was injured in the 2002 Bali bombings and wounded in a Baghdad suicide-bomb attack. I broke into Disneyland.

A colleague of Rodney's rocks up. Rodney tells him I'm writing a book and he says, 'Who reads books anymore?'

Great. This is the arc of my book. Act One, protagonist learns no one cares about Big Tobacco. Act Two, protagonist learns no one cares about corporations. Act Three, protagonist learns no one cares about books.

Still, I'll press on. I'm having too much fun.

Doctors prescribing medicinal marijuana could soon be helping fill Philip Morris's coffers. And while our Pharmaceutical Benefits Scheme does not yet provide rebates for it, one day taxpayers could be helping them out too.

Charades

Already in cigarettes, now they're in medicinal marijuana. Philip Morris provide you with leukaemia, then relieves you of the pain. It's a full-service business.

Why stop there, Philip Morris? Why not get involved in life insurance?

That's the joke, John? You're really going with that?

No, it's not the joke. Philip Morris has actually set up a life insurance company to ease their customers from coughing to coffin.

'Take a walk on the well side,' reads their website, winking at the Lou Reed hit 'Walk on the Wild Side'. I give that pun a B–.

By the way, Philip Morris, seeing as you bring it up, the year he died Lou Reed said, 'What I really want more than anything else is to quit smoking. That's what I want. I've quit a lot of things in my life, and this one's the worst.'

Anyway, launched in the UK in 2019, the life insurance company is named Reviti. Incredibly, they will lower your premium if you move from smoking cigarettes to using the IQOS. And they also discourage you from trying out the competition – switching to IQOS will earn you a 25 per cent reduction in your premium, while switching to vapes only gets you a 2.5 per cent reduction.

There's a lot going on here. Yes, yes, once again let's go in with an open mind and get the Florence Nightingale version of events out of the way: Reviti cares and wants to move smokers off cigarettes.

Perhaps. But here's a benefit to Philip Morris. As you'll recall, they're forbidden from marketing the IQOS as safer or healthier than cigarettes. That would be suggesting the IQOS is a medical device, which is a no-no unless proven and signed off by a government body.

What are Philip Morris to do? Say it without saying it. Like a person playing a game of charades, here they are, flapping their hands around madly, waiting for you to get what their lips are bursting to say and just go ahead and say it yourself.

Philip Morris tells you, through Reviti, that a customer's life insurance premium will drop 25 per cent if they switch from cigarettes to IQOS. That's saying it without saying it. And they promote this online, saying it without saying it to a wider world than only potential life-insurance customers.

Naturally, visitors to their website will need to bring an archaeologist to dig up the bit where Reviti reveal they're a Philip Morris venture. Like *Vice* and the Centre for Research Excellence: Indigenous Sovereignty and Smoking, here's a third party that can push their luck in pushing health claims that Philp Morris can't make directly.

PEOPLE FOR THE ETHICAL TREATMENT OF HOMO SAPIENS

Fine. I get it. Killing 8 million people per annum doesn't contravene the new moral code for some reason.

But good news! (Well, bad news.) Philip Morris *does* contravene edicts of the new moral code. I've been frustrated that Philip Morris are slinking along unnoticed, so this might be the way to rouse the people. I haven't caught a photo on Instagram of a Philip Morris executive hunting a lion, but I have found a sort of equivalent: Philip Morris has been testing the IQOS on animals.

Their science team released a study called 'Lung transcriptomic clock predicts premature aging in cigarette smoke-exposed mice'. I like how there's mice and a clock. Now I've got 'hickory, dickory, dock, the mouse ran up the clock' caught in my head.

Here's the gist of the study.

Hickory, dickory, dock,
the mouse smoked an IQOS.

Lungs got more old
on Marlboro Gold.
Hickory, dickory, cough.

So, a mouse fared better inhaling HeatStick discharge than traditional cigarette smoke. The usual caveat applies – this is a Philip Morris study, so for all we know, to make it appear that the mouse smoking the IQOS ended up healthier, they could have tipped the grandfather clock onto the mouse smoking the cigarette.

Here's how PETA, People for the Ethical Treatment of Animals, describe two of Philip Morris's experiments.

'Experimenters with Philip Morris stuffed thousands of rats into tiny canisters that pumped tobacco smoke directly into their noses six hours a day for 90 consecutive days. The rats were then killed and dissected to examine the harm caused to their bodies.'

'Philip Morris experimenters subjected 1000 rats to two years of breathing either diesel engine exhaust or second-hand cigarette smoke for six hours a day, seven days a week, just to compare the effects of the exposure on their lungs.'

I'm not eating meat with my friend Simone Stewart in a booth at a bar ten minutes from my home, towards the beach. Last time we caught up and didn't eat meat, I told her about Philip Morris and the mice. Knowing her love of animals, I hoped to gain an ally. She's since done further reading on the history of smoking experiments.

'They even put holes in the dogs' and the monkeys' throats and put a tube directly going into their lungs,' she tells me. 'I feel like I'm going to pass out just talking about it.'

She brings up the matter of empathy.

'Anyway, of course, that evoked in me a massive shock and reaction of disgust. Much more than thinking about people dying from the consequences of smoking.'

Simone has assumed my book will be full of stunts. I guess in my last book I did sneak into a far-right meeting disguised as a farmer. And she works in the theatre, so this is where her mind drifts.

'I thought if you're wanting to evoke empathy about *that* subject, in the palliative care wards of people dying due to smoking, you'd start dressing them up as animals.'

'The people who are already dying of lung cancer, you dress up as mice?'

'Yes.'

What a strange idea. Brand Human Being is so in the toilet we need to say 'they're just like mice' to get people to feel something.

I remember watching a news story with my grandmother in her flat. A community had rallied around saving a dog, raising money for an operation or pulling it out of a well, I can't remember the details. My grandmother said she had nothing against the dog, but where was everyone during the Holocaust? So that was my upbringing, my indoctrination. That's why I think people are more important than mice.

I ponder those PETA descriptions of Philip Morris pumping tobacco smoke into mice. Because that's the same thing they do to people! But people have free choice and the mice don't. Just as the lion didn't choose to take the bullet. But then, as Theodore Dalrymple told me, addiction is a measurable scientific phenomenon. People have free choice, but they don't.

Regardless of all these loose ends, I know where I stand on this vexed mice versus people issue.

Dr Alex Wodak told me about exit strategies, giving your opponent an honourable peace, like Kennedy did for Khrushchev. Let's apply that here.

So, you (well, some of you) think mice are more important than people and I think people are more important than mice. Let's meet halfway and agree that people are as important as mice. As Simone's stunt demonstrates.

'People will see their cute little ears,' she continues. 'And their little tails, as they get wheeled around the hospital. And maybe you could even put them in full fur suits the further on they go. Then people will really care and want to stop Philip Morris.'

'My friend Michelle Bennett,' I begin. 'She cares about animals, but also her father was in palliative care because of smoking. I'll ask her what she thinks about dressing Mr Bennett as a mouse. Yeah. I like it. I can see why you're in showbiz.'

'Razzle-dazzle.'

Strolling home from the bar, the idea of a stunt now planted in my head, I come up with my own. I'll dress up as a Generation X mouse in a flannel shirt and run through the Philip Morris building singing that Smashing Pumpkins song about not wishing to be a rat encaged, regardless of my rage.

That's not the end of the matter. I do some digging. While one arm of PETA is pummelling Philip Morris, another paw is handing them an award. How can this be?

Here we go again. Philip Morris have become financially involved with PETA.

In 2019, they joined with PETA to donate equipment to a US laboratory that conducts animal-free testing. Even though Philip Morris themselves conduct animal testing.

They've also contributed resources to an online database set up to stop animal testing. PETA has thanked them for this in the form of an award. So, despite them gassing animals, and PETA eviscerating them for this, they get to promote on their website and in the press 'Philip Morris International receives PETA award'.

Once again, Philip Morris never loses.

Under the sea

What other laws of the new moral code do Philip Morris contravene? Well, they're killing the environment.

Clean-Up Australia reports seven billion cigarette butts are littered around the country each year. These butts contain plastic, tar and other chemicals. One butt in 40 litres of water triggers 'a week of carnage' for crustaceans.

The organisation Break Free From Plastic placed Philip Morris International at number eight on their 2020 list of top-ten polluters. Seven of those ten companies have now signed The New Plastics Global Economy Commitment, dedicated to reducing waste. Philip Morris isn't one of them.

Here's a better idea. I'll run through the Philip Morris building dressed as eighties hit-maker Phil Collins, with cigarette butts and Marlboro packs stuck all over me, shouting, 'I'm Land*Phil* Collins!' crooning how I feel something coming in the air tonight 'and that something is your pollution, Philip Morris!'

The fuzz

Philip Morris torture animals, and they kill the sky and the ocean. What other laws of the new moral code do they contravene?

Let's move on from mice and crustaceans to men.

I think this one is quite the humdinger, considering the moment we're living through and what people care about.

Philip Morris has bought vehicles, high-tech cameras, protective equipment and sniffer dogs for the Romanian police. This is part of their $100 million project to buy themselves into law enforcement around the globe. They've brought in a former Senior Prosecutor for the US Department of Justice, Suzanne Hayden, to help run the project known as PMI-IMPACT.

I think about all those social media posts, rolling in non-stop: 'Defund the police!'

What's going on with PMI-IMPACT?

Philip Morris wants law enforcement to ramp up their efforts to destroy the cigarette smuggling trade. But to make it seem less cynical, I reckon – and to curry favour with the powerful – they're funding law enforcement campaigns that go beyond that.

They've bought high-speed boats and surveillance equipment for the National Coast Guard of Greece, who stop immigrants seeking asylum.

They've funded a counter-terrorism campaign run by the Royal United Service Institute. That organisation's president is the Duke of Kent, Prince Edward.

But I'm particularly interested in this. Beyond PMI-IMPACT, Philip Morris has signed a partnership with the California Narcotic Officers' Association, which trains police officers.

'Why do Philip Morris get away with this?' I say, flapping my arms at Scarlett-Jae, who is poking her fork into some tofu at my kitchen table. 'Why do they just get away with this? Help me connect the dots, so I don't sound like a madman. I'm so annoyed. Look at this. On the one side, everyone's, "Defund the police, defund the police." That's all I hear about. On the other side, Philip Morris *is* funding the police and no one's noticed!

'And Eric Garner, the Black guy who was killed, the Black Lives Matter one,' I continue. 'He was killed because the police were able to approach him because he was involved in the illegal cigarette trade. No one's connecting the dots. No one's protesting outside Philip Morris.'

I humph.

'You're right,' says Scarlett-Jae. 'You're not mad.'

Twenty minutes later she's on the balcony smoking a cigarette.

I stay inside and watch a YouTube video: 'PMI IMPACT Expert Council: In Their Own Words'. Talking heads lull us into the idea that corporations buying into policing is uncomplicated and (their word) 'holistic'. Like Buddha on a Pilates ball, but with cigarettes and guns.

'We can invent something new in the twenty-first century,' says Luis Moreno Ocampo warmly. He's a former prosecutor in the International Criminal Court.

'I'm convinced that the future is private and public,' adds Alain Juillet, former Head of French Economic Intelligence.

They appear to be in hotel rooms. For some reason I'm fascinated by whether they came in their own suits or if it's a supplied wardrobe. All the colours – the lounge, the walls, the suits – rest so pleasingly together.

My friend in the human rights biz later tells me these people are international relations superstars Philip Morris has poached. A former UN High Commissioner for Human Rights, Navi Pillay, is in the video too.

The only one not washed over with serenity is Suzanne Hayden, former Senior Prosecutor for the US Department of Justice. She looks like a terrorist is holding a gun to her just off camera. She says of Philip Morris and their foray into law enforcement, 'this is the first time I have seen anyone look at the problem holistically and say, "It's not about me."'

The QAnon conspiracy, that a shadowy elite is running the world and encroaching into every aspect of our lives, is spreading like wildfire on the internet. Meanwhile in this video Carlos Creus Moreira, whose company is 'deploying large scale digital identity ecosystems for people and objects using Artificial Intelligence', calmly talks up PMI-IMPACT. The video has been up for a year and at the time of writing has 108 views. About forty of those are mine. Where is everybody?

STATEN ISLAND, NEW YORK,
17 JULY, 2014

A cop wanders over to Eric Garner, a 43-year old Black American, standing outside a beauty supply store in Staten Island, New York. He accuses Eric of selling cigarettes without tax stamps, a violation of the law.

'You want to stop me [garbled] selling cigarettes. I'm minding my business, officer. I'm minding my business. Please just leave me alone.'

Within fifteen minutes the police have wrestled him to the ground, put him in a chokehold, and Eric has lost consciousness. Within the hour he's pronounced dead. The medical examiner rules it a homicide.

'They don't even go after murderers the way they went after my son,' says Gwyn Carr, mother of Eric Garner, down the line.

'The Marlboro people,' I say. 'Philip Morris – they've started funding police programs to crack down on people who are selling illegal cigarettes. And I just wanted to know what you thought.'

'I think that's just an attack on the Black community again. If they're funding police, you know it's profitable to them. Because they're not going to fund anything they'll lose money on.'

'So you're against Philip Morris funding police?'

'Right.'

So I'm not mad for thinking it's ominous that Philip Morris has bought into law enforcement. A woman who couldn't have more authority on the matter of police overreach and cigarette 'crimes' is against it. It's Eric Garner's mum and me versus Philip Morris.

Tangle

There is a tiny tangle. Not one that, if pulled, unravels the above, but a tangle nonetheless.

In 2020 the government of California plans to ban menthol cigarettes. This is bundled in with a proposed law to ban vape juice flavours. The logic is that the menthol cigarette is another flavoured nicotine product, and flavours are more likely to attract young people.

Like with the European Union's impending menthol ban, California would like to ban all cigarettes, but they have to start somewhere. But this isn't Luxembourg, this is America. It's a different country – a different planet, really – and there are different landmines planted in the soil.

Around 85 per cent of Black Americans who smoke choose menthol cigarettes, three times the rate of white Americans. So this proposed menthol-cigarette ban is striking a match in the close vicinity of race.

There's a commercial running in support of the ban. A stylised chalk outline of a human body snaps onto the screen, followed by a stylised human heart. Words slam on, in sync with the slam poetry of Tasha 'SixFootah ThePoet' Turner. Staccato and fast fast fast over a monophonic, haunting chord.

She says menthol cigarettes put her mother in the graveyard. Just as cops kill Black people, so do these cigarettes, so lawmakers are hypocrites if they say 'Black Lives Matter' but don't vote for this ban.

This commercial was paid for by Bloomberg Philanthropy, the powerful group who oppose Big Tobacco (as well as vaping, as I would have learnt from Dr Wodak at the vape expo if I hadn't spoken over him).

Meanwhile the other side of the argument are seeing this through the lens of race too, but in a totally different way. They say it's racist to ban menthol cigarettes, the choice of Black Americans, when you're not banning regular cigarettes, the choice of white Americans.

In the commercial trying to stop the ban, old white men in suits smoke cigars in an exclusive club. There's leather lounge chairs, a decanter of scotch on a mahogany table, the privileged chortles of the rich.

'Backroom deals with special favours for the rich,' the voice-over warns us. 'SB 793 criminalises the sale of menthol cigarettes, the choice of Black and Latino smokers.'

A silver-haired white businessman gives a self-satisfied smirk at an airport business lounge.

'Giving special treatment to the rich and singling out communities of colour. Tell your assembly member to vote No on SB 793. It reeks of politics.'

This commercial is brought to you by Reynolds American, makers of Camel, Newport and Lucky Strike. It uses stock footage, and

I think of the actor at the airport business lounge, who had no idea he would end up as the face of systemic racism. Cheer up, it could have been a paedophile prevention public service announcement.

So which side of the argument did Gwyn Carr, mother of Eric Garner, fall on? Is she for or against the ban on menthol cigarettes?

'I'm not a smoker myself, but I am against the ban, because it's going to cause a lot of problems in the Black and Brown neighbourhoods. It'll be another excuse for the police to come in and terrorise, brutalise and kill our people, because the majority of Black and Brown people are the ones who smoke the menthol cigarettes. They're not going into Marlboro Country and stopping them from smoking.' She's imagining the pale cowboy on those old billboards.

I remember Dr Marewa Glover telling me in New Zealand that laws against smoking were proxies for laws against minorities, the people most likely to smoke.

Gwyn Carr appeared in a promotional video opposing the ban, sponsored by the American National Newspaper Publishers Association (formerly the National Negro Publishers Association), who are working with the makers of Camel on this campaign. So her advocacy on this matter is something good, trying to keep her community safe from police brutality, that, as a side effect, is also good for the cigarette giants.

I play with my reflection in a Zippo lighter. Bulbous nose, then skinny nose. Pointy chin, then round. All these life-and-death cigarette matters bend this way, that way, a third way, all depending on the precise angle at which you hold them to the light.

LAST PICK FOR THE DEBATING TEAM

I fear I won't convince the world that Philip Morris are up to skulduggery again, this time passing off what is clearly a cigarette as not a cigarette. The guy writing the book can't – put – He's just bad at arguing his point.

Example.

'Did you set up poison stations?' Simone Stewart asks at our next meat-free nibble.

'The man did.'

'But you hired the man to set up poison stations around your apartment. Why?'

'Because I had – there's mice, and I have to get rid of them.'

'You don't use poison. It's so disturbing. It's a very slow death. They bleed from the inside out. And also other animals eat them sometimes, and then *they* die a slow death too. Like an owl or a magpie or a crow.'

I say nothing, but she can somehow read my face.

'You can't . . . No, no, no. You have to stop your relationship with the poison rat man.'

'Okay.'

'That has to end.'

She's still reading my face.

'It's all horrible. Why must you?'

A thought pops into my head that brings me over to her side of this issue.

'How can I paint Philip Morris as diabolical for torturing mice when I'm killing mice myself?'

I'm so bad at arguing that this argument in favour of her position turns her against it.

'Well, sometimes it's about the context,' she says. 'They're doing that on mass levels. You're just getting rid of one or two little mice in your house.'

TRUE CRIME

The Romanian dwarf who works at the prison, Nigel – you met him many pages ago – has called me up to talk cigarette smuggling. 'Everybody's making money because it's so expensive. It's such a valuable crop.'

I put him on speaker, laying the phone down on my coffee table. How have we become so lazy that holding a phone to our ear seems a chore?

Nigel continues. 'I met this guy who you should meet – a *yiddishe* guy. He got busted coming in from Vietnam with three suitcases full of cigarettes.'

Is this the sort of person PMI-IMPACT has in their sights? Perhaps literal gun sights?

'It's the mob, it's organised crime,' says Nigel. Exciting. 'But this guy's a simple guy. I know him. He's just a regular joe who needed some cash. He just went off the tracks.'

So how can I meet him?

'I'm not dropping names over the phone for obvious reasons. I think he's got issues at the moment. But that doesn't matter, because I know where he lives, so I can just lob up and fix it. He'll be hard to get to, but it'll be worth the chase.'

'We can go on a road trip,' I say.

'He can run but he can't hide.'

For some reason Nigel doesn't correct me, but no road trip will be happening. This cigarette smuggler, whom I'll call Reuben, lives a three-minute stroll from my apartment. Maybe two. I learn he has brushed past me over the years, at the 7-Eleven that's equidistant from our homes.

'They came from Hungary,' Reuben says. 'They weren't in the Holocaust, my mum's parents. They were able to make some connections, gather a bunch of US dollars together, to literally be able to flee the country. Ships in the night stuff. How are you with dogs?'

A full-size eighties arcade machine stands out among the furnishings and tchotchkes of his grandparents' home. There's black and white photos of men and women from the old country, 'the good crockery' behind glass cabinets, a painting of the Western Wall in Jerusalem. Thick carpet, soft to the feet; it's his grandparents' home so we took our shoes off at the door, but they have passed away and he lives here alone.

'Nothing wrong with dogs,' I say.

Reuben has brought another personal touch to the home, besides the arcade machine. Rainforest music, the type that you hear when you go to the chiropractor, softly plays.

'I have gone through addiction,' he tells me in the kitchen. 'I went through drug-induced psychosis. Having gone through that, the dark night of the soul, has allowed me to rehabilitate myself from the inside out. I'm completely drug free.'

He glances at the cigarette parked between his fingers.

'Except these fucking things. I've come close a couple of times to stopping. In fact, I did a ten-day Vipassana meditation course at the start of the year.'

I glance at his kitchen counter. We pick up our coffee beans at the same shop down the street. Although he buys decaf, shunning caffeine. He rejects meat, too. He says by eating meat you're, 'Consuming consciousness of death. By putting death and suffering into the body, that doesn't go away. That stays with you.'

'So we have the souls of the scallops and the lambs in our bodies?'

'And all the trauma and pain of the unnecessary production behind the machine.'

'The experience in the abattoir?'

'All of it.'

He gazes at his cigarette and sees the consciousness of death in that, too.

'I know when I give these cigarettes up, and the time's fast approaching – it's not just the cigarette itself, it's the whole – what you're working on, the lies.' Like Lliam the Māori shaman (and me) he thinks concoctions are cursed by the darkness of their maker.

'And I've got a list of people that I'd love to be able to take down, which . . . it's very, very difficult, because they're running the world. But Big Tobacco is one of them.'

'How can you take down a cigarette company?'

We're not quite at the end of the book. There might still be time.

'I've had this – this is a utopian dream, what I'm talking about here. I'm talking about assembling – this is proper imagination stuff – assembling an elite crack SAS force that can go deep undercover and just knock it all out, knock out their computer systems, blow up all their buildings. Take out all the documentations, take out all the powers that be, those at the top of the chain of their narcissistic leadership.'

'Can we take them hostage and deprogram them rather than —'

'Not possible.'

'Oh, we've got to take them out.'

He says we do. I move on to why I was drawn here.

'I hear you were busted at the airport.'

He sips on his decaf and we shift back into the lounge room.

'I got involved with a group of people, through a friend of a friend. They set up an operation based in Ho Chi Minh City in Vietnam. And I thought, it's a really sweet deal. They paid for the round-trip flights, paid for accommodation, paid cash for spending money. And all my job was was to come back into Melbourne and grab three suitcases off the carousel and walk them straight through customs.'

'And did you have to check those suitcases in?'

'Yes, I helped pack them,' he says. 'The money was really, really good.'

'What was the money?'

'Between $7500 and $10,000 per trip.'

I whistle and his little grey dog trots in from the other room.

'And were these counterfeits?'

'No, the genuine thing.'

This racket exists because the excise tax on cigarettes is so high in Australia. Smugglers can incur the costs of world travel and still make a tidy profit selling these cigarettes at a quarter of the price that Coles charges. Or even less.

'And what did they tell you would be the consequences if you got busted?'

'There were no consequences. That's why I did it. It's not illegal to do what we were doing.'

I arch my eyebrow at the dog.

'How can it not be illegal?'

'Because it's not an illegal product. So I had the choice at the airport, if caught, to either pay the duty on them, which means it's not illegal, or forfeit them.'

'Oh my God, it's so clever.'

Note for smugglers-to-be: the authorities frown upon syndicates. This loophole only exists for travellers bringing in cigarettes for personal use. So, if customs ask, that's what you have to tell them.

It's such a clever crime. In contrast, if you're caught with marijuana or coke, you're screwed. It doesn't matter if you convince the authorities it's just for personal use.

'All the money tied up for border security is going into counter-terrorism,' says Reuben.

Busting punters with too many cartons is not a priority. In so much as they're after anyone, they're only after syndicates.

'If they uncovered this, if they dug deeper, they would be able to find out what's going on. They could prosecute. And there are pretty serious fines. But there was a clear and simple rule: *These are for myself.* If nobody talks, then it's personal use.'

'So how many times did you do it?'

He says six times over the last eighteen months. 'And my sixth one was the one that they got me.'

Further note for smugglers-to-be: recently a new consideration has come into play, a heavy disincentive. Now if you get caught, it's a minimum $10,000 fine, even if it's for personal use. Reuben was busted just before this law rolled in. He forfeited his three suitcases bursting with cartons.

'You never heard from them again, after they took your cigarettes?'

He wanders from the room. The dog and I stand around awkwardly. He returns with the letter he received from Australian Border Force. It's not a summons for a court appearance, nor a fine, just a list of the items he had forfeited.

He says the smuggled cigarettes are sold to everyday shops in Melbourne.

'A lot of the black-market trade is purchased in certain suburbs where there's a concentration of Asian smokers.'

I remember these cigarettes came in from Vietnam.

'And were they Vietnamese Australians, the guys who were running this operation?'

'Nah, good Jewish boys, just like you and me. Russians.'

(Later I have an argument with Nigel the Romanian dwarf. He thinks I shouldn't mention that the syndicate is Jewish because the Jews have enough troubles. I argue that it's not a stereotype that Jews are cigarette smugglers – I spent over a year canvassing antisemites for my last book and it didn't come up once. In fact, come to think of it, cigarette smuggling is about the only thing not blamed on the Jews.)

Reuben's grandparents haven't just left behind figurines and tapestries. A neatly torn side of a Marlboro carton lies on the dining room table.

'My grandfather, my father and myself, we all smoked the same brand of cigarettes.' He picks up the side of the carton. 'My grandfather, he'd write lists of things on the back. On this one he was documenting, I think, a trip that he did with my nana in the car.'

The trail of cigarette smoke runs right back. His father drove a cigarette delivery truck and Reuben followed him into the trade with a job at Linfox.

'They had a warehouse full of cigarettes and the van was already packed. I used to drive out every day with $200,000 in the back. Alarms rigged up all over me and all over the vehicle. I also had the job of servicing, fixing and restocking cigarette vending machines.'

So he was once legitimate.

'And I rorted the hell out of it.'

Retraction: he was not legitimate.

'Just a pack here and there?'

He reaches for his pouch of tobacco from the dining room table. His forearm is inked with the words *Discepolo della Sperientia*. Disciple of experience.

'Much more, much more. On my run I had Crown Casino – they had twenty-four babies inside there, twenty-four machines. The highest selling machines in the country. I used to change the levels all the time and just change them by five, pocket five. A significant amount of theft. Which I was gleefully happy to engage in. Just given the nature of the, you know – I wouldn't steal from anybody but the tobacco industry. "I'm paying a fortune to

you arseholes for killing me. Fuck you. I'm getting some back."
Something for the good guys.'

Why am I feeling like I'm on Reuben's side here?

Let's pop away for a moment and head to the Philip Morris
International 2020 Annual Shareholders Meeting. A man has a
question.

'Last year on a tobacco farm that supplies Philip Morris
International, eighteen workers, who were facing wage theft and
unsanitary living conditions, joined a farm labour organising
committee. And they reached out to the Philip Morris International
supplier with a request to meet, in order to improve working conditions. The farm owner threatened union organisers and worked
to blacklist all the union members. So they have no jobs this year.
Question to the Chairman. Will Philip Morris International still
blacklist, in retaliation, workers exercising their rights for freedom
of association?'

The Chairman, Louis Camilleri, says the farmer was investigated
and was found to have done nothing wrong.

For Reuben, anything goes when it comes to cigarettes and
hoodwinkery, but who cares? Philip Morris is the ultimate anything-
goes business. They do what they like and it's apparently all legal.
Maybe that's fine, but that puts in place a moral framework where
it's hard to get worked up about cigarette smugglers, fare evaders and
shoppers who weigh the expensive tomatoes as cheap potatoes at the
self-serve check-out.

Reuben pets his dog goodbye and we head down the street. He
wants to show me how seamlessly the black market is absorbed into
the world. We visit two shops. In each one, he knows how to talk

the small talk that builds enough trust with the person behind the counter for them to pull out their illicit products.

And now I have a pouch of chop-chop – untaxed loose tobacco – in my Adidas shoebox, on the counter next to my fridge. It's tucked in there with the vape kazoos, IQOS and nicotine toothpicks.

PMNL

I'm writing 'PMNL' in lipstick on my bathroom mirror to remind myself each morning that no matter what happens, Philip Morris Never Loses.

The University of Bath runs a research institute called Tobacco Tactics. They accuse Big Tobacco of accommodating smuggling. 'Evidence shows that they are over-producing products in some markets in the knowledge that excess products will end up on the illicit market.'

Why would Big Tobacco want this?

A pack of cigarettes might be a couple of bucks in Vietnam and more than forty bucks here, but the vast majority of that goes to the Australian government.

So the accusation is that, in the overall scheme of things, Philip Morris doesn't care from which country you buy their cigarettes, the price differentiation largely coming down to excise tax they never see anyway.

On top of this, this brutal tax has meant a sharp drop in sales. So, the accusation continues, tobacco giants are accommodating smuggling, to continue selling cigarettes to people otherwise priced out of the market. Tobacco giants want their sale by any means necessary.

There's a saying, when you point your finger at someone, three fingers are pointing back at you. Reuben hated Philip Morris and saw smuggling cheap cigarettes as a little act of revenge. But Philip Morris got paid either way. When you stick your middle finger up at Philip Morris, three middle fingers are sticking up back at you.

OUT OF NOWHERE, COVID

Simon Dowding, my Philip Morris lunch date, emails me. He tells me that he can't believe society has melted down so quickly over toilet paper, pasta and rice. We're only in week one of lockdown. He adds that unfortunately COVID-19 has put a hold on all travel plans for the forseeable future.

Jesus. The worst of both worlds. I won't get to the cube in Switzerland and, if my hunch about that lunch is right, Philip Morris has a recording of me accepting a Big Tobacco junket.

WHAT WOULD JESUS DO?

I'm not able to leave my house, but it's not the end of the world.

I remember what that woman from the advertising agency said about Generation X in her presentation to Philip Morris. 'They are adaptive. They live by their wits.'

I start signing up for Zoom seminars.

Tonight, I click into one called 'Finance for Christians: Biblical Responsible Investing'. I'm thinking about my Philip Morris shares. If I keep them after the upcoming Annual Shareholders Meeting, at the very least it's going to be bad optics.

'For every webinar, when people are trickling in, I'm like, do I tell a joke, do I sing a psalm?' Enoch begins. Crisp shirt, nice smile, clearly free of sin. 'Does anybody have a joke?' He homes in on one gentleman. 'Okay, Sean, do you have a joke?'

Sean does not have a joke.

'Does anyone want to offer a joke?'

No one offers a joke.

'How about Maria? I think you have a joke you want to share?'

She does not.

'I can't think of any jokes,' Enoch concludes. He's addressing us from British Columbia.

'As any good Asian kid would do, you're either an accountant, a lawyer, a doctor or an engineer.'

He studied accounting and finance and was pumped for the real world.

'Having graduated and started to look into some different investment firms, I just felt so off. I was going to this penthouse party with a bunch of different finance people, hedge-fund managers, you know, the bee's knees.'

I like how he said the bee's knees.

'I remember walking in the front doors and the host saying, "Hey, I can grab you some coke." And I said to him, "Sure, do you have Diet Coke?" And he gave me a look, saying, what's Diet Coke? And I was like, "Oh, you're talking about *that* type of coke. Whoops!"'

Not the bee's knees after all.

Enoch decided to abandon that world and work at a non-profit.

'But then I started to learn that there's over 2300 verses in the Bible that speak about stewardship, money management, wealth. And Jesus himself talks about money over 700 times.'

Well, he was Jewish. (Sorry, Nigel the Romanian dwarf.)

'It got me thinking, if the Bible speaks so much about this, how come we're not speaking more about it?'

He comes to the crux of the matter.

'Here's your first key takeaway to do with stewardship mentality: God owns it all.'

He explains that as God owns it all, you have to invest your money as God would invest. By His moral standards, not yours.

Enoch asks us to type in our questions. I patter away at my keyboard:

I own shares in Philip Morris the cigarette company, should I get rid of them?

This question animates the congregation, who are eager to type replies.

Daniel: YES

Anonymous Moose: yes

Sabrina 'Princess': Yes

The brethren have spoken, the verdict is clear. I need to dump my shares.

But, hang on, not everyone's agreeing with Anonymous Moose.

Choi: How far into abstraction does this logic extend? What about investing in the paper that makes the cigarettes? What about investing in the company that makes the tools that the farmers use to harvest tobacco?

Choi makes a good poi— Oh, he's still typing.

Choi: What about the company that provides the cameras to the porn studio?

That is a vali—

Choi: What about the company that makes the raw silicone that the dildo company makes their products out of?

Yes, John, what about the dildos? You hypocrite.

At last Enoch takes note of my question. 'Ivan, did you want to tackle the tobacco one?'

His fellow host, also in a crisp shirt, takes a moment. He addresses me directly.

'I say pray. Pray about it. It's between you and God. If God is speaking to you about it, that you should divest, then listen to Him. But if you are going to keep at it, then that's your call.'

I handballed this to you, Ivan. Kick it to Jesus, don't handball it back to me.

'What are you doing with the money after? That's what God cares about more.' His eyes lock on me through the screen. 'If you take the money and invest in other people, and they're able to get a closer relation to God, I think that's what God would want us to do. Pray and see what God speaks to you about it.'

I check the NAB Trade app. I'm $316 up on the roughly two grand I put in.

'NOT ABLE TO LEAVE MY HOUSE, NOT THE END OF THE WORLD' — JOHN SAFRAN

As Enoch the Christian investor would say, 'Whoops!'

It's five weeks into hard lockdown. I crane my neck out through my bedroom window. I see a police car slow-rolling and pulling up beside a woman who's breaking Melbourne's 8 pm curfew.

I stopped typing weeks ago. Now I just burble into my audio recorder, falling into a funk. I miss the mice.

I couldn't judge vapers even if I wanted to – I'm drinking Red Bull from a can half full with Houndstooth gin. I gave up marking the dates on the gin bottles ages ago. I'm neither the bee's knees nor the cat's meow.

I don't want to get into it, I'm embarrassed, but hours before this months-long lockdown started I went to stock up on wine. I picked up six bottles of wine, to help me get through this apocalypse, this plague. But at the counter, I discovered three of the bottles I'd picked up were very expensive bottles of wine. I'd got confused by the price tags on the display. But it was too late by the time I was at the register. You know what I mean. I just had to buy them.

So now I have six bottles of wine, and three of them are very expensive. I'm too embarrassed to tell you how expensive. Just consider what I've done over my career – I've streaked through Jerusalem on TV – and then think about the fact that I'm too embarrassed to tell you how much these three bottles of wine cost. The other three were expensive too, but not humiliatingly expensive.

Anyway, that's the reason I'm drinking Houndstooth gin from a can of Red Bull. The bottles of wine are too good to drink. I defeated the purpose of buying them by buying them.

Holy hell, I bought that wine on day one of lockdown. When I should have been a bit frugal, because I had a couple of gigs lined up, but no idea what was happening after that. At that exact point, I bought the wines. They're in this no-man's-land; can't drink them and can't gift them. A wedding gift, for instance. Ironically, that person would think I'm low-balling them on a gift. *Oh yeah, thanks John. A bottle of wine.* They'd have no idea.

Another thing I might add – lying on floor, eyes affixed to the lounge-room ceiling – is that I have two smoke alarms unscrewed, resting on my coffee table. I burned dinner months ago and they wouldn't shut up.

This is just how stupid artists are. Look at me. Over-ruminating on all the angles of the dangers of smoke. Catching a plane to Adelaide, then Launceston, to have scientists help me understand this, for my book. It's like, okay, that's fine, but considering your concern over the danger of smoke, perhaps put the batteries back into the smoke alarms and screw them onto your ceiling.

There's piles of pages beside me, spread out on the floor. Print-outs of this manuscript. What if I never get out of the house, what happens to the book? There's definitely not an ending. Do I break curfew to get one? Sneak past the patrol cars? To what end? I can't jump in a shipping container to Switzerland. I've got what I've got. I take another swig of Houndstooth. I'm reading and reading, and crossing out bits where I sound like a jackass.

William, in the IQOS booth in Auckland, tells me, 'Normally when a journo comes in, we're like, okay, what kind of stitch-up are we about to walk into?'

Nothing close to the stitch-up after the tumour is cut out of one of your customers, William.

Do I sound like a jackass? I think so. I'll change it. Or am I paranoid? I'm not changing it. I'm not changing a single word.

Here's the deal. You are not allowed to side against me with William, Rhenu or any Philip Morris employee. No 'they were just doing their job, trying to get through the day, like any working person, and you were annoying them, or making a remark about their haircut'. You have to be on my side in this. I am David and they are Goliath. I am Jonah and they are the whale.

THE SCIENCE AND TECH START-UP

Simon Dowding, my lunch date from Philip Morris, shoots me another email. He informs me that Philip Morris International co-owns a biopharmaceutical company called Medicago, and they're developing a vaccine for COVID-19.

It soon becomes apparent that this isn't a Philip Morris trick. Canadian prime minister Justin Trudeau announces his government will contribute $173 million to help Medicago develop the vaccine and build a plant in Quebec to produce it.

I put down my glass of one of the three expensive but not humiliatingly expensive bottles of wine and take this in.

Philip Morris has been evangelising about healing the world, and I've been calling them out, eyeball-rolling and zinging, for 275 pages. But now it seems they're up to something not diabolical.

On top of this, the idea behind the vaccine could only have been spawned by a company like Philip Morris. Vaccines in the past have relied on chicken eggs, growing the necessary virus samples in the yolk. For whatever reason, this doesn't fly with the coronavirus.

So what did the scientists at Philip Morris's Medicago come up with? What did they look to, to inspire a substitution?

Tobacco.

They are working with a tobacco-related plant, *nicotiana benthamiana*.

The *Financial Post* explains 'the plant has a weakened immune system that allows it to easily host genetic material and develop particles that mimic a virus'.

It seems Philip Morris will soon be saving lives, and in a way only they could, because of their tobacco past.

Flick back not too many pages. I was throwing peanuts from the peanut gallery at a Philip Morris executive for claiming, at an innovations festival, that she works for 'the science and tech start-up called Philip Morris International'. But what is this if not an innovation, a life-saving one, from a science and tech company?

This is Philip Morris doing . . . good. I can't come up with any downside.

Jesus Christ, and the plant is replacing eggs, so it's vegan, too.

The best snark I can conjure is this. The plant they're using, *nicotiana benthamiana*, is an indigenous Australian plant. So . . . cultural appropriation.

I reach for the bag of peanuts by my laptop and feed one into my mouth. The taste is bitter on the tongue.

Doctors and nurses

Week ten of hard lockdown. I'm rearranging the books on my book-shelf by width. I'm taking 2 am showers and drawing Mickey Mouse in the steam on the glass. I'm giving up on push-ups after managing six. My beard is growing a beard.

I crack my knuckles and email the Australian Medical Association. What do they think of all this? Doctors and research-ers, working with legitimate science and medical ventures, funded by Philip Morris. And if the Australian government asks them 'should we purchase the Philip Morris COVID vaccine', what are they going to say?

'John, I've been asked to reply on behalf of the AMA. Your ques-tions are (unsurprisingly!) challenging and ones we have never been asked before.'

I think of my enemies stewing as they read that compliment – the ones who hate me enough to hate-read my book.

'The AMA does not have any specific policy on tobacco company funded health research. The AMA acknowledges that for a medical association, it is reasonable that we are uncomfort-able with the idea of tobacco companies funding any health and medical research.'

No, they'll turn that on me too. My enemies, I mean. They'll be like, 'Jesus Christ he actually kept in the compliment. Speaks to his character. Narcissist.'

'In weighing up the risk versus benefit in the current pandemic, the AMA position is that it is not unreasonable to let that research happen at this time and not to oppose it simply because of the tobacco company investment.

'Once this COVID-19 crisis has passed, the government, the AMA and others can consider this issue in more depth. When that time comes, it should not be limited to tobacco company investment, as there are other equally "offensive" industries/companies whose investment in health and medical research would be questionable (such as those with poor human rights records, those associated with war/weapons, fossil fuels, etc).'

Quit fretting over your enemies, John, don't lose your bearings. Focus on Philip Morris. The AMA says, after the pandemic subsides, they'll be pondering over the matter of complicity.

Yes, Philip Morris, I've snitched. The AMA is going to be discussing you. I bet now you regret paying for my lunch.

BUCKET

I have a craving. I dig into my stash of nicotine knick-knacks in the Adidas shoebox. I find the pods for one vape device, but I've lost the kazoo itself. I grab another vape but I've sucked out all the juice in that one. I cycle down a near empty street to the vape shop and discover they're shut due to Covid. Turning back, I notice Chemist Warehouse. I haven't tried nicotine gum yet.

Back at my laptop in the lounge room, I've been chewing a piece of nicotine gum for a few minutes and already I'm getting a bit of – I feel a rush in my arms. I chuck another piece in my mouth.

Ten minutes later, I'm feeling 3 per cent, 4 per cent, 5 per cent like I want to throw up.

I feel compelled to take the chewing gum out of my mouth. I press the glob to my bookcase and wander to the bathroom to stand over the sink.

This is not a perfect experiment because I've had maybe five black coffees this morning as well. Who knows what's what?

I go back to typing in the lounge room, but now with a red bucket next to me. This is the first book I've written where I've needed a bucket. That says something, doesn't it?

An hour rolls by. I like the gum. I keep chewing . . . something's off.

I spring from my chair, shoot straight to the bathroom, skipping the red bucket – cutting out the bureaucracy. Up come rice and blueberries.

But I didn't think it through. Sinks don't have that big hole anymore. They've got that metal stopper screwed over it, permanently fixed. So it was a bad decision. Now I've got the mop and have to transfer the sick to the red bucket.

I finally make it to bed. That night I have continuous, monstrous nightmares.

POLITICS

The next morning, Savvas calls with news. In recent days, federal health minister Greg Hunt had proposed a ban on importing nicotine vape juice and devices. This is the only way to procure these products in Australia, so this would effectively be a ban on vaping.

George Christensen and Matt Canavan, politicians from Hunt's own Liberal National Party, struck back. They drafted a petition objecting to this ban and found nearly two dozen fellow Liberals happy to sign it. Hunt is apparently seething over this revolt.

And here's the news: a Senate inquiry has been announced, a 'Select Committee on Tobacco Harm Reduction'.

Following this inquiry, the committee will recommend either opening the doors, so businesses like Vapoureyes will be allowed to sell their nicotine juices and devices in shops around Australia, or they'll ban vaping businesses entirely and Vapoureyes goes kaput.

'I hope you get to talk at the inquiry,' I tell Savvas.

'I will.' I hear the click-clack of his prayer beads down the line. 'I have God on my side.'

JUICY FRUITING

Stretched out on the couch, I haven't learnt my lesson. I'm back on the gum. I want the nicotine even though the taste is somehow both bland and nasty. I have a Eureka moment inspired by vapers and their zany flavour mixes. Why not mix this with flavoured chewing gum? Hubba Bubba, that sort of thing.

It's 11.30 at night so I can't head down to the shops, because of the curfew. Is this a thing no one's thought of before? I'm going to google it. Have I invented a new subculture of drug taking? Am I like Hon Lik, the man who came up with vaping in a dream one night?

The next morning I go to the shops and get a pack of Juicy Fruit, Extra Watermelon, Extra Tropical and Extra Raspberry and Lime.

First I try chewing the nicotine gum and Juicy Fruit at the same time. *Chew chew chew*. It really improves it. Have I invented something? I need a word to describe it, like 'vaping'. 'Chewing'? How about 'juicy fruiting', there's a pleasant pop to that.

And I looked this up on the internet and it isn't a thing –
I couldn't find anything. There's not already a subculture of juicy
fruiters. I came up with it.

Time for experiment number two. I cut the nicotine gum in half.
I've read the history of vaping, and it's hard to pinpoint when it all
started, but I've got it right here. The very moment that juicy fruiting
begins.

Chew chew chew. Oh, yes! This is closer to what I'm trying
to achieve.

Imagine all the rituals that will develop from this. Little tools to
cut your nicotine gum in two. Facebook pages where we exchange
our concoctions, blending this and that flavour, calling them Bubble
O' Bills and Bazooka Josephines. Camps form – are you a Nicorette
or Nicobate juicy fruiter? Oh! And like vapers blowing vape rings on
Instagram, juicy fruiters blow bubbles.

I'm placing half a nugget of 4-milligram Nicorette on a stick of
Extra Tropical and wrapping it up like Pig in a Blanket. This might
be the way to go. *Chew chew chew.* Yeah. I can feel the nicotine in
my face.

WELL, WELL, WELL

So often people have derided me for my sarcasm. My *lingua materna*, my native tongue. A co-worker called me Captain Sarcasmo. Sarcasm is dismissed as the lowest form of wit, but I've always felt in my bones that was wrong. Now I learn it is something much more powerful than even I had thought.

Upon learning Philip Morris is developing a Covid vaccine, I joked that their use of an indigenous plant to make it was cultural appropriation. But my wisecrack was a *wise* crack.

I learn this *is* a hidden and simmering issue. Plants and indigenous intellectual property rights. I spend the afternoon on the phone.

Dr Steve Wiley from the WA State Agricultural Biotechnology Centre, based at Murdoch University, has taken a special interest in the plant Philip Morris has chosen. He's not happy.

'It's been seventy years since John Cleland, a botanist at Adelaide University, picked *nicotiana benthamiana* from the Granites, up north of Alice Springs,' Dr Wiley says. 'And he sent it over to a colleague in the US. The Aboriginal people that have used it probably for tens of thousands of years have never had any say in its use.'

He says traditionally the leaves were baked in the sun, mixed with ash from wattle and rolled up in a fresh leaf. 'And then it was stuffed into the gap between your teeth and your gum. The alkaloids, including nicotine, would come out and infuse into your body. People got a buzz out of it.'

So it turns out someone has invented juicy fruiting before me. (I've stuck my blob of watermelon Nicorette on my mug of coffee so I'm not chewing in the academic's ear.)

Importantly for the issue at hand, it was also considered a form of currency. So not something you can just come and pluck at will.

'There seem to be no regulations at all,' Dr Wiley says venomously. 'You can just walk in and basically pillage the genetic heritage of this country as much as you like.'

My friend John Clarke is General Manager for Biocultural Landscape at the Eastern Maar Aboriginal Corporation. The Eastern Maar are Traditional Owners in south-western Victoria. He's also not happy.

'Far too often we get people that come in and they ask all these questions of community members about species of plants. And they take that information away and we don't know if they're doing it for commercial reasons. The legislation doesn't protect Indigenous intellectual property rights.'

This is because the law is built around individual, not communal, ownership.

'Multinational companies are exploiting it to the hilt,' he warns.

What a mess. Philip Morris is snaffling a sacred plant. Even when they're doing good there's a shadow of no good.

What else have I learned from this? This insight began with a sarcastic quip about cultural appropriation. I am the oracle. Sarcasm is soothsaying. The wisecrack from my lips, a compass pointing to something deeper.

I commit to being twice as sarcastic, thrice as often.

A NEW DAY

The news reporters announce the easing of Covid restrictions. The sun streams through the window. I sweep scores of bottle tops and corks from the windowsill above the kitchen sink into a green Glad bag. I swing it over my shoulder and head to the bins out the back of my apartment.

Pull yourself together, John. Alcohol is a drug, and that windowsill tells quite the unflattering story. Enough with the glugging and justifying it, after the fact, as character development or a storyline.

You love those Theodore Dalrymple books, and remember what he said about writers and their addictions. 'In modern society the main cause of drug addiction, apart from the fact that many people have nothing to live for, is a literary tradition of romantic claptrap. It encourages histrionic self-dramatisation, to the detriment of real character.'

BETRAYAL

The wooden spoon swirls the cooking porridge. Savvas is about to make a phone call to the 'Select Committee on Tobacco Harm Reduction' Senate inquiry. These inquiries usually take place in a room at Parliament House in Canberra, but due to Covid the authorities have shut the borders. Savvas sits at my kitchen table instead. I'm making him breakfast.

'I'm going to give them a bit of a perspective from somebody in the industry. So far, they haven't called any businesses to testify. I sent Hollie an email the other day. I was like, how come you haven't had businesses on? And so, she invited me.'

Hollie Hughes is the Liberal Senator who called this inquiry. Long addicted, she is weaning herself off cigarettes with vapes.

'That's nice,' I say, porridge thickening. 'But it does seem a bit disorganised. Why didn't a lobbyist from the vaping industry sort something out?'

'We're not paying a lobbyist at the moment.'

I splash in more milk.

'What's the purpose of this inquiry? It's in aid of what?'

'If you want to be truthful about it? I suppose the purpose of the Senate inquiry is to disrupt what Greg Hunt is trying to do.'

I'm refreshed by his frankness.

Health Minister Greg Hunt wants the 'prescription model'. This would require vapers to visit a doctor for a nicotine prescription, then pop down to the pharmacy for a vaping device. Savvas says most doctors won't want to prescribe nicotine, so this would be, in effect, a ban on vaping. And deliberately so.

In contrast, the vaping industry wants the 'consumer model'. Vapers would be able to buy nicotine juice and devices from supermarkets, 7-Elevens and the like. No prescription required.

Hollie Hughes backs this consumer model and will steer the inquiry towards it, according to Savvas. 'The lobbyist that I've been speaking about, they went to Hollie Hughes and said, you need to do this so that we can stop Greg Hunt from going ahead. And she said, no problem, I'll play ball. She called the Senate inquiry.'

I'm confused. Savvas said Vapoureyes hasn't been paying a lobbyist at the moment. Who's this lobbyist he's talking about? The conversation's moved on.

'So it's a disruptive tactic. The Liberal Party is internally split on this issue.' It's not just Hollie Hughes, George Christensen and Matt Canavan. As mentioned, more than twenty backbenchers have publicly opposed Greg Hunt's prescription model.

Savvas thinks Prime Minister Scott Morrison sides with the backbenchers but, equally, doesn't want a fight with Greg Hunt.

'He needs some sort of pretext to say to Greg Hunt, "Look, for the good of the party, you're going to need to set this aside." Right? This Senate inquiry is that pretext. If the Senate inquiry goes our way, he can lean on that and take the steps necessary to push aside this prescription model.'

'You're allowed these, but not honey?' I point the wooden spoon towards the fruit on the kitchen bench, next to a jar of honey. Savvas is a vegan.

'That's it.'

I double check.

'You have nothing against blueberries, strawberries or bananas?'

'Well, I don't eat bananas. Not a big fan of the texture.'

In my head, I do that carnivore thing of getting embittered by vegans. If you're already ruling out pretty much everything, just eat the banana. Also, what's up with the no honey? Does he think bees are led into a slaughterhouse and bolt-gunned?

'And what about sugar?' I say, masking my fury.

'I'm happy about it.'

The first sitting of the inquiry was six days ago. This is the second sitting. Despite being chaired by Senator Hollie Hughes, who's friendly to the cause, Savvas says it's not going well.

Six senators sit on the panel: three from the Liberal–National coalition, two from the Labor Party and one from the teeny-weeny Centre Alliance party. At the very least Savvas expected all the Liberals would be on their side, but it hasn't played out like that.

'Sarah Henderson, she's a Liberal senator. But the problem is that Greg Hunt has gotten to her. She's sitting in a room in Canberra, surrounded by a bunch of Greg Hunt's staffers, who are writing her questions to ask the witnesses who are appearing.'

The two Labor senators, too, are hostile to vaping, or at least the consumer model.

'I don't know how it's going to go today. They've been pretty vicious.'

An Ampol spokesman was torn apart for saying their convenience store attendants could offer health advice to customers about the benefits of vaping. Apparently it's a big no-no to suggest the guy picking his nose by the hotdog rotisserie could offer medical guidance.

'I'm kind of wondering what the gotcha questions are going to be today. I'm wondering how they're going to try and fuck me up. It's making me slightly anxious. I think I've got all the answers to anything they might ask. Fingers crossed, I guess.'

He slurps a spoonful of porridge.

'What's the most gotcha question you can think of?' he asks.

I poke the blueberries in my porridge.

'Why are you trying to kill children?'

Savvas laughs. 'You say that, but it could be an actual question that Henderson asks. In that kind of way as well.'

He is concerned they'll accuse him of Vapoureyes marketing their products to kids, but that's not the only vaping controversy related to children.

'What about the kid who died?'

In Melbourne, in 2019, a 19-month-old toddler swallowed nicotine juice. The mother, who was trying to quit cigarettes, had imported it from the USA.

'That was tragic and it highlights the reason why regulation is so important. In New Zealand, we sell a bag which is designed to hold nicotine in. It's a lockable bag with a zip and padlock.'

I'm feeling uninhibited. Now we're cosplaying senator and witness.

'Another way that the kid wouldn't have died is if vaping was banned outright.'

'That death should never have happened,' Savvas pushes back. 'It was absolutely tragic. But in the amount of time that I'm going to be appearing before you today, two Australians are going to die as a result of tobacco. That's just in the half an hour that you and I will be speaking. This year, some 20,000 Australians are going to die. What are those lives worth?'

Fair enough. I can see Savvas has prepared thoroughly for this. But what's wrong with Greg Hunt's prescription model? 'Then why are you objecting to this going through doctors and pharmacists? You're saying you want this to be regulated, and that's really good regulation.'

'It is regulation, but it's overregulation. You're making access to vaping harder than access to smoking. Why is it okay for those people to die and not have access to a safer alternative to tobacco?'

Safer. That bendy word, 'safer'.

'The whole premise of all of this is that vaping's safer. How so? It might be safer in so much as you're not inhaling carbon monoxide and smoke. That is true. But what about respiratory issues that are unrelated to smoke? We don't know enough about that. You could be sending people to a death sentence.'

Savvas puts down his spoon.

'I'm going to disagree with the statement that we don't know enough about it. I think there is plenty of medical evidence already to suggest that vaping is safer than smoking. That much is undisputed.'

I put down my spoon too. I remember one of Simon Chapman's allegories.

'They'll say it's like – you're not jumping off a twenty-storey building, you're jumping off a fifteen-storey building or a ten-storey building. So it's safer, but you're still jumping off a building.'

'No, no, I disagree with that characterisation,' Savvas rebuts. 'It's jumping off a one-foot building. That's the difference in magnitude, in terms of the proportional risk. Twenty thousand Australians will die this year of smoking. Zero will die as a result, or at least the direct result, of vaping.'

(What about the baby?)

I search my mind for another gotcha question.

'How many trans people are on the board of Vapoureyes?'

He says there are no trans people on the board. 'We have one person of colour. So, does that count?'

Oomph

Savvas settles into a chair in my lounge room, squeezing his iPhone buds into his ears, my shelf of exorcism books running behind his bushy head.

'We're going to do this, John.'

It's his turn next. He hears Simon Chapman wrap up his evidence to the inquiry.

'Chapman's a fucking idiot.'

When his turn comes, the chair of the inquiry asks Savvas for a brief opening statement.

Savvas puffs out a cloud, places down his vape, and furrows his brow.

'I've never seen our customers so angry and frustrated, and, frankly, frightened, as they are by the, frankly, insane proposal to make vaping less accessible than cigarettes through this bizarre and unworkable prescription model.' Oomph, he's going in full throttle. 'Our customers can't stomach the idea of having to go through the rigmarole of convincing a doctor who may have an ideological opposition to vaping that they deserve to be allowed to quit smoking.'

Defying stereotypes, he has quite a lot of energy for a banana-less vegan.

'The thought of putting control of their lives into someone else's hands as though they're not competent enough to make that decision for themselves is honestly pretty insulting.'

Liberal senator Hollie Hughes opens question time, lobbing Savvas a softball. She asks how many people Vapoureyes employs. The answer is about thirty in Australia, forty in New Zealand.

'And how many different types of vaping machines do you sell?'

Hey, Hollie? This isn't an infomercial. I went harder on Savvas while playing senator over porridge.

Nationals senator Matt Canavan takes over, and he's also a big old softy with Savvas.

Then the honeymoon ends. Now Labor senator Tony Sheldon pipes in. He hounds Savvas, claiming that his interests align with those of Big Tobacco. Savvas says that's not true, that he wants to disrupt the cigarette giants.

'Well, you say that you want to disrupt the tobacco companies. That's from a commercial point of view. Isn't that correct?'

'It's not just from the financial point of view but from a moral one. I have friends and family members who have died of smoking-related illnesses. Why wouldn't I want to disrupt the tobacco industry?'

Senator Sheldon is going somewhere with this. He circles back to whether the rise of vaping, a boom for Vapoureyes, will really be detrimental to the tobacco giants.

'Are you aware that last week a paid editorial in the *Australian* newspaper from Philip Morris International was published?'

This paid editorial asked the reader to be open-minded about e-cigarettes. The senator's point? If vaping is genuinely going to disrupt Big Tobacco, as Savvas is saying, why is Philip Morris arguing the same case Savvas is arguing? That is, why is Philip Morris saying bring on vaping, and dump the prescription model and go with the consumer model?

'Well, I presume because they do have devices that they are trying to bring to market. But again, I represent a completely different industry. The model of vaping that I'm advocating for has nothing to do with heat-not-burn devices. I'm sure you've seen them, the IQOS.'

Senator Stirling Griff from the Centre Alliance party swoops in. He stands sternly against libertine impulses. He doesn't suffer sinners lightly. Along with vaping, he is pushing to ban Japanese anime and manga, for their sexual imagery.

'Mr Dimitriou, isn't the real issue that you have with the prescription model that you won't profit from it?'

It is true that under that model, vaping devices would be sold by pharmacies rather than businesses like Vapoureyes.

'No, not at all,' Savvas says. 'The problem is it's not going to meet the needs of Australian vapers.'

Labor senator Anne Urquhart tags in.

'You had made a statement in your submission that tens of thousands of Australians would most certainly have been saved had they had the opportunity to switch to vaping. I'm asking where the reference to that is. And why you put that in your statement without a reference point.'

'I'm referring simply to the indisputable fact that vaping is less harmful than smoking and therefore if people's predilection goes to vaping, rather than smoking, fewer of them will die.'

'So you actually don't have a reference point to substantiate the statement that you're putting in your submission,' she snipes. 'Chair, I have no further questions. I'm happy to defer the rest of my time.'

Next in line is Liberal senator Sarah Henderson, Greg Hunt's proxy, according to Savvas. She, too, takes a swipe at his motives.

'You're characterising our position as only coming from a position of profit,' Savvas snarks.

'Please don't tell me what I'm saying,' Senator Henderson countersnarks. She returns to one of the earlier points. 'You've stated in your submission that your entire business model is about stealing big tobacco's customers, and yet Philip Morris and others are on the public record advocating for exactly the same position as you and using exactly the same arguments. You're saying this is a remarkable coincidence?'

'If they happen to have arguments that aligned with what I'm saying, then all well and good for them, but that's not really my business. I'm here to advocate for vaping. I'm not here to advocate for the tobacco industry.'

The puppet master

Savvas plucks the buds from his ears, looking dark.

'How did that go?' I ask.

After that escapes my lips, I remember stepping off stage after live performances. The question 'how do you reckon it went?' always sent shivers of paranoia up my spine. Why didn't the person say, 'Oh my God, that was so good!'

'I don't think that went very well.' Savvas is puffing his vape, staring out of the floor-to-ceiling window, eyeing the cacti on my balcony. 'I feel like I was spinning my wheels a lot and didn't really have an opportunity to make any worthwhile points. I really didn't enjoy that. I'm going to have a quick call now with Matt Stafford, who's the uber lobbyist. This is the guy. This is the puppet master. I'm going to have a quick chat with him.'

I remember Savvas telling me over porridge that Vapoureyes weren't paying a lobbyist at the moment. So who is this Matt Stafford?

'You're welcome to sit here and listen in, but again, don't quote any of this or anything like that.'

Stop the book.

That sentence Savvas just spoke?

He said 'don't quote any of this' only *after* he said, 'I'm going to have a quick call now with Matt Stafford.' So, at the very least, I can write about that. His request can't go backwards in time. But what's the expiry date of 'don't quote any of this'?

Legal advice will dictate I can't quote Matt and Savvas's phone conversation, which I wasn't even listening in on. At this point I don't appreciate how influential Matt is. And even if I had chosen to listen in, I would have only heard Savvas's side of the call.

Savvas paces around my coffee table for around fifteen minutes, phone to ear, while I spool through Twitter, checking out if anyone's dissing me.

'Well, that's good,' Savvas says eventually, sliding his phone back into his pocket, happiness in his voice. 'I feel better now. He was very complimentary.'

Can I point out that I'm holding a fluffy shotgun microphone the size of Muppet. And wearing headphones so large and puffy I'm basically Princess Leia. And I'm writing a book about vaping and smoking. And Savvas knows this.

'So Matt Stafford, I think I've mentioned him to you before.' If he has, I don't remember. 'He's the guy from BCW, the big lobbying firm. He's the puppet master. He's the guy who has co-ordinated everything you know about in vaping, in terms of lobbying, that's happened. Like, Senator Canavan and Christensen.'

Matthew Canavan and George Christensen, you'll remember, were the first to rebel against Greg Hunt. They produced a petition and convinced more than twenty Liberals to sign it.

'When they had their petition, that was him. This inquiry? That was him. All the various lobbying firms that are working, whether they are part of BCW or not, all of them, they take their directions from him. So he's the one that organised for this to happen. For me to appear as a witness.'

My mind is fluxing, trying to pull the pieces together. This Matt Stafford works for BCW – what does that stand for? And he's a lobbyist? But not for Vapoureyes?

Matt Stafford heard Savvas's testimony on the live feed on the parliament website. 'So he's basically just going through it and saying

I got all the points that I need to get across. I came across as credible and confident, humanised it. He said he was getting text messages from various other lobbyists. He said Philip Morris told him I did very well.'

If I was drinking coffee, I'd spit it out right now. Did he just say Philip Morris?

'Which is an interesting thing to have happen, to have a tobacco company compliment your work. And that's just such a weird feeling, because I really don't like Philip Morris. But he's involved with Philip Morris, of course, because they are lobbying and he's the one that does their lobbying.'

Woah, woah, woah.

Is he saying what I think he's saying? This Matt Stafford orchestrated an Australian government Senate inquiry on behalf of Philip Morris?

I later do a google to fill in the holes, but let me flesh it out for you now. BCW stands for Burson Cohn & Wolfe, a multinational lobbying firm. Their head office is situated in New York City. Philip Morris has been a long-term client. Matt Stafford is president for the Asia-Pacific region, which includes Australia. And he's an influential person beyond this; for one, he was cabinet secretary under Liberal prime minister Tony Abbott.

Savvas was on the phone to this man. His first call after appearing at the inquiry. Philip Morris was in the inquiry without being in the inquiry. Damn.

I ask Savvas what's in it for Philip Morris, but he doesn't know.

'It's difficult. There is a very complex network of relationships happening behind the scenes in all of this. You could take a step back from the vaping perspective and think, why are they doing all of this? Why are there millions of dollars going into lobbying in favour of the model that would be most successful for us and not necessarily for the big tobacco companies? Right? If you're the big tobacco company, you would love it if vaping gets crushed but the IQOS gets approved. What's in it for them to see us succeed? I don't know the answer to that question, but it's happening. Millions of dollars are getting spent on it.'

I tell him what I think. 'One thing is the loosening of the laws brings things a bit forward. If you're approved and your devices are approved, that makes it a little easier, that's a little footstep, to the IQOS.'

'So kind of like hide the IQOS among all of the other things? Sneak it in?'

'Yeah.'

'That's a good point.'

I ask him if he's being used.

'Oh, I am,' he happily concedes. 'I'm fully aware of that fact. But the point is that I'm using them right back.'

I take this to mean that Philip Morris are successfully living in two realities, both of them true. On the one hand they are toxic and shunned. On the other, they have money, power and connections far in excess of those in the nascent vaping industry.

Matt Stafford got Savvas into the inquiry, according to Savvas. 'It's in my interest to make sure that I get a voice in things like this.'

Savvas is being pragmatic, living in the grey, like anyone with a job has to live in the grey.

'That's why I think there probably should be far more restrictions on lobbying in a fair and just society,' he says. 'Companies like ours – not just ours but, of course, much, much bigger companies – have a disproportionate influence over government because we can afford to access lobbyists. Whereas in a fair and just society, you would expect that every member of that society would have the same, equal access to their politicians.'

Philip Morris slithered into the inquiry. And I know this, and no one else does. Not even the senators on the panel who were suspicious of exactly this.

I head to the kitchen and make myself a coffee with the vegan almond milk Savvas brought over.

'It's going to be interesting to see how this actually turns out,' he says. Greg Hunt still wants the prescription model. 'The whole purpose of the Senate inquiry was to stop that from going ahead. If this inquiry doesn't come down in our favour, we are fucked. And I'm worried that that's where we are at the moment.'

There's no point in getting drunk – even those three bottles of expensive red wouldn't black out what I now know.

Bubbles

The following evening, I message Savvas for a fact check.

'The day before you went to the Senate inquiry, who did you practise questions with? Your girlfriend? Matt, from BCW? Vapoureyes employees?'

Text message bubbles bubble.

'Just to be clear, I would rather you didn't mention Matt in any way, shape or form.'

Bubbles bubble.

'I really, really want to be clear on the subject of Matt. I only mentioned him and BCW for that matter in confidence, to give you an idea of what happens behind the scenes. So, if you mentioned him in the book, it will completely and totally fuck me up.'

Mental health check

I think back to Mandy. You mightn't recall the name, but you will remember her. I had put the call out on social media for anyone working for cigarette and vape companies to get in touch.

Mandy worked in upper management at a vape giant, and she piped up. She was the one who had lunch with two of Philip Morris's external affairs managers while I was next door getting nervous drunk.

After her lunch she told me: 'It seemed clear to me that what they wanted was a puppet. One of the guys even said it: "There are things that we can't say, and people we can't meet, that you can meet and you can say."'

It seems to me Philip Morris did orchestrate an Australian Senate inquiry, using the vaping industry as cover.

Although both sides have claimed otherwise, it appears Philip Morris and vaping have been in bed together.

This is definitely a thing. I'm not mad.

GUILT

I'm driving Simone Stewart home, the woman who grilled me over my mouse traps, after some late afternoon cake on St Kilda beach.

'If you had invited him over just for breakfast, that wouldn't be so brutal. But the fact that you invited him over for porridge and berries – that's so wholesome and nourishing, and it creates an absolute environment of safety. And that's what you invited him into.'

Kids, trekking back from the beach, are mooning passing cars.

'It's not like you invited him for eggs and bacon. That's a masculine breakfast. That's something where you're going, "We're two individual men where we can hold our own ground." But you invited him for porridge and berries. That's like, "When two become one." That's what porridge and berries is. It's vulnerable. It's a vulnerable breakfast meal.'

I turn from the wheel. 'To be fair to me, I was happy to have eggs, but he's a vegan.'

'No, no, no.' She's not letting me off the hook. 'Did you actually mention that you had porridge and berries in the invitation?'

'Yes.'

'At the start?'

'Yes.'

'On the phone?'

'Yes.' I break down exactly what happened. 'I said, "I have mini bagels and porridge and berries." And he said, "I'll bring over the vegan butter and the almond milk."'

'See, that's a very shared experience and a shared meal. My initial response was that you can out all of this information. But now this is feeling like a much more intimate experience than what I initially thought it might've been.'

'Okay. I agree with you. The only thing, to be fair to me, that doesn't make me a jerk, is I had *no* idea he was going to unload any of this information.'

And! The Senate inquiry was public, streaming live on the internet. That underscores (I think?) that there was no pretence that my home provided some cloak of privacy. And my Muppet shotgun mic!

'For days after, the almond milk was still in my fridge,' I say. 'And I was still having it. And I felt like he was breastfeeding me.'

'Whilst you're plotting his demise,' Simone needles. 'This is deep. You've gone very deep. This is becoming very Freudian.'

'I had no idea he was going to reveal these things. Unless I sensed it in the universe. Subconsciously.' Did I? 'The good thing is, I've got it all on tape and you can goddamn hear I'm not trying to trick him. I couldn't even trick him into anything, because I had no idea —'

'Of course, that that was going to play out. Oh, hell. You've dug yourself a good old grave here.'

I open the car window for air.

Journalism 101

Mahmood Fazal and I wipe our noses and walk out of the toilet cubicle in a wine bar in Prahran, two train stops up from mine.

'Like, what are the ethics of – like, it's going to fuck him over.'

Mahmood you'll remember from the shisha lounge. Please also remember that he's been awarded a Walkley, Australia's top journalism prize, for his reporting. His take is, 'Who gives a fuck. He's agreed to speak with you.'

'I think he just lost his bearings.'

'That's too bad. If he's doing the wrong thing, it doesn't throw the ball into your court.'

We perch on a low wall in the beer garden.

'I did not hide from him, at all, the angle of the book. So why did he tell me that and not expect me to use it? I didn't even – this all rolled out —'

'He's giving it to you. He sounds like he wants to reveal something from within Philip Morris. Like, he feels a bit insecure about what he's doing and he wants to reveal the truth. Is that what it feels like to you?'

'There's that element. But I'm kind of betra—'

'It's not betrayal if it's in the interest of the greater good. That's my whole perspective on any issue that I tackle in my journalism.'

Yes. If I keep it under my cap, that doesn't solve the question of betrayal. By not betraying Savvas, I'm betraying you, the reader. Because I know this piece of information and you don't.

This is newsworthy. It's a Senate inquiry. Philip Morris are using the vape industry to sway government policy, without people knowing, including politicians sitting in the inquiry. And what's the endgame? To get their IQOS onto shelves and into lungs.

'This is how big companies get away with so much,' I say. 'They set up this situation where you feel inhibited to attack them because they put normal people on the frontline. When your laptop breaks down, you don't end up ringing Jeff Bezos from Amazon or Tim Cook from Apple, you end up on the line with some normie in a call centre.'

'He isn't on a call-centre salary if he's having meetings with Philip Morris,' Mahmood says, meaning Savvas, whose job title is General Manager. 'He's not on minimum wage. I haven't read the Bible, but this dude sounds like he should be crucified.'

I like that vivid descripti— hang on. Does that make him Jesus? And does that make *me* Judas?

'Sometimes it's hard,' Mahmood says. He tells me about a piece he's writing right now. 'I'm in Rome. I'm having a great time. I see some of my Muslim brothers, I want to hang out with them. I give them some money, cash, because I have money and they don't, and they're refugees. And then they dance with me, which was the most heartbreaking fucking thing. One puts his arm around me and then I walk off, and I was like, they were great guys. And then I feel for my phone. And I've got my phone. But where's my fucking wallet gone? They'd stolen my wallet.'

He chased them down, catching the younger cousin of the pickpocket.

'But I'm a piece of shit,' he continues. 'I'm not a good person. My nature is – in the area that I grew up in, in Dandenong, it's a struggle to survive. So if someone takes advantage of you, you have to make them feel the repercussions of that, which is generally with force. And so I pull his younger cousin over the bridge and I threaten to drown him and throw him over. And I would have thrown him over the bridge, because they robbed me and they took advantage of me when I trusted them.'

This was not the story he wanted. Ideally it would have been asylum seekers, and him, looking squeaky clean. But he says he's still going to write it up as it happened.

'I'll write that because it's the truth. You're not a journalist if you don't do that, right?'

Where does this leave me?

'I think you have to throw him under the bus, if it's in the interest of the greater good.'

Mahmood thinks his pickpocket story serves the greater good. 'I'm going to write that because these refugees go to these places and they can't get jobs. They're desperate and they'll rob anyone that they can. That's the story. Your situation, the way I would look at it, is how would I sleep better at night? Knowing what I know, and I've kept this one dude safe? Or knowing what I know, and all these people are out there, smoking cigarettes and killing themselves? Like what would make you sleep better at night?'

The magic pudding

Father Bob's eyes are watery from an operation on one of the sockets. It's not just his face, his old man body is in slow collapse too, sinking into his chair in his office. Part Bob, part blob.

'He's part of the pudding,' Bob says of Savvas. 'Part of the magic pudding, and he can't get out of it. You can't take bits out of pudding.'

'Ah, yeah, I see what you mean,' I say. Bob talks in a magical language adjacent to English, but I always understand what he means. Although I want to confirm I have it right. 'He's part of the pudding of Philip Morris and their wily ways. And, therefore, we can't pull him out of the pudding.'

'Yeah, I would have thought.'

So, Bob's with Mahmood. This information needs to be in the book.

'What would your lot say in the synagogue?' he asks.

Australian story

I catch Rabbi Gutnick down my street, opposite the fruit shop. And by opposite the fruit shop I actually mean in front of the bagel shop, but typing that, I thought it came across as fake and hammy, even though it's true. Sure, John, a rabbi in front of a bagel shop.

It's funny to me that a reader might think I've put too much Jewish colour into this book when the truth is I've downplayed it all over the shop, but it just squeezes out everywhere. (Considering the context, maybe 'hammy' should be 'non-hammy'.)

Rabbi Gutnick says it's not as simple as Mahmood and Father Bob would have me believe. It's relevant that Savvas told me what he did in apparent confidence.

'If you were to triage what the key ethical principles are, being loyal and keeping a secret are right up there.'

So it seems at the moment it's two in each column, Simone and Rabbi Gutnick on one side, Father Bob and Mahmood on the other.

He gives me a serious look and takes a bite out of his . . . Vegemite sandwich.

Shrink

Next I stroll to Scrabble cheat Jeremy Weinstein's home, not to see Jeremy but to speak his wife, Caroline, a psychologist.

Mahmood had proposed that Savvas 'sounds like he feels a bit insecure about what he's doing and he wants to reveal the truth'. That makes sense. But I want to check how likely this is with someone who knows about these things.

I've brought along a bag of Bazooka Joe bubble gum because that's the only way to temporarily glue the Weinstein children's mouths shut when I want to talk to their parents.

'Maybe he feels guilty and he wants it out there,' I tell her, as she cuts cantaloupe in the kitchen. 'Even though he's claiming he doesn't want it out there.'

'I was watching a training film around trauma,' she says. 'And this woman was describing how our subconscious rules our behaviours and our thoughts 95 per cent of the time. So I think things do leak out and we don't realise we're really wanting to say them.'

Yes. This is perfect.

'If I'm feeling guilty about something, and it's hidden,' I say, hypothesising, 'I just keep on pushing it and pushing it until it's out there in some way, shape or form. I'm the criminal who wants to be caught.'

But something still doesn't sit right.

'It's this dude I've hung around with, on and off.' I tell her we've spent time together in Melbourne and New Zealand, partying and laughing and shooting guns. Not to mention the Hobbits. 'So it feels like more than – I met him for forty-five minutes and he happened to screw up. I feel like I'm undermining someone a bit closer than that.'

'Oh God.'

Simone Stewart gave me an 'oh God' too.

'This is the spot he has put me in.' I accept a slice of cantaloupe. 'If he revealed something about his own industry, the vaping industry – like, they're smuggling guns in the vats of vape juice – I could conceivably go, "I don't want to screw him over." But he knew I was writing a book about Philip Morris and the book was about how they weasel their way into little spaces and manipulate things. And then he tells me something about *them* and about *that*. So there's no way I can't put it in the book.'

Regardless, how am I the bad guy? Savvas is the one who put me in this spot. I can't unknow what he told me.

Pandering to the base

'It's kind of ironic that Savvas's gotcha moment was you,' Scarlett-Jae says from the kitchen table, putting down the manuscript.

'True,' I say as I stir the stir-fry of kangaroo, broccolini, chilli and capsicum. 'He was worried what was going to happen in the Senate inquiry. But he said it to me.'

'It's a vindication for you. "Look, I told you Philip Morris were awful. It's not in my head."'

My glee is short lived.

'I've got this stuff in there already. Like, "Aha! I've proven *Vice* is in cahoots with Philip Morris." And I'm thinking, that's a great punchline to a section. And then I learn that's a Gen X thing and no one else cares.'

'I would care about this more,' Scarlett-Jae says, meaning Savvas's revelation. 'Because it just shows you the influence that lobby groups have on laws. And that kind of frightens me.'

'Oh yeah.' I perk up again. 'My audience all hate the Liberal Party. And this makes the Liberal Par— yeah, this is good. Cos they all want to hang shit on conservatives. And this is dragging the conservatives into all of this and making the Liberal Party look corrupt. They'll like that. Even though they don't care about Philip Morris, they hate the Liberal Party and they hate Scott Morrison. It's like when Borat got Rudy Giuliani – no one cares about the specifics, it's just that he stuck it to one of Trump's people. So maybe people will like me.'

Scarlett-Jae looks at me strangely.

'Yeah, I think they definitely will. And it also paints Scott Morrison in a pretty poor light. Greg Hunt is trying to be the hero of the country at the moment because of Covid. And then there's all this sneaky stuff, people undermining him, going on behind the scenes.'

Scarlett-Jae thinks this is all good for another reason.

'Is there anywhere else in the book as big as this where you have the vaping industry working with Big Tobacco? Because they've presented themselves as pitted against it in the past.'

I'm the one with the intel. Philip Morris, the invisible man, sat in the Senate inquiry.

'Oh God.' I'm thinking of Savvas again. He was slurping porridge in the chair in which Scarlett-Jae now sits.

'Why, why, why?' I clang the wooden spoon against the pan on each 'why'. 'Why can't things be simpler?'

'I knew that you were closer to him than other subjects, but I didn't think that you were like *friends* friends.'

'Imagine if it was important for me to put in the book that it was you who snorted cocaine on my coffee table? What would you think about that?'

'I think I would just say it was someone else, but you just used me to amalgamate characters.'

I dish stir-fry onto her plate.

'When this book comes out and you've betrayed Savvas, do you think your other friends will be very wary around you?'

Shut up, Scarlett-Jae.

MY NEW CRUSH

I reach into the Adidas shoebox of nicotine knick-knacks by the fridge. At the moment I'm trying out John Player Special Crushball Blue. I'm going to have to see whether it takes, but out of everything I've tried, from the vapes to the IQOS, to the cigarillos, to the gum, to the toothpicks, to the other cigarettes, this is the one that I'm enjoying the most. I think because of the Crushball. They look like regular cigarettes, but there's a little ball in the filter that you get to click, and it snaps open, releasing a menthol. That's tactile. I like that. I like combining that with fidgeting with my Zippo lighter, because then I've got the two fidgets.

Same same

I check the news every day. Weeks later, the Senate inquiry returns their report. Four out of the six senators favour Greg Hunt's choice, the prescription model. Liberals Hollie Hughes and Matt Canavan dissent – they want the consumer model.

This report isn't a binding ruling, it's a recommendation. Greg Hunt and the Therapeutic Goods Administration have final say.

But finally, behind-the-scenes sulking, whining and horse-trading has returned a result. The prescription model will go ahead. Businesses like Vapoureyes will not be able to sell their nicotine products in Australia.

In what seems like a concession, however, they'll be able to continue selling them to Australians from New Zealand. Just like before. The vape industry is neither elevated nor banned. So, the same.

Savvas tells me that his business will remain in a grey zone. They can continue to operate but, at the snap of the fingers of powerful enough politicians, it could change overnight. Just like before.

So what was the point of all this?

RIGHT OF REPLY

I tell Senator Hollie Hughes that I have three friendly questions and one antagonistic one. We're being led through an exclusive lounge in the sky, forty-seven storeys up at the Sofitel hotel in the Melbourne CBD. Considering its exclusivity, I wish it more closely resembled the Illuminati lodge in my head. Chandeliers, softly lit, Siamese twins playing a grand piano, guests in Venetian masks. Instead there are enormous windows. Couldn't be letting in more of that best disinfectant.

'I remember back when we were kids, cigarettes were less than five bucks a packet,' she says. We sit on a set of couches that form a circle around a flue, which draws up smoke from a glass-sealed fireplace. We're served wine and cheese. 'We're not talking about the sixties, we're talking about in the eighties and nineties. When I quit, 150 days ago, they were $58 a packet. Benson and Hedges Smooth 25s.'

She retrieves a kazoo from her handbag.

'This is mine. It's $15 or something for two pods. A $7 pod's a lot cheaper than a $58 pack of fags.'

It could have gone so much better for Hollie at the Senate inquiry. The recommendation could have been to allow nicotine juice and vapes to be sold in Australia. Instead, people will still need to import them from New Zealand. Hollie says, quite apart from anything else, that means the New Zealand government will be the ones to reap the tax on these items, not the Australian government.

'I send all my money to Jacinda, and that annoys me no end. I'm not a supporter of hers or her government and —'

'I was neutral, but then I found out she was following me on Instagram —'

'Ooh, you're busy and important —'

'Before I followed her.'

'Ooh, you're a bit special.'

The Senator darts her eyes around the lounge.

'If it wasn't for those people there, I'd be sneaking a vape right now.'

After the three friendly questions, which were just there to cushion the antagonistic one, I forward announce what will be happening next.

'Here's my hostile question,' I kindly introduce.

'Aha,' she says warily.

'Someone involved in the inquiry said that Matt Stafford, on behalf of Philip Morris, lobbied you to get the inquiry up. Because they thought in the long term —'

'Do I know Matt Stafford?'

'I don't know. This is what they told me. That —'

'Who told you this, sorry?'

'Just someone involved in the inquiry.'

'I don't think I know Matt Stafford. And if I do, I don't recall who he is. Certainly, there was absolutely no pressure from anyone.'

I'm feeling more awkward than usual but push on.

'Not from Philip Morris? Because the argument was that Philip Morris benefits in the long-term, so maybe not immediately —'

'There's this sort of obsession that anyone who supports vaping must be the shill of Big Tobacco. Philip Morris had zero influence, impact, discussion, knowledge, advice around the setting up of this inquiry, in any shape or form.'

I find out someone else has been digging around.

'So, you know, whoever's telling you that is clearly one of the mischief makers, who's probably been talking to the *AFR* and trying to dump on me from a great height.' A journalist at the *Australian Financial Review*, Neil Chenoweth, has apparently found a social media snap of her fraternising with a lobbyist.

'A friend of mine that I went to school with, his husband owns a lobbying firm and apparently he does work for British American Tobacco,' Senator Hughes explains. 'I have never met with British American Tobacco. I was there at their place on Christmas night having a drink.'

Was it mead? I learnt at Hobbiton that just having a drink doesn't exculpate yourself from the accusation that you're under the influence of lobbying.

Maybe sometimes it's about being paid off, but other times it's not that. It's a hazier situation. They might be friends you want to help out. And even if they're not, you don't want to rock the boat when it's full of people you know.

She tells me about another friend, Brian Marlow from Legalise Vaping Australia. They describe themselves as a 'grassroots advocacy organisation'. I will learn later that Philip Morris funded a lobbying operation with them.

Senator Hughes fills me in. 'The Legalise Vaping lobbyist's office is in the same building that I live in.' She thinks it's ridiculous for her opponents to make something of this. 'Which is a 38-storey building.' She rolls her eyes. 'I'm a separated mother of three. And, yeah, I'm going to choose the building I live in – when I get death threats – based on which lobbying firm is there. As opposed to, you know, it's got a good concierge and full-blown security.'

A waiter appears, a silver tray perched on her fingers.

Hollie and I move on to our third, fourth, fifth glass of wine?

'No more nasty questions?'

'No, no, no,' I murble. 'There was only one nasty question.'

She pulls out her vape, takes a puff and passes it to me. I take a puff. A peace pipe.

'Greg literally threatens to resign, every time, if vaping goes through. But I mean, he says this, it's like this sort of grand gesture. No one believes him.'

She takes another puff.

'This is off the record.'

Oh God, I am not going down this path again.

So that was her right of reply.

I email the lobbyist in question, Matt Stafford, from Burson Cohn & Wolfe. He does not respond. Hurtfully, my LinkedIn invitation to him remains pending.

WIN/LOSE

I win. This isn't my usual bullshit where I buzz the white supremacist's doorbell and he creaks open his front door and I spot an Asian baby crawling in the hallway and his Asian wife peeks in from the lounge room, and I'm like, 'Exposed! Fake racist.'

No, it's different in this book. I've revealed something bigger. Philip Morris was likely pulling the strings behind the 'independent' government inquiry into vaping. They turned it into a taxpayer-funded buffoonery, unbeknown even to most sitting on the inquiry. All in aid of the IQOS.

And yet.

Because of the betrayal, I feel filthy. Wind back the decades to me returning home from parties at 3 am, cigarette stink in my clothes, in my hair, hard to wash out. That's what it feels like now. I will never forgive you Philip Morris for this stink of shame left on me.

An eye for an eye, a tooth for a tooth, a lung for a lung. Vengeance.

KILL PHIL

'This can be a tale of revenge, modelled on those Quentin Tarantino films I love. *Kill Phil* boings into the ear as pleasantly as *Puff Piece*.' — *Puff Piece*, page 51

Let's say Philip Morris is right. Let's go along with their word games. Let's say the HeatStick isn't a cigarette, it's a HeatStick. Let's say the HeatStick's smoke isn't smoke, it's aerosol. Let's say its tar isn't tar, it's Nicotine Free Dry Particulate Matter.

Let's concede all those points to Philip Morris. I've slowly realised they're all misdirection. And one killer omission.

Let's ask something else of them. Forget the yellow-stained fingertips, the hit to your hip pocket, the stink in your hair. Why do people hate cigarettes? Why do you denounce them? Ultimately? Because they give you cancer.

Strip everything else away. This is the only question that counts: can you get cancer from HeatSticks?

It's clear to me now. The Smoke-Free Future, the 'unsmoke the world', the websites, the billboards, the gambit, the employment branding, the dancing around the meaning of words, the speeches, the Shadowland, the Babushkas, the labyrinths, the double-speak, the sleek metallic-looking device itself, it's all in service of Philip Morris's ultimate desire. Don't bring up the word 'cancer'. Whatever happens, don't let the word 'cancer' be pinned on HeatSticks.

Foreign arthouse Zoom

'Hello, everyone, and welcome to Philip Morris's Open Science Event. My name is Gizelle Baker, and I'm so glad that so many of you were able to join us from all over the world today to take part in our very first ever virtual science update.'

Gizelle Baker is Director Global Scientific Engagement. She looks quite a lot like New Zealand prime minister Jacinda Ardern, who followed me before I followed her on Instagram. Gizelle says Covid has made Philip Morris adapt. Thus, this online event to discuss the science of the IQOS. It's past midnight in Australia, jet black out my lounge-room windows.

'We're going to present some of the latest scientific research on our tobacco heating system, which is currently sold in over fifty markets globally under the brand name of IQOS, with over 14 million smokers globally using IQOS and over 10 million of them completely leaving cigarettes behind.'

There are six speakers, all women, various ages, various heart-melting European accents that remind me of the beautiful women in the one million foreign arthouse films I watched in my university years.

'We're finally at a place where we can start looking at some of the longer-term end points and assess the potential of these products to impact the health of the population.'

Gizelle throws it over to Christelle Haziza, Global Head of Clinical Research and Execution.

'Execution'? Finally some straight talk about the role of Philip Morris executives in society.

Christelle 'The Executioner' Haziza begins. Her topic is smoking and cardiovascular disease. It takes me a few minutes to absorb what she's getting at, her science lingo a challenge to my layman's ears. But when I do absorb it, I laugh and slap the table, rattling my cup of tea.

Get this. Cardiovascular disease is the leading cause of death in the United States, and smoking is responsible for one in four of these deaths. So, imagine, you're speaking for the largest cigarette company in the world. You say you're interested in reducing cardio-vascular disease in the community. What's your angle?

I have a shelf of Gideon Bibles behind me, from Japanese to French, and I swear on them all I'm not making this up.

Christelle's angle? Weight gain is a big contributor to cardio-vascular disease. And when you quit cigarettes, you put on weight, 4 to 5 kilograms. So quitting smoking contributes to cardiovascular disease!

But don't worry, Philip Morris are here to help. Their tests show that for smokers wanting to quit, switching to IQOS addresses this concern. Unlike quitting outright, if you switch to the IQOS, your weight will remain roughly the same as it did when you smoked cigarettes. Thank you, Philip Morris, for fighting the scourge of heart disease caused by people quitting smoking.

We're asked to submit our questions in preparation for the Q&A session following the speakers. I patter away at my keyboard.

Next, Betty Blue talks about the science of smoker's cough. I fall in love each time she says *cuff* in her French accent. Then La Femme Nikita discusses IQOS use in Japan.

Finally, question time begins. They roll through a few.

'So, the next question we want to address is the following. "The worst thing about cigarettes is that they give you cancer. Can you get cancer from using IQOS?"'

Oh, it's mine. Exciting.

Gizelle, Director Global Scientific Engagement, fields it.

'When you look at smoking, smoking exposes you to large quantities of carcinogens, and a large number of them. When you look at IQOS, it does not eliminate the carcinogens. Carcinogens are reduced compared to cigarettes. But we don't have the data today to go to "what does that mean for cancer?"'

Bang.

Philip Morris can't say the IQOS won't give you cancer.

As far as I know, they have never said this out loud before.

'It's not a cigarette, it's a HeatStick. Unlike a cigarette it heats-not-burns!' they proclaim.

So what? Who cares what car the hitman was driving on his way to your home to kill you?

I wipe the blood from my yellow leather jumpsuit and return my samurai sword to its sheath.

The last babushka

I click out of the Philip Morris Open Science event. By my laptop, next to a pencil, lies a HeatStick. I pluck it up and roll it in my fingers.

Early on I thought that it took me between a week and three months to realise I'd been duped by some claim Philip Morris made. Now I realise I was flattering myself; sometimes it takes me much, much longer than three months.

Philip Morris, explaining why they want to unsmoke the world, say that what makes cigarettes so harmful is the smoke they produce.

This is at the same time true and, ingeniously, leads you up the garden path, through a field full of strawmen, to a river overflowing with red herrings. I realise the precise truth is that what makes cigarettes so harmful is the *tar* in the smoke they produce.

The Australian Department of Health spells it out: 'Tar produced by conventional cigarettes is the main cause of lung cancer.'

Because Philip Morris brought up smoke, and the alleged lack of it in HeatSticks, I've been wild-goose chasing smoke this whole time. Is it smoke? Is it not? But it's all been one more misdirection. Who cares, given *whatever it is* produces the same deadly agent as smoke, which is the reason smoke is deadly in the first place? I should have been chasing tar.

The question, the clincher, the salient point, the deal maker or breaker, is not 'Does the HeatStick produce smoke?' It's 'Does the HeatStick produce tar?'

That wouldn't have been much of a book. It would have been slimmer than a novella, briefer than a pamphlet. In fact, *Puff Piece* could have been sold in the form of a Chinese fortune cookie. Nibble the cookie and unroll the message within:

Yes. Yes, the HeatStick produces tar.

In their submission to the FDA Philip Morris compares the amount of tar produced by a cigarette to that produced by a HeatStick. I point this out because, Philip Morris, if you're going to throw a bucket of marbles at my feet to try to trip me up and claim that the type of tar in a cigarette is different to the type of tar in a HeatStick, you're not arguing with the nicotine-gum vomiting fool, you're arguing with *you*. You've listed it as the same constituent in both. And you say a HeatStick produces 22 per cent less of it. Which is the best way you can put: a HeatStick produces 78 per cent of the tar produced by a cigarette.

Philip Morris, the Marlboro cowboys, have one bullet left in the chamber when it comes to this matter. They could double down, insist a 22 per cent drop in tar is a meaningful drop.

This is a shot I predict they won't fire. Because, boy, have we been here before.

Billion-dollar lawsuits against Philip Morris have circled around this old claim that low-tar cigarettes were safer. You can read how one of those cases ended on their very own website.

'A Federal Court has ordered Philip Morris USA to make this statement. Many smokers switch to low tar cigarettes because they think low tar cigarettes are less harmful. They are not. All cigarettes cause cancer, lung disease, heart attacks, and premature death. There is no safe cigarette.'

So they'll be keeping the gun in the holster, I reckon.

Tar. Philip Morris must know this is cancer to their IQOS story. When compiling their PMI-58 list, all but one constituent is given their ordinary name. Carbon monoxide is carbon monoxide, mercury is mercury. Only tar is scrubbed out, reworded as 'NFDPM' – Nicotine Free Dry Particulate Matter.

I've sulked that people aren't thinking hard enough about Philip Morris and their HeatSticks. Why am I the only one flapping my arms? But I'm coming to understand that the opposite plays into their hands too – people like me overthinking it. Making something complex that need not be. Maybe it's easier to grapple with and battle in its simplicity.

What we have here is a low-tar cigarette. It's that simple.

Doing the laundry

By comparison, tar is absent from vapes. So whatever other dangers they pose, vapers can fairly say that the main cause of lung cancer from cigarettes is absent from vapes.

So this is why Philip Morris hitches its wagon to the vape industry. Create a fog in which both vapes and the IQOS are 'e-cigarettes'.

During the Senate inquiry Philip Morris bought advertorials in *The Australian*, arguing our government 'is increasingly at odds with other countries, where alternatives like e-cigarettes are legally available'.

In this laundering of language, the IQOS emerges untarred.

Bucket of marbles

I reckon I know Philip Morris's next move.

I've been scaling a skyscraper, their twenty-storey high submission to the FDA, and a little snake peeked through a crack. 'Aerosol Chemistry' study, section 6.1.1.3.2, table 5, footnote 8.

For the PMI-58, they presented the NFDPM (tar) in cigarettes and HeatSticks as the same constituent, so they could brag that there was a lower rate of it in HeatSticks. But squinting at this footnote, I see they're contradicting that here, claiming the tar in a cigarette and a HeatStick have a 'different constituent make-up'.

'Blah, blah, blah, it's not the same type of tar.' That will be the new misdirection.

Once again, I don't have the mice and monkeys and Bunsen burners to corroborate or debunk this. But once again, who cares?

Does this supposedly different tar produced by HeatSticks *not* give you cancer? Will it *not* activate gene-mutation of a normal cell, turning it into a cancer cell, dividing itself, over and over, cultivating a tumour, spreading to tissues, metastasising, the army of cancer cells now breaking away, travelling through the bloodstream to eat away at bones, the brain, the liver, the lungs and Michelle's father's face?

Tell us that, Philip Morris.

THERE WILL BE NO ESCAPE

The 'Unsmoke Your World' campaign trumpets 'the best choice any smoker can make, is to quit cigarettes and nicotine altogether'. So we are left with the impression that Philip Morris wants to wean us off cigarettes and move us to IQOS. And, following that, put down the IQOS and be free of nicotine addiction forever. But hold up, do they really want us free?

I remember back to my trip to New Zealand. After a long day at the vape expo, I was sitting with the Vapoureyes emperor, Morris Lazootin, on the floor of his garage. We could hear the dings from the backyard – guests firing bullets into a gong, deep in the pine trees.

He said Philip Morris have a duty to keep us addicted.

'You were talking to William?' he asked, meaning William Churchill, the freshly washed man manning the IQOS booth.

'His angle,' I told Lazootin, 'is there might have been a previous generation of Philip Morris trying to kill people, but the new generation, his generation, they're trying to get people off cigarettes.'

'Why?' Lazootin said, cracking up at the notion. In a beat he turned as serious as a heart-attack. He was concerned I'd been sucked in. 'Why are they trying to do that?'

'They'll say it's some regular, human being, moral thing.'

'But they legally can't do that.' He rested his drink by the tyre of his Tesla. 'They're a publicly traded corporation. They can't lose money because they feel like it – they have to make money. They have a fiduciary duty to make money for the shareholders. You can't bring in, "Philip Morris wants to help people." Philip Morris can't be motivated by feelings. There's no way, legally, they can.'

So Philip Morris is obliged to *not* let IQOS be a pathway to quitting. The IQOS must keep people hooked. That's the law.

You won't hear them say this out loud, though.

To have them disclose that this is the plan would be nice.

To try to get them admit it, I'll need to ask the question as an investor who's worried they're not following their fiduciary duty. Lucky I have the shares despite the optics. That has bought me a ticket to their Annual Shareholders Meeting conference call.

On this call, I shall say thusly: 'I have a question about the long-term viability of IQOS and HeatSticks as revenue earners. Do you see customers who move from cigarettes to HeatSticks, remaining long-term customers of HeatSticks? Or only temporary users of HeatSticks, then moving on to not using tobacco products at all?'

The ex

I've been whining on the phone to Philip Morris International, trying to get a sixteen-digit code that I'll need to punch into the phone to ask a question during the Annual Shareholders Meeting. Which is tonight, Australian time.

I've been thrown all around. Philip Morris say I have to ask my brokerage firm, which is NAB Trade. NAB Trade say they don't have the sixteen-digit code. I chase up Computershare, which runs the shares for Philip Morris, but they don't know either.

I might not even get to ask the goddamn question. So annoying.

Jesus, why didn't I try to sort this all out before?

I try emailing Philip Morris International Investor Relations. 'Hello, A company of whom I'm a director, Your Ex-Boyfriend Pty Ltd, holds shares in Philip Morris International. How can I find the 16-digit code for the Annual Meeting of Shareholders? Regards, John Safran.'

Yes, my company is called Your Ex-Boyfriend Pty Ltd. I thought it was funny when I had to come up with a name decades ago.

Cut to the chase: even though I pissed in my sock, compromising myself by buying the shares, no one can tell me my sixteen-digit code, so I don't end up asking my question at the Philip Morris Annual Shareholders Meeting.

Adding salt to my sock to my wound, I *can* listen in. And pretty much everyone who asks a question is some rabble-rouser who has only bought shares to ask a trouble-making question. None of them the question I, a concerned shareholder, need to ask.

A question from a man who remembered his sixteen-digit code

'I'm a Filipino physician, living in Manila for over thirty years. I've met many smokers who began smoking in their teens, whose lives have now been forever transformed by their addiction. Some have died prematurely from heart disease and cancer. Others now live with lifelong disability. Philip Morris talks about transformation and "unsmoked", and it's now rolling out heated tobacco products. However, it is misleading and hypocritical to claim corporate transformation if your company, now admitting cigarettes are harmful, continues to make those same harmful cigarettes and continues earning most of its profits from them.'

Their past is their present.

'While claiming to promote a Smoke-Free Future, Philip Morris joined a consortium to sue a small town in the Philippines when that city council passed smoke-free ordinances aimed at protecting young people from cigarettes. If the transformation plans by Philip Morris were genuine, you would be taking responsibility for continuing to sell these harmful products. So I ask when, and how, will Philip Morris implement a global product recall for cigarettes?'

'Thank you for your question,' says Louis Camilleri, Chairman of Philip Morris International. 'We are very, very committed to a Smoke-Free Future and comments such as yours, or criticisms, will not deter us. So thank you very much.'

Rude.

Briefcase

My sulky communications eventually break them down and James from Philip Morris International Investor Relations agrees to a call with the director of Your Ex-Boyfriend Pty Ltd.

'I'm hearing a lot about moving to IQOS and HeatSticks,' I say, trying to sound like I'm wearing a suit and have a paperweight on my desk. 'And it's just occurring to me, are those people who move on to IQOS going to remain loyal customers or not? Because I guess that makes a huge difference to the whole unsmoked strategy.'

'We do have consumer panels in a number of markets and we do track this,' James says, in a voice that sounds like he's wearing cufflinks and has a letter opener. A consumer panel, I learn, is a group of customers chosen for research and feedback. 'We track how many consumers that we switch from smoking to using IQOS then go on to quit overall. There are roughly the same amount of people giving up cigarettes as there are giving up IQOS.'

He gives the example that in some markets, in a given year, 98 per cent of cigarette smokers might remain smokers. And this mirrors IQOS users. In the same given year, 98 per cent will remain IQOS users. Or, put another way, they'll remain addicted to IQOS.

Being from Investor Relations, and talking to a shareholder, this is presented as reassuring.

But James wants to reassure me further. He tells me something I haven't heard before. There 'tends to be a one-to-one' replacement between cigarettes and HeatSticks. If you smoke twenty cigarettes a day, you'll be smoking twenty HeatSticks a day.

Or, put another way, moving from twenty cigarettes to twenty cigarettes.

IQOS use 'doesn't seem so far to be changing the rates of cessation, or quitting tobacco use altogether'.

Experts funded by Philip Morris, like Dr Marewa Glover, pitch the IQOS to the public and politicians as a path to quitting.

But now that I'm behind closed doors, businessman to businessman, Philip Morris does not look at the IQOS that way. It's a panicky strategy to retain customers, currently smokers, who otherwise might quit. And James says they have research – consumer panels – to back up that this strategy is working.

You get a very different conversation when you're a shareholder than a writer. They're happy to confirm Lazootin's theory. They would be breaking their fiduciary duty if they let addicts escape.

PUFFERY PIECE

Philip Morris and I sit in agreement. The precise words chosen, to tell their story, are critical. That's why they fret if people call a HeatStick a cigarette, refer to its discharge as smoke, or point out that its Nicotine Free Dry Particulate Matter is tar. And why they are erasing 'cigarette company' and writing instead 'science and tech start-up'.

But, I learn, Philip Morris has an escape hatch. They believe these claims and their opposite at the very same time. At any given moment they can claim the words that *they* chose are not, in fact, critical at all. They're only words.

This is made clear by two investment companies who have decided to sue Philip Morris International. In their court papers, filed with a New York district court, they say Philip Morris misled investors about the success of IQOS clinical trials.

They are relying on the testimony of Tamara Koval, a former Philip Morris scientist. She has complained of irregularities in the trials. She says urine samples collected in a Polish study exceeded the limits of what a human being can produce. Several subjects reported 12 to 18 litres of urine in a day when the normal urine samples produced by humans are between 2 and 4 litres.

And, during a session in Tokyo, Tamara says protocols were presented in English yet some of those involved couldn't understand English. 'I was like, Jesus, what are we doing here?'

The suing parties say Philip Morris sent a 'threatening letter' to the bosses of independent researchers who found higher levels of several toxic compounds in IQOS than Philip Morris had claimed. Apparently, a letter like this is highly unusual in the scientific community.

Despite all this, Philip Morris had proudly claimed that they were 'following a rigorous scientific assessment program', with CEO André Calantzopoulos saying, 'We are producing the best science you can produce in the field today.'

Tamara squealed to the press and, on that day, the company's stock price fell US$3.75, a loss of US$5.8 billion in market capitalisation. This is why the investment companies are suing. If they had known what Tamara knew, they might have invested differently. (They also complain that Philip Morris misled investors about the future success of the IQOS in Japan.)

So how is Philip Morris defending themselves against claims they made false and misleading statements? By dancing around the meaning of 'false and misleading'.

Philip Morris say their statements weren't false and misleading, they were 'inactionable puffery'. Puffery defined as 'an optimistic statement that is so vague, broad, and non-specific, that a reasonable investor would not rely on it'.

They're saying that words don't mean what they mean.

They point to legal precedent, saying puffery 'permits companies "to operate with a hopeful outlook", because corporate offices "are not required to take a gloomy, fearful or defeatist view of the future"'.

As such, statements that they were 'conducting extensive and rigorous scientific studies', 'drawing upon a team of world class scientists', following a 'thorough and systematic approach to smoke-free product development and assessment', 'producing the best science you can produce in the field today', are mere puffery and 'could not amount to a guarantee regarding the quality of Philip Morris's studies'.

On 4 February, 2020, Judge Ronnie Abrams returns her ruling. She sides with Philip Morris.

Philip Morris stood accused of making false and misleading statements about the IQOS, but were not required to prove that their statements are true.

Philip Morris never loses. They can shrug it off as puffery and walk away whistling.

IN YOUR CLOTHES,
IN YOUR HAIR, EVERYWHERE

After graduating from the University of Melbourne, Dr Bronwyn King scored a job in the lung ward at the Peter MacCallum Cancer Centre. 'Everybody had lung cancer, nearly all smokers or ex-smokers. I was the person making those horrible phone calls in the middle of the night, saying, "Look, I'm terribly sorry, but you need to come in now because I don't think your dad is going to make it through the night." I was twenty-five years old and I was the classic brand-new, shiny doctor planning to save the world.'

I've pulled over to the side of the road to take Dr King's call, and over the trees in my eye line is a grey-brown building marked 'Peter MacCallum Cancer Centre'. Weird.

When Dr King and her husband decided to buy a house, she needed to know how much she had squirrelled away in superannuation. She sat down with the superfund representative for employees at the Peter MacCallum Cancer Centre and he told her that she was invested in the 'default option'. She was curious what that meant.

'He said, look, there is this one other "greenie option", for people who have a problem investing in mining, alcohol or tobacco.'

Was he saying what she thought he was saying?

'I said, "You're telling me I'm currently investing in tobacco?" And he said, "Oh, yes, everyone here at the Peter MacCallum Cancer Centre is."'

Philip Morris is omnipresent. So quiet and stealthy, the oncologists at the largest cancer centre in the southern hemisphere were unwittingly investing in the company killing their patients.

'I knew nothing about the finance sector or superannuation but I just knew that I couldn't continue when my money's being invested in Big Tobacco.'

She convinced her superfund to divest from Big Tobacco. That superfund, then called First State Super, controlled tens of billions of dollars. Now called Aware Super, they serve hundreds of millions of people around the world, all of whom aren't invested in Philip Morris, thanks to her.

Dr King has definitely been more annoying to Philip Morris than me, rocking up to the IQOS booth at the vape expo. I flatter myself that I'm a pebble in their shoe.

Half chicken, seasonal mushrooms, herbs and jus

I mention Dr Bronwyn King to my dad, who's sipping coffee at my kitchen table. Investment is his wheelhouse. He's a retired Certified Practising Accountant, although he has one sole client remaining: me. Every few months, I pass him my shoebox of receipts. It's next to my Adidas shoebox of nicotine knick-knacks.

The evening after I tell him about Dr King's campaign to convince her superfund to divest from Big Tobacco, he texts me: 'Philip Morris is the 28th largest holding in the 100 largest companies held in the iShares Global Fund. It sits between BP and McDonald's.'

Interesting. Did he merely research this for research's sake or does he own shares?

I text him: 'And you have an investment in this iShares Global Fund?'

He texts back: 'YOU DO.'

Damn. And I was stressing out over the free lunch. I was complicit even before I knew I was complicit.

Philip Morris, so slippery, invisible and everywhere. Long before I typed the first word of this book examining how they're slippery, invisible and everywhere, I was funding them. I'm a long-term investor in Philip Morris.

And you know what that means?

I paid for the lunch.

THIS IS NOT A EUPHEMISM

Professor Ghil'ad Zuckermann is Chair of Linguistics and Endangered Languages at the University of Adelaide. Linguistics is the scientific study of language, and I want to talk to him about the way Philip Morris have been manipulating language.

When I arrive at his office, I see that cheeky humour is one of the endangered languages he spends his time with. He's in trouble for sticking a poster to his door that promoted etymology – the study of the origins of words – which joked that the origin of 'studying' is not 'student dying'.

'Just my door. It was not put up around the university.' He's defending himself over the phone to a higher-up on campus. I gather they're concerned it will trigger students, perhaps plant suicidal thoughts in them, like an Ozzy Osbourne record spun backwards.

But students wishing to leap out of a window will have to find someplace other than Professor Zuckermann's office – his window is blocked by piles of books, as he's run out of space in the floor-to-ceiling bookcases that stretch along the walls.

Over the next three days he'll drive hundreds of kilometres, along the coast, to Port Lincoln. He hopes to convince school principals to begin teaching a local Indigenous language, Barngarla. He has spent the last ten years working with Barngarla people on a dictionary.

After sitting through one more conference call about the 'student dying' poster fiasco, we climb into his SUV and he backs it out of his parking spot.

'We had a party for our son,' he says, turning onto the road. Professor Zuckermann may be a pointy headed intellectual but his face is round, and he has a ponytail. 'We had 200 people, but none of them were Aboriginal, because my Aboriginal friends are eight hours from here. And my wife had a birthday cake.' She wanted to light the candles. 'I asked 200 people, none of them had a lighter, none of them had a match. None of them smoked. The next day I was in Port Augusta, teaching a class in the Barngarla language to fifty Aboriginal people. Then we had the break. Yeah. Fifty people smoked.'

Professor Zuckermann has more. As we leave the city, he talks of a friend, an Aboriginal man. 'I was at the hospital visiting Simon, who was dying of lung cancer. I came and I was the only whitefella there – five people around the bed, his son, nieces, nephews. The doctor comes and says, I would like to explain to you the situation. Simon smoked for fifty years and this is why he's dying now. And now it went to the oesophagus, he cannot eat. He will die in two days. Then the doctor leaves. Everyone's shaken up and anxious. And one of his nephews was, "Okay, we need a break." So we go to the patio of the hospital and everybody gets a smoke. And I said, "What?" He says, "Yeah, we've heard a horrible story, we need to calm down with a smoke."'

I remember my John Player Special Crushball Blues. I left them in Melbourne and I couldn't tell you where they are. On the balcony? On the floor of my car? They didn't take.

We drive for hours and stop in Whyalla. My dolphin history has been a series of people excitedly pointing far into the ocean, but I can never see them. Here on the pier in Whyalla, they're so close I could lie down and reach them with my hand. I finally see dolphins. I'm pretty happy.

'Is there any precedent for this?' I ask Professor Zuckermann. 'I always assumed that what happens is people on the streets, regular people, they start expressing themselves in certain ways. And then that gets codified after the fact by highbrow dictionaries. But maybe I've got that wrong, or maybe it's different now.'

'Your question about this manipulation by Philip Morris is a wonderful question, touches upon a number of huge things in linguistics.'

That flattery is going in the book. I look down and note the timecode on my recorder.

'One is called Whorfianism.' The theory is named after linguist Benjamin Lee Whorf. 'It's the idea that language dictates slash influences the way we think.'

Professor Zuckermann speaks with an Israeli accent and I mishear 'slash' as 'flesh'. I prefer my mishearing: language dictates flesh!

After all, that's what I felt in my bones upon first hearing the word HeatStick: 'The word's not grassroots and organic, it's top

down and calculated. Created and deployed to change the meaning
of what a cigarette is and isn't. Which in turn can change facts in the
flesh and blood world.'

Language dictates flesh!

A world-renowned linguist agrees with me, provided I mishear
him.

The dolphins squeak and Professor Zuckerman tells me about
a colleague of his who's looked into words bending our perception
of reality.

'I have a friend who conducted research about the word "bridge".'
Unlike English, many languages assign genders to objects. 'The word
'bridge' is masculine in Italian (*il ponte*). In German, it is feminine
(*die Brücke*). This friend of mine, she found out that, subconsciously,
when Italians talk about a bridge, they describe it as sturdy, as strong.
When Germans speaks about a bridge, they describe it as elegant, as
beautiful. And she argued that it's because of the gender, the gram-
matical gender. 'Brücke' makes you feel that bridges are elegant and
'ponte' makes you feel that bridges are sturdy.'

Without knowing it's happening, reality is morphed by the
words that we hear. They bend what we see with our eyes.

He has another example of words bending perception. He was
born in Tel Aviv, and he says that Zionists did this when establish-
ing the modern state of Israel in 1948.

'"Mishkan", in the Bible, was the place where you worship God,
where the Temple was, where the Ten Commandments were,' he
explains. 'What Zionism did is they took this word that evokes
sacredness and they decided to use it to describe the building
where the Knesset members sit.' The Knesset is modern-day Israel's

national legislature. He says that the word 'Mishkan' draws Israelis to subconsciously feel that a sacredness and divinity hangs over the Knesset. Something they wouldn't feel if it was just named 'the Knesset building'.

Zuckermann presents this as top-down 'lexical engineering'.

I came to discuss a corporation, but he won't stop talking about religion to explain how language is used to lull us into someone else's reality.

'What is religion? Religion, if you want, is the control of language to achieve power.'

We stroll to a lookout and look at the ocean through mounted binoculars. I feel we've done this the wrong way around, because nothing beats getting nose-to-nose with a dolphin.

'When they found a suicide bomber in Israel, he was fourteen years old, and they saw that his penis was wrapped with white cloth,' he says. 'And the army asked him why. He said, my mother told me that when I go to paradise, I need my penis to be ready for the seventy-two virgins.'

But he explains that there might be a misunderstanding at play. 'Now the word "houri" is usually considered to mean "a virgin".' He says some linguists claim it never meant this. Rather, it meant 'raisins'. 'In the time of the Qur'an, white raisins were very rare in Saudi Arabia. So they said, okay, you will get seventy-two white raisins.'

Professor Zuckermann locks his eyes on me.

'If that is true, do you understand the implications on world history?' He brings up September 11. 'All the suicide bombers that did it because they believed that they were going to get virgins?

I mean, you would have had many less people doing all this bullshit, because they'd say, I'm not going to do it for sultanas.'

We start wandering back to his SUV.

'Language is so much more powerful than the layman understands. And I think that religious leaders, politicians – and Philip Morris – they understand it more than the layman. And this is why they manage to control.'

He can see things from Philip Morris's perspective.

'I can understand they just want to survive. But obviously there is a very big manipulation here. And the only good thing you can say about it is that the manipulators understand the nature of language. And the nature of language is such that it gives you power, if you know how to use it.'

The sun bears down. A bug kamikazes into my side of the windscreen.

Combustible

We draw closer to Port Lincoln.

Professor Zuckermann says sneaking in and flipping 'cigarette' for 'HeatStick' could be seen as Philip Morris simply engaging in the art of euphemism. It's been a while since we consulted a dictionary: 'a mild or indirect word substituted for one considered to be too harsh or blunt'.

'But it's not only a euphemism. When you say, I'm not going to "shit", I'm going to "number two", then everybody knows you're going to shit. So this is a euphemism. Or, I'm not going to "fuck her", I'm going to "make love to her". So everybody knows that you're going to penetrate her with your penis. Those cases, they change our perception of reality through a euphemism. But in this case, with the HeatStick, I would argue that this euphemism is even more than changing our *perception* of reality, it's changing reality.'

The difference? He says that the public knows what a shit is but not the nuances of tobacco, nicotine, smoke and tar.

'I think that in the case of Philip Morris, there is a very good combination of scientific cluelessness by people and linguistic manipulation. It's very combustible.'

He's pulled it all together for me. Even threw in a nice allusion to cigarettes.

A FINAL BLESSING

It rattles me that Philip Morris might slip 'unsmoke' into my Torah, my Qur'an, my Ramayana: the Scrabble dictionary. Don't laugh. They've already got it into the online Urban Dictionary.

Unsmoke:
To 'Unsmoke' means to rid smoke from your life.
Danny has been a cigarette smoker for 15 years. He's Unsmoked his life by switching from cigarettes to a smoke-free alternative.
Contributor: Philip Morris International, April 08, 2019.

Despite my many attempts, I'm not a smoker. For smokers who want to quit, Philip Morris slinking into the Scrabble dictionary is not their top concern.

I pull up around the corner of the Father Bob Maguire Foundation and bleep my car shut. I make my way past the cake shop with the meringues in the window. Green ones that are frogs, and white ones that look like mice from one angle and Klansmen from another.

I push the door open and pass the trinkets in the Collingwood Football Club shrine, a mirror of the Papa Gedi voodoo shrines I remember from Haiti.

I salute the woman at reception and head to the boardroom. Although it might not seem like it, I always start off my projects trying to be a fly on the wall. That's what you're meant to do as a reporter, or whatever it is I am. But then by page 5 the fly has developed a lisp and by page 12 the fly has grown to 5'7", come down from the wall, and it's sipping tea with Father Bob.

I pull up a seat.

'Do you know anything about addiction?' I ask him.

'Addiction? What do you mean? Everybody knows about bloody addiction.'

By the time of this visit Father Bob's body is so old and melted that he might as well be a puddle on the floor.

'I was just thinking, cos I'm writi—'

'Addiction is – you've lost emotional control. You know it's doing you no good, but you feel you want to smoke. You feel that you want to drink. You feel that you want sex. You feel that you want whatever. Our feelings and imaginings – our emotions – they've got to be treated with the greatest respect. Because they're the things that make us colourful individuals.'

I have the responsibility; I am the Bob whisperer. I need to make sure that he's saying what I think he's saying.

'The reason you shouldn't be addicted is you have to respect that you have feelings? And if you let those feelings go out of control, that's no good for yourself?'

'And no good for others.'

I look down. Without noticing I was doing it, I've slowly torn a page from my notepad into a dozen pieces. I don't know what that means or why I do that. But I realise now that I must come across as a lunatic to others. To Sarah from Quit Victoria, to Dr Alex Wodak, to everyone I've spoken to.

'So why do you reckon people can't just stop smoking?'

'You've got urges, U-R-G-E-S, urges. You can either teach yourself, or your mother will teach you, how to restrain yourself.'

He mimics the part of the mother. 'This is not going to do anybody else any good, my son.'

Now he's the son. 'But I want it, because it's gonna do me good.'

Now he's either the mother or himself. 'I said, darling, there's more here in this universe than you.'

'That's a very good way of looking at it,' I reason. 'Because, addiction – you can always rationalise it. "Oh, this is only damaging me —"'

'It's not!'

'You're damaging others,' I say. 'Even, like, you're not going to be around, because you're addicted.'

'Yes! And they need to have you around. "No, they don't. Nobody's interested in me. My name's nobody."'

Someone's clanking cutlery in the kitchen next to the board-room.

'I said, no, no, no, darling. Just because others haven't naturally expressed themselves, give them time.'

The microwave bleeps from the other room.

'You need to make sure you learn to think and act in accordance with the plan. You were born in the image and likeness of good slash God. Don't waste your energy on yourself.'

The black poodle trots over and licks the puddle on the floor.

TOOTLES

Let's circle back to the beginning, with the European Parliament decreeing: from Wednesday 20 May, 2020, menthol cigarettes will be forbidden.

This should have been one big celebration. All those lungs that will go uncoated in tar, all those tumours that will never sprout, all the leukemia that will never be.

What actually happens that morning?

Whistling, with a spring in their step, Philip Morris tootles around the ban with their HeatSticks, just like that.

In fact, that is understating the scope of their triumph. On the day the EU bans menthol cigarettes, Philip Morris launches – alongside its two existing menthol HeatSticks – two more menthol variants.

Change the word and change the world. On the day this Fortune 500 company, who cultivate cancer from lips to lungs, the biggest player in an industry that snuffs out 8 million lives a year, pulls this off, I can't find one media story pointing out they've trickily replaced a cigarette with a cigarette.

Some of the campaigners against Big Tobacco whom you've met, Michael Daube and Dr Bronwyn King, had their thoughts why this is so. Cigarettes have slipped out of the zeitgeist. It's simply an old, old, issue. As old, yellowing and weathered as a Winfield ad in a box of seventies *Women's Weekly*s forgotten in a garage. There's no novelty in it.

They're right. That *is* what many people think. But what a cop-out. It's like going, 'Black Lives Matter? Ugh, that's *so* Mississippi, 1964.'

Philip Morris is committing double homicide. They're killing us with cigarettes, but they're also lulling us into apathy – we're bored to death by the matter.

Actually, that's not quite right. Yes, they're responsible for the cigarettes, but if we're going to zone out and let them rewrite the dictionary, that's not on Philip Morris, that's on us.

ACKNOWLEDGEMENTS

Much appreciation to Nikki Christer, Johannes Jakob and all at Penguin Random House; Kevin Whyte, Georgina Ogilvie, Clare Harrison and all at Token Artists/Creative Representation; and Scarlett-Jae.